THEY SHALL NOT PASS

*The French Army
on the Western Front
1914–1918*

IAN SUMNER

Pen & Sword
MILITARY

First published in Great Britain in 2012 by
PEN & SWORD MILITARY
an imprint of
Pen & Sword Books Ltd
47 Church Street
Barnsley
South Yorkshire
S70 2AS

ISBN 978 1 84884 209 0

A CIP catalogue record for this book is
available from the British Library

Typeset in Ehrhardt
by Chic Media Ltd

Printed and bound in England
by CPI Group (UK) Ltd, Croydon, CR0 4YY

Pen & Sword Books Ltd incorporates the imprints of
Pen & Sword Aviation, Pen & Sword Family History, Pen & Sword Maritime,
Pen & Sword Military, Pen & Sword Discovery, Wharncliffe Local History,
Wharncliffe True Crime, Wharncliffe Transport, Pen & Sword Select,
Pen & Sword Military Classics, Leo Cooper, Remember When,
The Praetorian Press, Seaforth Publishing and Frontline Publishing

For a complete list of Pen & Sword titles please contact
PEN & SWORD BOOKS LIMITED
47 Church Street, Barnsley, South Yorkshire, S70 2AS England
E-mail: enquiries@pen-and-sword.co.uk
Website: www.pen-and-sword.co.uk

Contents

Introduction and Acknowledgements...iv

Map of the Western Front vii

1   'To Berlin!' – 1914 1

2   'Nibbling at the Enemy' – 1915..46

3   'They Shall Not Pass' – 1916..96

4   'Hold' – 1917..143

5   'Victory!' – 1918 183

Appendix: French and British Army Ranks....................................221

Bibliography and Sources 223

Index...239

Introduction and Acknowledgements

In August 1914 France went to war confident of victory. Over the next four years, despite huge casualties and enormous costs, the nation struggled to drive the invader from its soil. The First World War took a massive toll on the French people. From a pre-war population of 38 million, France mobilized around 8.5 million men, of whom 1.5 million were killed, 800,000 severely disabled and 3 million wounded. On average, 890 French soldiers died each day of the war.

In addition to mobilizing its armies, the nation had also to transform its industrial base to render it capable of supporting the enormous military effort required for victory, supplying not only its own forces but those of its allies as well. Despite the appalling level of casualties, and the damage inflicted on industry and agriculture in the north and east of the country, France shouldered the heaviest burden in obtaining that victory. The eventual result was an exhausted nation, unable or unwilling to wage war in the same way again.

Who, then, was the soldier who endured so much? In August 1927 Pétain, by then a Marshal of France, asked himself the same question on laying the first stone of the ossuary at Verdun:

> From what kind of steel was forged this soldier ... ? Was he blessed with some particular gift which naturally resulted in heroism? We who knew him, knew that he was just a man, with all his strengths and weaknesses; one of our race whose thoughts and affections ... remained attached to his family, his workplace, his office, his village, the farm where he grew up. But ... these individual links, which taken together formed his attachment to his homeland ... imposed upon him an obligation to protect the people and things most important in his life. ... Other feelings also played their part: affection for the land in the peasant ... submission to the will of Providence for the believer; the defence of an ideal of civilization for the intellectual.

The aim of this book is to tell the soldier's story in his own words; how, as

Pétain put it, did he accustom himself to the battlefield and experience the conditions of the struggle? Contemporary testimony provides an immediacy often lacking in more formal accounts, but it is not without its dangers. Events and emotions remembered years after the event may be recalled imperfectly or coloured by later experience. Preference has therefore been given to letters, diaries, newspaper reports and accounts written during or shortly after the events they describe. Little of this material has previously been available in English; all French texts have been newly translated for this book.

The majority of the men quoted in these pages served in the infantry. In 1914 most infantry regiments comprised 113 officers and 3,226 men, organized in three battalions of four companies each. Two regiments made up a brigade; two brigades, a division. The light infantry (chasseurs à pied and chasseurs alpins) were single-battalion units of 30 officers and 1,700 men each. Soldiers changed rank and units during the course of the war; those cited are contemporary with the quotation.

A word about wages and prices. In 1914 a private soldier earned just one sou (5 centimes) a day, and a corporal 22 centimes. Men were supposed to be paid every ten days, although wages often arrived late. The basic pay was quintupled in October 1915 to 25 centimes a day, a sum further boosted by war pay of 10 centimes a day (payable to all those in uniform) and combat pay of 50 centimes a day (payable only when in the front line). By 1917, therefore, a front-line soldier could receive a maximum of 85 centimes a day, or approximately 25 francs a month. During the war the exchange rate used by the British army to pay its soldiers valued the franc at approximately £0.04p. At its 1914 value one franc is today worth approximately £2.65; at its 1917 value just £1.65.

In contrast to the poorly paid soldier, factory workers in Clermont-Ferrand, employed largely in the rubber industry, received between 40 and 45 centimes an hour in 1914, and 55 centimes by the end of the war. Pay was higher in Paris, where the equivalent figure was one franc. Women workers in Clermont received 25 centimes, later 35 centimes an hour; those in the capital, 65 centimes. Wages in munitions factories were higher still: in 1918 men received between 8.50 and 18 francs a day, women between 7.50 and 12 francs.

How much did this buy? Prices too rose substantially in the four years of the conflict. In Tours a litre of milk cost 30 centimes in 1915, but 2 francs three years later. Beef cost 2.20 francs a kilo in 1914, but 6 francs in 1918. In Paris a kilo of carrots cost 12 centimes before the war, 80 centimes in 1915. Wine sold at 15 francs per hectolitre in 1914, 80 francs in 1918.

Ingredients for cabbage soup (bacon, cabbage, carrots, turnip and leek) cost 2.05 francs in 1914, 5.60 francs four years later.

The headings for each chapter are taken from songs popular at the time. For 1914 the *Chant du départ*, composed in 1794 by Etienne Méhul and Marie-Joseph Chénier; for 1915 *Chant des Girondins*, composed in 1848 by Alexandre Dumas, Auguste Maquet and Claude-Joseph Rouget de Lisle, with music by Alphonse Varney; for 1916 *Le Régiment de Sambre et Meuse*, composed in 1870 by Robert Planquette and Paul Cezano; for 1917 the anonymous *Chanson de Craonne*; and for 1918 *La Madelon de la victoire*, composed in the same year by Lucien Boyer and Charles Borel-Clerc.

I would like to thank everyone who has helped in the production of this book: reader extraordinaire Katherine Bracewell, the staffs of the Service Historique de la Défense at Vincennes, the Bibliothèque Nationale and Archives Nationales in Paris, the municipal libraries of Albi, Dijon, Meaux and Tours, the British Library and East Riding of Yorkshire Libraries. And last, but by no means least, my wife Margaret for her considerable help with the research, translation and editing.

I must also acknowledge the work of numerous French scholars in unearthing and analysing wartime accounts, in particular Gérard Bacconnier, Rémy Cazals, Roger Laouénan, Jules Maurin, Jean Nicot, Jacques Péricard and René Nobécourt. Every effort has been made to avoid infringing copyright and all omissions are unintentional. If this has occurred, please contact the publisher who will include a credit in subsequent printings and editions.

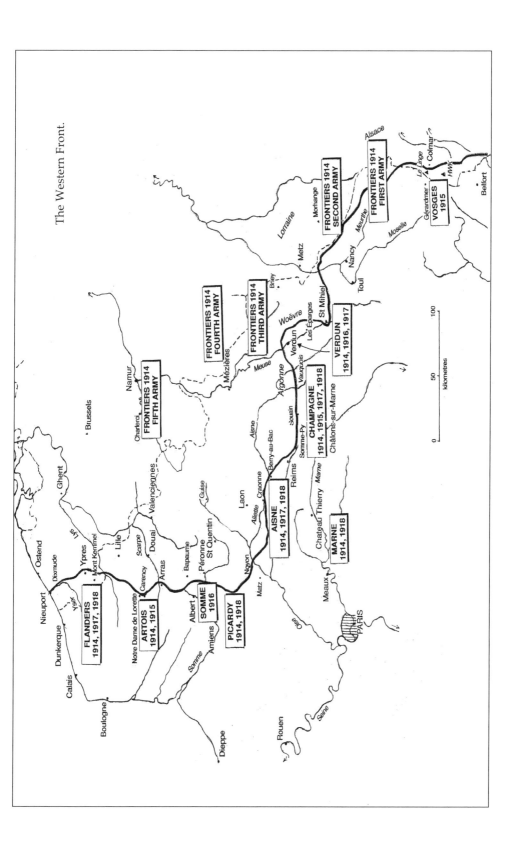

The Western Front.

Chapter 1

'To Berlin!'
1914

Chronology

28 June	Archduke Franz Ferdinand of Austria is assassinated
1 Aug	French order general mobilization
3 Aug	German armies invade Belgium; Germany declares war on France
7–25 Aug	Battles of the Frontiers: two French offensives into Alsace are repulsed
14–25 Aug	Battles of the Frontiers: the French and German armies collide in a series of meeting engagements (the battles of Lorraine, Ardennes and Sambre)
14–25 Aug	Battle of Lorraine: First and Second Armies advance south of Metz; they are halted and then driven back
22–25 Aug	Battle of the Ardennes: Third and Fourth Armies are driven back with very heavy losses
22–23 Aug	Battle of the Sambre: Fifth Army is forced to withdraw from an over-extended position on the French left flank
29 Aug	Battle of Guise: Fifth Army counter-attacks its German pursuers, forcing the enemy to halt
5–10 Sept	First Battle of the Marne: after several days of intense fighting the Germans retreat
10–13 Sept	The Germans withdraw to the Aisne and defy allied attempts to dislodge them
18–24 Sept	Battle of Picardy: Second Army is transferred from Alsace and halts a German advance on the Somme

20–25 Sept	The French drive off a succession of attacks on Verdun; however, the Germans manage to create a salient around Saint-Mihiel
26 Sept	The French repulse a German offensive between the Oise and the Meuse
16 Oct–30 Nov	Battle of the Yser: French and Belgian forces prevent the Germans from capturing the Channel ports
30 Oct–24 Nov	First Battle of Ypres: French and British forces prevent the capture of the town
6–17 Nov	The Germans make further attempts to capture Ypres and Dixmude

'The Republic is calling us' – mobilization

Late afternoon, 1 August 1914. In towns and villages across France gendarmes and municipal employees were hard at work. They were busily posting notices on the walls of public buildings – notices which proclaimed general mobilization for the following day. Despite German demands to remain neutral in the event of war with Russia, France was coming to the aid of her ally. Reservists between the ages of 24 and 38 were recalled with immediate effect; the 20-year-olds due to be called up in October would follow later in the month.

This development was not entirely unexpected. The countries of Europe had been preparing for war for the past decade, and speculation had only intensified after the assassination of Archduke Franz Ferdinand in late June. On 31 July and 1 August anti-war demonstrations attracted thousands of participants in cities from Denain to Avignon, from Brest to Lyon. But it was also the height of the holiday season and other news demanded its share of the headlines. On 28 July Madame Henriette Caillaux, wife of the minister of finance, had been acquitted of murder after the trial of the summer, her actions judged a *crime passionel*. Madame Caillaux had shot Gaston Calmette, editor of *Le Figaro*, after he published a letter damaging to her husband's reputation. Three days later Jean Jaurès, leader of the French socialists and an ardent pacifist, was assassinated while eating a strawberry tart in a Paris café.

Deep in the countryside, news that the country was mobilizing might come as a complete surprise. As one smallholder in rural Languedoc recalled: 'We didn't take any newspapers [and] we seldom left the village, plus it all happened very suddenly.' Rural schools too did little to introduce their pupils to the wider world. One future infantryman (96th Infantry) remembered his teacher's comment on the assassination in Sarajevo: 'This could be an excuse for war'. But he was the exception; few of his comrades knew anything about the crisis brewing in 1914. And these southerners were not untypical. A survey conducted in 1906 had previously revealed just how little serving soldiers knew of recent French history; indeed, many were unaware that Alsace and Lorraine had been lost to Germany in the war of 1870–71.

Serving soldiers had received their marching orders on 28 July. Two days later Bandsman Meyer (74th Infantry) was with his unit in Rouen, where 'many of the men were drunk'. Trooper Henry Videau (5th Cuirassiers) was in barracks in Tours, with just enough time to dash off a letter to his parents. 'Don't be too down-hearted ...,' he told them:

> We're mobilizing, those on leave have been recalled, and so has the class of 1910. They've mobilized the whole of the east, so it's no joke. We must hope it'll go no further than that but I'm not confident. We're all confined to barracks and the trucks are waiting at the station to take us away. ... Don't worry though. If war does break out, better for us if it happens now than in four or five years' time. Right now I'm the only one with the colours [and] Raoul [his brother] won't be called up. I'm writing in haste since time is short.

Joseph Lintanf (19th Infantry) was home on leave in the Breton village of Plestin-les-Grèves (Côtes d'Armor), celebrating his sister's wedding. The mayor gave Joseph and his cousin Théophile permission to stay the night before they reported back for duty. Ernest Etienne (3rd Zouaves) was still in bed when he received his recall: 'On the morning of 31 July I was still fast asleep when my sister suddenly appeared in my room ... the gendarmes had just [called to] ask me to return to my regiment as soon as possible.'

In Mirepoix (Ariège), close to the Pyrenees, the town-crier toured the streets with news of the mobilization order. Lost property was his normal stock-in-trade and his voice rapidly failed. 'Nobody could hear him,' reported Marie-Louise Escholier. 'A crowd gathered round his silver-braided kepi and [started to] heckle: "Hey, we're not lip-readers! What a carry on!" ... At every street corner, the same hostile ring formed around him. He was as miserable as a bullock dogged by a cloud of angry flies.' In the countryside church bells or local officials broadcast the news. The bells were normally used to warn of hailstorms or fires. When people in the Limousin heard them ring, they looked up, puzzled, into a clear blue sky; elsewhere the fire brigade turned out, searching in vain for flames and smoke.

In the tiny Alpine village of Granon (Hautes-Alpes) the harvest was in full swing:

> When we heard the bells ringing, we wondered what was happening ... It was the *garde-champêtre* who brought us the news. 'We're at war, we're at war!' he told anyone he bumped into ... 'But who are we fighting?' 'Why, the Germans of course!' Once the mobilization orders and itineraries arrived, the reality of the situation began to hit home. Every able-bodied man received his papers; parting, that's what the war meant to start with. It turned the village completely upside down. Some people made a joke of it all. You'll get a summer holiday out of it. We've never had one before; make the most of it. But others were worriers, always looking on the black side. The war seemed like the end of the world for them and they wanted no part in it. Some lads went and hid in the forest. [But] in the end everyone went. In just one week the village had changed completely. There were no men left between the ages of twenty and thirty.

Conscripts had made up the bulk of the French army since 1798, with every 20-year-old male liable to spend three years with the colours. 'Young people didn't balk at military service,' recalled one stretcher-bearer from the class of 1915. 'It seemed normal to wear uniform for as long as was needed to guarantee peace.' Each January the *commune* posted a list of those deemed eligible for service, and these men then went before a board to assess their suitability. Every man was measured and weighed by a medical officer, and some were rejected immediately on medical grounds – for example, lack of stature or congenital infirmity. Serving prisoners were not excused; on completing their sentence they were sent off to the Infanterie Légère d'Afrique to man remote desert garrisons. Nor were there exemptions for conscientious objectors. It was also possible to volunteer in advance of the call-up – for three, four or five years, or for the duration. Just over 26,000 men did so in the first flush of enthusiasm in 1914. But by the following year that number had plunged to under 11,000.

In a tradition which dated back to the earliest days of conscription, towns and villages gave a big send-off to those selected for service each year, dressing them in distinctive costumes with ribbons and flowers, and giving them a special flag to carry. During wartime this custom became rather more muted, but it never disappeared entirely. As late as March 1918 Captain J.C. Dunn, a medical officer in the Royal Welsh Fusiliers, noted: 'Going on leave, I saw in Steenwerck the latest class of French conscripts leaving home for their depots. Dressed in their Sunday best, beflowered, beribboned, beflagged, befuddled, they were calling at every friend's house and being given liquor. Poor boys.'

After three years with the 'active' army, conscripts then spent eleven years in the reserves, a further seven in the territorials, and a final seven in the territorial reserves – a total of twenty-eight years in all. On mobilization in 1914 each infantry regiment and each chasseur battalion raised a reserve unit. These units were initially intended to man garrisons and lines of communication. But in the event they had to take their place in the line alongside serving soldiers: 'There is no such thing as reserves,' said Commander-in-Chief Joseph Joffre in 1915.

Some contingents of reservists set off for the front amid celebrations; others departed amid sadness and tears. On 2 August the men of the Pyrenean town of Bagnères-de-Bigorre marched to the station, led by a band and applauded by their fellow townspeople. But later that morning another contingent arrived in the town from the nearby village of Gerde. They too made their way to the station, but behind came their wives, mothers and sisters, weeping. In distant Lorraine the town of No). close to the German frontier, witnessed similar scenes: 'A noisy troop paraded in front of the Prévot works at half-past seven in the morning, singing the *Marseillaise:* it was the men from the villages ... [of] Raucourt, Abaucourt and Mailly, off to join their units. The Noméy men soon followed: women wept, children clung to their fathers, but the men kept their farewells short and their tears unshed.'

The territorials were intended only for very local, static defence. Some regiments did see action during the conflict, in emergencies such as the Race to the Sea in September 1914, but for the most part those not guarding lines of communication were used as works battalions – making and maintaining trench systems, roads and railway lines – or to guard prisoners of war.

The peacetime army contained 817,000 men, a figure increased on mobilization to 2,944,000. Altogether almost eight million men were called to the colours during the war.

Those who were small and light might qualify to join a cavalry regiment; those with any technical expertise – of railways, public works, shipyards or telecommunications – the artillery, engineers or air service. But most men went into the infantry; normally around two-thirds of all recruits, but rather more in 1915 in response to the losses sustained in the first months of the war. Around three out of every four infantrymen were peasant farmers and agricultural workers; the remainder were factory workers, small craftsmen, shop assistants, teachers or clerks. The engineers and the aviation service continued to demand appropriate qualifications, but the huge expansion of the wartime artillery quickly opened up that arm of service to a wider range of recruits. An artillery posting – indeed any posting away from the front line – was highly prized. Louis Lamothe (339th Infantry) was certainly envious of two acquaintances who went straight into the artillery in 1915: 'Perhaps they were right. Someone gave them good advice. It's much less dangerous than it is in the infantry.'

The army was structured on a local and regional basis. Each regiment recruited from a number of specific areas, and regiments from the same military region were brought together to form divisions and army corps. This system could be a source of weakness, as the British were later to discover with their Pals battalions. But its great strength was that it allowed soldiers to serve with men from their immediate locality, an advantage at a time when outsiders found regional accents or patois difficult to understand. Two country lads from the Pyrénées-Orientales ended up with the Algerians of the chasseurs d'Afrique. 'Their accent made them almost incomprehensible,' reported their sergeant, 'but they did have the gift of great good sense.' On transferring from 1st Hussars to 18th Infantry in late 1915, one soldier from Béziers felt very much alone, 'surrounded by Béarnais all speaking their own patois, with only a Toulousain and an Aveyronnais [for company]'.

A Savoyard from 108th Territorials – all from the Chambéry area – told the tale of a similar, and potentially more dangerous, experience late in 1914. He and his pals shot a partridge which fell to earth between the lines. That night the would-be hunters set off to retrieve the bird and were challenged by a sentry: '"In the name of God," [I] said. "Let's get the hell out of here. We've lost our way somehow. Whatever he's speaking, it's not French!" And did we scarper, I can tell you!' But in the light of day they realized that in fact they had never left their own lines. They had simply failed to recognize anything resembling French in the thick south-western accents of the neighbouring 129th Infantry, from Agen.

Speakers of patois were often reluctant to speak French, preferring their native tongue. Several trench newspapers continued to print articles and poems in patois, some as late as 1917: *Poil ... et Plume* (81st Infantry; Montpellier), for example, published items in Occitan; *Hurle obus* (12th Territorials; Amiens), in the Picard dialect. But personal preference did not always carry the day. Soldiers usually had no option but to speak French because that was the language used by their officers. In 1915 the future Communist leader Jacques Duclos recalled a Basque who spoke not a word of French, 'but events would force him to learn it'.

Problems of language between men from different regions were sometimes compounded by an undercurrent of prejudice and suspicion. Anxious parents sought reassurance that their loved ones were serving with men from their own area and not among 'strangers'. Georges Faleur, a medical officer in 52nd Division, came from Hirson, near the Belgian border. Faleur had mixed feelings about one man in his ranks: 'a grand lad, very obliging. His main fault was ... that like most southerners he remained an inveterate braggart: he was a know-all.' Raymond Garnung (60th Artillery), a native of Mios (Gironde), was rather more generous in return. Shortly after volunteering in 1915, Raymond reassured his sister: 'The northerners aren't as cold as people try to make out ... [they're really] very kind when you get to know them.'

Medieval historian Sergeant Marc Bloch (272nd Infantry) had little time for Bretons: 'In our view men from inland Brittany were no great shakes as soldiers. Prematurely aged, they seemed worn down by poverty and alcohol, their ignorance of [French] only adding to the impression of stupidity. To cap it all, they came from all over Brittany, so each man spoke a different dialect, and even those who knew a little French could seldom interpret for the rest.' Another officer marvelled at the hardiness of the Bretons and their ability to defy the wet of the trenches. He put it down to their native climate, living as they did 'amid fog and mist'.

The main part of the army consisted of French conscripts serving on French soil (conscripts were prevented by law from serving abroad in peacetime). However, France could also call on a number of other regiments, all raised specifically to serve in her overseas possessions – particularly in Africa and Indochina – but also available for service at home if required. Unique in offering opportunities for combat experience, these regiments were particularly attractive to energetic career officers and volunteers reluctant to spend their days mouldering in a dusty French garrison town. In 1914, therefore, they were the ones with the most recent combat experience. But the French high command largely ignored their expertise, dismissing skills gained in colonial warfare as irrelevant to any future European conflict.

XIX Corps was made up of regiments raised in north Africa from a mixture of conscripts and volunteers. The zouaves, tirailleurs and Foreign Legion were infantry regiments; the chasseurs d'Afrique and spahis, cavalry. The zouaves were conscripts raised from the white colonists, while the tirailleurs were raised among the indigenous peoples of Algeria and

Tunisia, using volunteers and a limited form of conscription. The cavalry was made up entirely of volunteers – the chasseurs recruiting from French colonists, the spahis from native Algerians.

Then there were the colonial regiments. These were of two different kinds: volunteer units recruited among French citizens in France and its colonies, and regiments raised by a system of quotas among the indigenous peoples (those from west and equatorial Africa were styled 'Senegalese', whatever their country of origin). Their main depots were in the principal French naval ports – Cherbourg, Brest, Toulon and Rochefort – and most volunteer regiments were on hand to take the field in 1914. A corps of three divisions, including regulars and reservists, became part of Fourth Army. The indigenous regiments were based overseas and none was immediately available on the outbreak of war, although they took part in increasing numbers as the conflict ground on.

Foreigners who volunteered to serve with the French Army (perhaps as many as 80,000 over the course of the conflict) were directed into the Foreign Legion. They offered their services for a variety of motives. The Swiss writer Blaise Cendrars did so out of hatred for the Germans: 'I can't abide the Boche,' he admitted. Others, like Pierre Goldfarb, a Jew of Polish extraction, joined up for love of France: 'France was for me a friend. This is why I defend her with the greatest courage.' But American Alan Seeger fought 'for the glory alone'.

'Leave model warriors!' – departure for the front

On 3 August 1914, two days after mobilization, Germany declared war on France. That evening Charles Péguy wrote to his wife with characteristic enthusiasm: 'Anyone who didn't see Paris today and yesterday has seen nothing.' Crowds of people crammed the streets of the capital, shouting 'To Berlin!' 'Down with the Prussians!' 'Bring back the Kaiser's moustache!'. In an excess of zeal, some Parisians turned on the premises of companies with German-sounding names, among them Singer sewing machines (American) and Maggi soups (Swiss).

The 41-year-old Péguy had volunteered as soon as war broke out and was commissioned as a sous-lieutenant in 276th Infantry. A socialist writer and philosopher, Péguy fought for the highest of principles: 'I leave [for the front] ... in the cause of universal disarmament and the war to end all wars,' he wrote in one of his farewell letters. 'If I don't return,' he advised another friend, 'remember me without sorrow. Thirty years of life is as nothing compared with what we'll be doing over the next few weeks.'

Others saw the war as an opportunity to reunite France with Alsace and

Lorraine, lost to Germany in the war of 1870–71. Philippe-Jean Grange, just 17 years old, was eagerly anticipating the call. 'For over a year,' he boasted, 'I had never gone to bed without first swearing the oath to liberate Alsace and Lorraine.' In Rennes Lieutenant Paul Valle (74th Infantry) was buoyed by the enthusiasm of the locals, who he normally found quite indifferent to the subject: 'Everyone is longing for war. ... After forty-four years of humiliation the hour of revenge is nigh.' On 31 July the military academy at Saint-Cyr held an improvised passing-out ceremony for the class of 1913. Newly commissioned officer Jean Allard-Meeus chose to recite a poem to a small group of his peers:

> Soldiers of our illustrious race ...
> Sleep, beyond the frontiers
> Soon you will be sleeping at home.

Some members of Languedoc's small Protestant communities found the idea of war attractive for another reason. They saw it as a necessary precursor to the moral regeneration of France: 'God willed the war for our own good, as a reawakening, to force self-discipline upon us.' But Sergeant Robert Hertz (44th Territorials) reported that one of his Catholic comrades found this kind of thinking hard to accept: 'The idea that one of us could embrace this war as a salutary event and welcome it as the culminating moment of his life seemed to him like mystical nonsense.'

Others believed in the justice of the French cause: 'We have right, reason and justice on our side. There's no question about it: it isn't France that wants war.' Or they fought from simple patriotism: 'I was happy to go and defend my country,' said one reservist (58th Infantry).

Corentin Carré, barely 15, was the youngest of nine children born to a poor peasant farmer of Faoüet (Morbihan). Adopting the identity of an older refugee, he volunteered and found himself in 410th Infantry:

> I didn't join up so people would talk about me, so they would say there's goes a brave man. I prefer to remain anonymous and seek my personal satisfaction from doing my duty ... one more soldier cannot save France on his own but he can play his part! France needs all her children. We must all be ready to lay down our lives. I couldn't survive under the yoke of an enemy forever flaunting his superiority ... A full life is the only one worth living.

But not everyone was enthusiastic about the war. In the Limousin, as in Granon, some men talked about taking to the woods to escape mobilization. At Tostat, near Pau, the village priest preached an inflammatory sermon. 'It's our own fault if we're at war,' he claimed. He went on praise the Kaiser and Emperor Franz Joseph, and to vilify the French president, Raymond Poincaré, as a puppet in the hands of the prime minister, 'that rogue' Viviani. He was arrested that same afternoon.

A small minority of leftists opposed the war wholeheartedly and continued to do so, adopting Lenin's dictum that 'The proletariat has no country'. In the Jura 36-year-old day labourer Paul Petit addressed a crowd some 200 strong: 'If France needs men, let her go out and buy some; anyone who answers the call-up is a coward, a fool or an idler. We shouldn't consent to it; I certainly won't!' Petit too was arrested and immediately handed over to the provosts to be taken to Besançon for court martial. However, the main parties of the left fell into line to support the war. The socialists argued that they were fighting imperialism and German militarism, rather than the German nation. As leader of the CGT, France's largest trade union, Léon Jouhaux gave an improvised address at the funeral of Jean Jaurès: 'We rise up to repel the invader [and] to safeguard the legacy bequeathed to us by history – a legacy of civilization and generosity of spirit.' The influential socialist writer Gustave Hervé also rallied to the cause: 'National defence first. They have killed Jaurès. We will not kill France.'

In an address delivered to Parliament on 4 August, President Poincaré invoked for the first time the idea of a sacred union: 'In the war now beginning France ... will be defended heroically by all her sons. Nothing will break their sacred union in the face of the enemy.' Organizations from left and right flocked to support this non-partisan approach to the conduct of the war. In Albi local socialists agreed to postpone an anti-war meeting arranged in honour of Jaurès, a local man. 'I called the organizers to a meeting in my office,' explained the prefect. 'They recognized that the mobilization order had changed the situation and promised to advise their comrades to disperse voluntarily and abandon the demonstration. They kept their word. No demonstration took place.'

Victorin Bès was a 19-year-old socialist from Castres, the birthplace of Jaurès:

> It's important for me to believe that our politicians want peace. It's true to say that moral responsibility for the current state of affairs rests with the capitalist regimes of the countries involved, the armed peace, the conflict of interest between industrialists and mine-owners. But who declared war? Germany. Who was attacked? France.

Conscription was all-encompassing, drawing in men of every political opinion, so the army naturally included committed pacifists, like Louis Barthas, as well as militarists. Barthas, a 35-year-old cooper from the village of Peyriac-Minervois (Aude) was recalled to serve with 125th Territorials. In his opinion, mobilization was 'the greatest scourge of all, the source of all [our] ills'. It was 'the prelude to war, vile, accursed war, bringing disgrace on our century, besmirching the civilization of which we were [so] proud.' But Barthas went on to serve throughout the war. Like him, most men simply resigned themselves to their lot. 'I was unhappy, but I fell in,' commented one veteran of the class of 1912.

In the countryside there were other preoccupations. With men and horses gone, who would bring in the harvest, till the land, and sow the seed for next year's crops? Shortage of labour quickly became apparent in the Côtes-du-Nord. 'We are feeling the lack of manpower,' reported the prefect, 'and on the big farms many fields have been left fallow.' At a smaller Provençal farm news of the call-up immediately halved the workforce: 'When the gendarmes came ... grandfather, Uncle Victor, father and me ... were in the barn, putting the hay in the loft ... Uncle Victor went with them, and so did my poor father. That only left grandfather and me.' And back in Plestin-les-Grèves Joseph Lintanf's parents were left to work their Breton farm with their three daughters and a 13-year-old boy.

Many communities in the Lot 'organized themselves ... to fill in for the farmhands leaving [for the front]'. In the Yonne women and old men were to the fore. 'The women', reported the prefect, 'have gathered up their husbands' scythes ... loaded the sheaves, spread the manure, guided the harrow. Some have even taken over the ploughing. But it's the old men in particular who are back at the head of the family, keeping an eye on the children and young mothers, and running the farm. They're out ploughing again, threshing the grain and driving the sheep to pasture.'

But the work was hot and tiring – even for those with machines to help them. In Brittany the Lintanfs had just acquired a reaper-binder, one of the first in the area: '[but] we still hadn't got used to it,' reported 18-year-old Léonie, '[and] the grain was heavy'. In the Gard 'the grape harvest didn't suffer. It went off as normal, or as near as matters ... [But it] was nothing like previous years: no whoops of laughter, no saucy stories, no dancing in the shade of the trees to the sound of clarinet and oboe: silence reigned. At mealtimes people chatted about the war or read newspapers out loud.'

The war did not just strip the countryside of its young men. Horses too were needed in enormous numbers; in 1914 alone 750,000 were requisitioned. Horses remained the backbone of farm life and giving them up was hard to bear. 'Farmers boasted to us of the[ir] qualities, of their docility, they told us how we should handle them,' recalled one officer. 'Then they went away quietly, heavy of heart, not daring to turn around ... Most of them were older men ... [who had also] seen their sons leave for the war.' A contemporary comic postcard showed a woman pleading with the requisitioning officer, 'Keep my husband at the front as long as you like but don't take my mare!'

After the initial excitement, Marc Bloch found life in Paris

> quiet and rather sombre. There was much less traffic, and with no buses [and] few motor taxis the streets were almost silent. There was little sign of the sadness deep within each heart, just lots of women with red, swollen eyes. People chatted in the streets, in the shops, on the trams; there was a general feeling of togetherness, visible in words and gestures which were clumsy and naïve but touching nonetheless. ... Few men were cheerful; [but all] were resolute which perhaps was more important.

A member of 2nd Engineers recalled the scene at their Montpellier barracks: 'Officers shook hands cordially with the lowliest privates. I made my farewells to a medical orderly, scarcely managing to keep a lid on my emotions; we took leave of each other without any fuss. There was no great outpouring of enthusiasm, but good cheer vanquished our underlying sadness. It really was a grand sight.'

Captain Alphonse Grasset (107th Infantry) was struck by the eagerness of his men as they prepared for war: 'Still only young people here and the most intense delight evident on most of the faces. I must say I've never seen such enthusiasm for a field day in the woods of Issy-les-Moulineaux!' But emotion still had to be tempered by discipline. When the mobilization order was read out to a parade of the 2nd Foreign Legion Regiment in Morocco, one man cried out *'Vive la France!'*. He promptly received thirty days' confinement for talking on parade.

Newly torn from their jobs and families, many reservists were reluctant soldiers. In Rodez, for example, Gratien Rigaud bedded down with some reservists in the barracks of 122nd Infantry: 'They weren't cheerful like us,' he recalled. 'No need to [say] why.' Jules Besson-Girerd was planning to marry on 18 August. Instead he found himself on his way to the front with 27th Chasseurs. 'I've been posted to the regulars,' he wrote to his sister on 8 August, 'and we're marching to face the fire in the front line. It's hardly what we'd want but what can we do? France is asking us to lay down our lives and we're all willing to do so.' Signing himself as 'your brother who believes his life destroyed', Besson-Girerd died in Lorraine later that month. On 2 August Joséphin Adam (112th Infantry) was in good spirits as left for Toulon: '[I'm] full of hope because instead of being first to march to the front line I think the 112th will be heading for the Italian frontier.' Joséphin was wrong – his regiment went straight to Lorraine; nevertheless, he appears to have survived the war.

The 31st Infantry was part of the Paris garrison. On 7 August the regiment marched out of the city's Tourelle Barracks to the sound of the stirring old tunes *Sambre et Meuse* and the *Chant du départ*. Corporal Jean Galtier-Boissière remembered 'women tossing flowers [at us]; we stuck them in the muzzles of our rifles'. In the Vendée a special mass was celebrated in La Roche-sur-Yon for the men of 93rd Infantry. The Abbé Rousseau described the scene: 'The whole regiment filled the huge nave. Many of those who tomorrow would be heroes wished to make Christian preparation, certain they would conduct themselves bravely in battle. Local priests who had been called to the colours heard the confessions of their comrades.'

Chaos reigned at the main Paris railway stations. On reaching the Gare d'Orsay, Captain Grasset found dense crowds blocking the surrounding area: 'Cars and buses, improbably overloaded with parcels and trunks, were forcing their way through, with no accidents that I could see.' A further surprise lay within: 'As if by magic, the train had been strewn with flowers and flags. It was impossible to guess where they'd all come from – they seemed to have fallen from the sky.' In Bordeaux, too, confidence was high: the trains were all painted with slogans – 'Luxury train to Berlin', 'The Bordelais to Berlin'.

Elsewhere in the hubbub, the newly minted Sous-lieutenant Marcel Carpentier, straight out of Saint-Cyr, was also struggling to reach his train:

> We worked our way with difficulty through the crowd, greatcoats rolled across our shoulders, each carrying a laundry bag with everything listed in the instructions for mobilization. I had scoured the shops in vain for a sabre and a holster for my revolver ... I drew a greatcoat myself [and] got my sous-lieutenant's braid sewn to my Saint-Cyr kepi. My lieutenant lent me a sabre ... If only I'd known how little use I'd make of it!

Once on board the train the regiments headed eastwards.

In the haste to mobilize, Carpentier was not the only soldier to leave his depot without the proper equipment. En route to joining 2nd Chasseurs in Lunéville, Sous-lieutenant Michelon had to take advantage 'of a short stop in Nancy to buy an infantry officer's sabre and a stout pair of hunting shoes at the Dames de France [department store]'. Michelon had also forgotten to acquire trousers in the regulation dark blue-grey of the chasseurs; to his shame he had to parade for the first time with his men in the red trousers of the 'ordinary' line infantry, contrary to all the traditions of his new unit.

The Naval Brigade, commanded by Admiral Ronarc'h, was raised from naval reservists. Rushing to garrison Paris in the first days of the war, the Brest unit set off in cattle trucks – no straw, no benches, just the bare floor to sit on. And transport was not their only problem: 'We left Brest in our jumpers. We didn't have greatcoats at that time. We even had to make our own equipment braces out of string. The captain had no holster for his revolver and carried it on a lanyard. And the rifles from the arsenal at Brest looked fine from the outside, very well-maintained; but in fact half of them had broken springs.'

At trackside and station, civilians gathered to sing patriotic songs – the *Marseillaise*, *Chant du départ* or *Chanson des Girondins*. In the spa town of Contrexéville Louis Donati (55th Artillery) was happy to find 'elegant ladies handing out sweets, cigarettes [and] fresh water'. Victor André (111th Infantry) was equally grateful: 'Throughout the journey, every station, every halt was full of women and girls giving us wine and grenadine to quench our thirst, for it was very hot in those trucks.' But Marcel Papillon (356th Infantry) was a little embarrassed by all the attention showered on his regiment: 'At Nancy they gave us all kinds of things – oranges, lemons, fruit pastilles, drinks, mints, tobacco, cigarettes – we couldn't get away from civilians.'

From the commander-in-chief to the lowliest private, the French went to war in 1914 believing that the fighting would be over within weeks. Issued in 1913, the French field service regulations argued the case that 'in any future war, the size of the forces involved, the difficulties of resupply [and] the interruption of the social and economic life of the nation [will] all encourage the search for a decision in the shortest possible time so as to end the fighting quickly'.

One man from the Beauce, south-west of Paris, was equally optimistic. Quizzed by a friend, he was confident that his military experience would be a short one:

'When are you off?' asked his pal.

'I'm leaving on the second,' he answered.

'The twenty-fifth for me,' said the friend.

'Oh, that won't be necessary,' the man reassured him. 'We'll be back by then.'

In one Languedoc village a neighbour came visiting: '[he] came round to say goodbye to us, certain he'd be back in a fortnight.' Sergeant-Major Paul Fontanille (6th Chasseurs Alpins) was rather less sanguine: 'Tears when we said goodbye. Personally, I'm not at all apprehensive, but who knows what the future holds. There are lots of rumours doing the rounds already. The war's going to last a fortnight etc. Myself, I reckon two months at least.'

In any short war the opening battles would be crucial, so Joffre's first objective was to get the maximum number of men into uniform as quickly as possible. By 8 August he had assembled four armies along the Belgian, Luxembourg and German frontiers, with a fifth kept in reserve. Joffre placed his armies in a relatively central position, in theory allowing him to strike in a variety of directions. But in practice a number of political constraints limited his freedom of action. In the east he had to attack; the imperative to free Alsace and Lorraine, lost in 1871, and French treaty obligations to Russia compelled him to take the offensive. In the north, however, the opposite was true. Despite the very real threat of a German attack through Belgium, Joffre was hindered by the need to respect Belgian neutrality. Britain had promised to intervene in the event of a land war. But how sincere were those promises? Invading Belgium might be enough to provoke perfidious Albion into withdrawing its much-needed support.

Joffre was also constrained in his planning by reservations over the quality of his troops. Training in peacetime had been conducted almost entirely within the regiment. Lack of money and a shortage of large training grounds had limited the number of large-scale field exercises, and no conscript served through the entire four-year cycle of manoeuvres – with exercises at brigade level in years one and two, army corps level in year three and army level in year four. One pre-war inspection report summed up the results: 'As I have said elsewhere, and as these manoeuvres have shown, the soldiers of XVI Corps are lively, intelligent, polite, sober and tough, but they have to be led.'

The training offered to reservists and territorials was even more limited. Reservists were recalled for forty days each year, in two periods of twenty-three and seventeen days, and spent much of their time in barracks, thanks to the shortage of suitable exercise grounds. The territorials had one nine-day training period a year; the territorial reserves, one day only. In Nevers (Nièvre) Lieutenant Gaudin (64th Territorials) took the desperate step of committing suicide on the outbreak of war, 'fearful of the responsibility of commanding, at a time of mobilization, a regiment which in his opinion was inadequately prepared'.

Gaudin was not alone in his concerns. Joffre was reluctant to place his reserve units in the front line, fearing they would crumble under the stress of combat. A member of 118th Infantry noticed an immediate difference between regulars and reservists: 'a 25-kilometre march was no problem for the regulars. [However,] our reservists, unaccustomed to this sort of game, dragged their feet the whole way and were forever asking the MO to see to their grazes and blisters.' After their first taste of action, Marc Bloch wondered how his troops would react to the sight of a wounded comrade: 'I covered [the] terrible wound with a cloth, anxious to hide it from my men. We think of farm workers and factory hands as tough but often they're quite sensitive.'

Lack of confidence in his reserve units now led Joffre into a serious error of strategy. Assuming the enemy reservists to be no more reliable than their French counterparts, he concluded that the Germans would lack the numbers needed to push through Belgium and consequently focused his resources further south – in Alsace and Lorraine. Even when French intelligence provided a complete German order of battle, Joffre remained unpersuaded. But he was wrong. In fact, well-trained reserve formations played a key role in German invasion plans, and the enemy had ample troops to drive its main attack through Belgium.

In the rear areas spy-mania was at its height. Unsuspecting individuals came under suspicion for the most trivial of reasons. Warned to be wary of German spies, Robert Deville (17th Artillery) and his fellow officers were enjoying their after-dinner coffee on the evening of 8 August. Suddenly in walked a civilian, 'quite tall, with a blonde beard, a pipe in his mouth, wearing a green cap. We fell upon him and placed him under arrest. On further interrogation he turned out to be from the local highways department. What the devil was he doing wearing a green cap?'

There was another narrow escape at Pont-sur-Sambre, near the Belgian border. *Garde civile* [an auxiliary policeman] Désiré Hounière was at home when he heard a knock at his door. He found a woman standing there, scared out of her wits: 'There's a Prussian,' she cried, 'there's a Prussian at the gate. Shoot [him], shoot.' Hounière went outside and saw a man in uniform: 'I fired. I didn't know who I was shooting at.' His target retaliated, hitting the *garde* in the chest. 'I realized that I'd fired on a captain in the Customs,' continued Hounière. 'I sincerely regret my mistake. I've no idea how I could've done such a thing.'

The *Express du Midi* ran a real scoop on 13 August. Mysterious car drivers had reportedly appeared in several villages deep in the countryside of the Corrèze and the Lot, 'handing out poisoned sweets to children as they pass by. At Figeac seven individuals disguised as women threw their deadly sweetmeats to the little ones.' Seventeen such cases had been reported and in Cahors one child had died. 'Everything leads [us] to believe that we're dealing with Germans,' concluded the *Express*. 'An absurd tissue of lies,' snorted the prefect; but the stories carried on circulating for several months thereafter. And suspicion continued to fall on the Swiss-owned company Maggi: on 10 September *Le Correspondant* warned that pre-war German spy-rings had put up posters for Maggi soups and Kub-brand bouillon cubes to mark points of great strategic significance. The newspaper advised its readers to tear them down immediately.

Such episodes have an air of black comedy. But in the febrile atmosphere of the time events could quickly turn sour. Luigi Barzini, a journalist for the Italian newspaper *Corriere della Sera*, was travelling behind the front when a gendarme stopped him and asked to see his papers. 'We have to be very careful,' said the gendarme, 'because we're surrounded by spies. We shot three here just yesterday morning, one of them a woman. I was the executioner, I presided over the court-martial and we didn't hang about.' The whole incident was over in less than half an hour.

'The trumpet of war signals the hour of the fight' – the Battles of the Frontiers

Having assembled his forces, Joffre now revealed his strategy – to isolate the German right flank in Belgium and pin the enemy left in Alsace, before going on to rupture the centre. Joffre deployed his troops accordingly: while a small force advanced into Alsace, First and Second Armies would move into Lorraine, south of the fortifications of Metz-Thionville; Third and Fourth Armies would advance north of Metz-Thionville into Belgium and Luxembourg; and, finally, Fifth Army would cover the left flank in Belgium.

Clashes had already taken place on the Franco-German frontier. A German cavalry patrol crossed the border on 2 August, even before the official declaration of war. Near Jonchery, just outside the fortress town of Belfort, they encountered a detachment of 44th Infantry. A bullet hit Corporal André Peugeot, a teacher in civilian life, who died of his wound later that morning. Corporal Peugeot was the first French soldier to be killed in the conflict.

The French met with no resistance when they first crossed into Alsace and Lorraine. In Alsace units entered Mulhouse and reached the outskirts of Colmar. And all seemed quiet when a battalion of chasseurs alpins (alpine troops) arrived in the town of Dieuze (Moselle). 'Our men were light-hearted,' reported Georges Bertrand (6th Chasseurs Alpins). 'They were keen to try their hand at reading the shop signs and said they'd be speaking German within a fortnight. There's nothing funnier than hearing these country lads from the Basque provinces, the Cévennes, the Dauphiné, the Alps or Provence ... doing their best to twist their tongues around the language of the northern barbarians.'

But the Germans soon put a stop to these diversions. The chasseur battalion was one of the first French units into combat, and also one of the first to suffer at the hands of well-handled German machine-guns:

> Every time a machine-gun opened up nearby, the men strained to hear whether it was one of ours or one of theirs. And each time someone said, 'It's the coffee-grinder', a little shiver ran through the ranks. The German machine-gun certainly deserved its nickname. It couldn't change speed, which was actually a weakness, and when fired it made a steadier noise than ours. I can't think of anything more disheartening in the midst of battle – when everything is noise and confusion ... than the remorseless sound of this instrument of death.

As the French advanced, they collided with the Germans in a series of disastrous encounters. Antoine Biesse (143rd Infantry) found himself in action on 20 August:

> From my position behind a tree, I fired and kept on firing. To increase my rate of fire, I emptied out two packets of rounds by my side and took them straight from the pile ... We were so strung out that we couldn't for a moment stop and think about what was in store for us ... In front of the platoon, Sous-lieutenant Marty continually urged us on. Sabre in his right hand, revolver in his left, he marched straight at the enemy. We followed very close behind but alas we [soon] had to stop. We had scarcely covered ten metres when our beloved sous-lieutenant fell, mortally wounded. Impossible to go any further and without hesitation we dropped to the ground.

Biesse, too, soon lay wounded between the lines. 'I lost all hope,' he recalled. 'You couldn't breathe; the smell was foul because [so] many were dead. The crows ... were already there, all over my comrades. It was truly horrific.'

Father Ernest Brec (77th Infantry) was a cleric serving as an infantryman: 'The ordinary soldier knew nothing and I got the impression that our officers didn't know much more either.' But Brec felt there was some virtue in this ignorance. As he and his pals went into action on 23

August, they were 'strung out in a skirmish line in fields of oats and lucerne, hearing bullets whistle past for the first time. There was no emotion in the ranks because we didn't realize the danger. It was a different kettle of fish when 77s from the German field artillery began to burst over our heads. Then there was a bit of panic, which our good captain quickly brought under control.'

Some officers tried to encourage their men by a show of coolness under fire. Charles Chenu (226th Infantry) was close at hand when one of his officers was hit by a shrapnel ball: '"It's nothing," was all he said. "A bit of shrapnel in the back. Nothing serious. Who's got the tweezers?" ... And right there and then, in the face of our invisible enemy, the bugler picked out the fragment, and the captain put his shirt on again without a word.'

Captain Ferdinand Belmont (11th Chasseurs Alpins) was astonished to survive his first taste of action: 'How did I get to the wooded hillock our alpine battery and our machine-gun were occupying?' he wondered. 'At the very least how did I avoid being wounded that day? It was a miracle; I noticed afterwards that four bullets had hit me: one just nicked my knapsack, another went through my aluminium water-bottle, a third went right through my pack; and the fourth hit the butt of the rifle I was carrying in my hand. [But] thanks be to God I came out safe and sound.'

Reservist Germain Cuzacq (234th Infantry) went into action at Delme on 20 August: 'It was 08.30 am. Everyone was scared stiff. [They] didn't know where to put themselves.' One anonymous Marseillais (141st Infantry) later described his experience of combat in Lorraine in a letter to his local newspaper:

At dawn we returned to our regiment, close to the marshes at Bénestroff. That was the start of the most violent attack [imaginable]; the whole of XV Corps was deployed and advanced in the face of artillery, machine-guns and Mausers. We were up to the waist in water and mud [and] many men drowned there. Things seemed to be going our way, but around 10.00 am a remarkable change took place; the enemy guns were firing at no more than 3,300 metres and we had no cover. Meanwhile the Boche army was firmly entrenched on the heights. ... Around 11.00 am the chasseur battalions which launched the attack began to give ground with appalling losses. The order was given to fall back to Dieuze, so we started to withdraw under the fire of 210s and machine-guns. But still the buglers ... continued to sound the charge.

Men were scattered all over the heavily wooded countryside, searching desperately for their regiments. The Marseillais found a companion and together they scoured the countryside around Dieuze looking for their battalion: 'But when we found them they were even more lost than we were. You must realize that absolute chaos reigned in that small Lorraine town – infantrymen, artillerymen dragging their bulky caissons, first- and second-line transport, the shining cars of our shining staff – all met up there, uncertain what to do or where to go. If this wasn't a retreat, we were at the very least falling back in a hurry.'

Troops of 322nd Infantry also took part in the retreat from Dieuze. Around Lunéville, recalled one infantryman, 'the ground [was] strewn with red trousers'. As the troops pulled back,

> Machine-gun bullets fell upon a rabble which no longer bore any resemblance to an army ... villages [were] completely destroyed, burned, ransacked and deserted. Hens, cattle, horses and goats wandered everywhere ... The dead weren't buried quickly enough. By the side of the road dead horses gave off a foul smell. The medical corps was found wanting. We had a lot of wounded, among them many officers and sergeants ... so the men were left rudderless. At the least sign of danger they ran every which way; it was all extremely demoralizing.

Yet an underlying discipline still remained. It only needed a few provosts to take action, providing a rallying point for each regiment, for the units to reassemble.

Further north, Third and Fourth Armies were faring little better. Jean Galtier-Boissière (31st Infantry) was part of Third Army. By 24 August his regiment had been fighting in the Ardennes for two solid days, never catching a glimpse of the enemy but sustaining a constant stream of casualties from German artillery.

Then came the order to attack: 'In front of us the hillside is stripped bare: not a tree, not a wall, not a fold in the ground ... Bullets whistle, shrapnel flies; great shells raise huge fountains of earth ... Deafened, ears ringing, I can't hear the orders being shouted ... Deaf, dumb, drunk with dust and noise, I walk on as if in a trance. Just one idea, one purpose in mind ... Forward! Forward!'

Suddenly the bugler sounded the charge:

> Now we're moving forward in bounds. At a signal from the adjutant we stand up ... run straight ahead, weighed down by our packs, hampered by pouches, waterbottle, haversack ... then we throw

ourselves to the ground ... Some men stumble as we run, others are hit in the head as they get up. The bullets come in quick succession, very low down ...

Another bound! ... We still can't see the enemy machine-gunners. We haven't fired a single round yet. There's only about a dozen of us left ... I stay absolutely still, crouched down between two big mounds of earth. I hear the coffee-grinders close by: tac-tac-tac. The bullets stream past; what a hellish din. 'This one's mine,' I think every time I hear a shot ...

Suddenly I hear someone shout, 'Fall back. We're withdrawing!' Bewildering. But it's right ... The adjutant signals that we should crawl towards a small potato-field. I move forward on my elbows, on my thighs, my forehead hard up against the hobnailed boots of a comrade. Made it! All around bullets are whipping up the earth, chopping down the hay ... We're about twenty metres from a main road bordered by trees ... The ditch alongside is salvation. But we've got to cross an area swept by fire ... One man leaps up, takes a few steps, then collapses without a sound, face to the ground ... Another flings himself forward and gets halfway, rolls over like a stuck rabbit, and clutching his stomach shouts '*Oh là là ! Oh là là!*' A third man sets off, comes to a dead halt, swings round, his face covered with blood, and collapses, moaning like a small child, 'Mother, oh! Mother' ... I'm the last, I run as hard as I can, jump into the ditch and huddle down there: I'm safe! I'm afraid our losses are very high. The lieutenant-colonel, the battalion commander, and three-quarters of the officers are [all] out of action ... We approach each other with doleful countenances. We talk in hushed tones. The regiment appears to be in mourning.

Galtier-Boissière continued,

Ever since we left Paris, the *Bulletin des armées* has upheld in us the blessed illusion that war would be a snap. We all believed the line that the Boche would surrender for a *tartine*. Convinced of the crushing superiority of our artillery and our aircraft, we imagined in our innocence that the campaign would be nothing more than a military parade, a rapid succession of brilliant, easy victories. By showing us the terrifying disparity between the engines of death and the puny soldier ... today's crack of thunder suddenly brought it home to us that the struggle just beginning would be a terrible ordeal.

Battle made particular demands on the artillery: 'Our artillerymen, under fire for the first time, showed admirable courage and coolness,' reported Robert Deville. 'They had no possibility of taking action, they had to await their orders. They never wavered in their effort to remain steady. I was proud of them and proud to be their leader. Deep down I knew they were setting me a fine example and I tried to do the same for them. I was already aware that I wanted to be worthy of the generations of soldiers from whom I am descended. I learned today that one must also be worthy of the men one commands.'

But Paul Lintier (44th Artillery) wasn't feeling cool, simply frightened and confused:

> The infantry platoons deploy on the slopes of a horseshoe of hills and advance in bounds. With no warning the men stand up and immediately start to run; then suddenly, to an inaudible word of command, they fall down, they disappear as if through a trap-door. The infantrymen move off. Just for a moment we can see them still, dark silhouettes passing over the crest of the hill ... And now the column stops in this potato field so churned up by machine-gun fire that it's hard to pick a path between the shell-holes for the wagons. What are we waiting for? At least let's deploy our guns ... Let's fight back! ... In these desperate moments I think we would be gripped less by fear if we could hear our 75s firing. Don't let's bleed to death ... Come on, let's fight! ... [But] here we stay, stock still ... I'm sweating ... I'm scared. Yet I know perfectly well that I won't run away, that I'll let myself be killed right here ... But come on, let's fight!

Lintier's battery eventually deployed in a field of oats, just below the ridgeline: 'But the captain, down on his knees amid the crops, out in front of the battery, field-glasses raised, can't make out a thing. There still seems to be a thick mist hanging around down there, over the great woods of Ethe and Etalle occupied by the enemy.'

As the retreating infantrymen began to stream past in ever-increasing numbers, the officers conferred: 'But what do you want to do? ... we've no orders, no orders at all,' said the commanding officer.

The battery eventually pulled out. 'We've lost the battle,' thought Lintier. 'I don't know why or how. I didn't see a thing.'

Alphonse Grasset vividly described an infantry attack: 'Among the bodies stretched out on the ground, [I] could no longer tell the living from the dead: the former, eagerly concentrating on their task, the others, motionless, still in the position they occupied when surprised by death.

The only frightening sight was the wounded. Some raised themselves up to their full height, in the midst of the fire, covered in blood, a few of them quite hideous. They ran aimlessly, arms out before them, eyes fixed on the ground, turning round and round.'

On the left the Germans were flooding through Belgium in much greater strength than anticipated. On 21 August medical orderly Dr Georges Veaux (41st Infantry) watched a German attack develop east of Charleroi: 'We had an excellent view of it all, without being in any great danger ourselves, because the German attack column passed without stopping at Mornimont and went into action at Ham-sur-Sambre, defended by 1st Battalion. The sound of frantic gunfire rang out, volleys alternating with independent fire. We were horrified to see flames everywhere: everything was on fire – villages, forests, isolated farms. The German artillery began to fire back in the direction of Ham.'

Among those defending the village was Yves-Marie Conan:

> There was another railway line in front of us and behind that an enormous meadow – our 75s had already found its range – which stretched as far as the village occupied by the Germans. [They] started to crawl across this meadow ... unaware that our machine-gun section had taken up position thirty metres behind us ... When the Boche arrived within fifty metres of the railway embankment ahead of us, our machine-guns opened fire ... the German battalion was in the meadow, out in the open, with no cover, swept by bursts of shellfire, mown down by our machine-guns, and picked off by the rest of us. After half an hour there was nothing left ... but the dead and the dying.

However, the victory at Ham-sur-Sambre could not stop the enemy advance; the Germans simply crossed the river further west, forcing the 41st to withdraw. Paradoxically, Joffre took heart from the ferocity of the German attack. Surely they must have weakened their centre to strengthen the right, so making it ripe for his decisive thrust? But events were proving Joffre disastrously wrong. In fact, the Germans were present in far greater strength than anticipated all along the line. Even now Joffre was slow to recognize the reality of the situation, and the shortcomings of peacetime training began to make their effects felt. The French armies blundered into their opponents without undertaking proper reconnaissance, and senior officers were so wedded to the idea of the offensive that formations and units were thrown into the attack without proper artillery support, and suffered accordingly.

The French cavalry expected to take action in the traditional grand style. On 4 August an officer of 11th Cuirassiers reminded his men: 'under no circumstances does a cuirassier have anything to fear from an infantryman and he should always be first to charge his opponent. Always use your sword by pointing it. Don't slash, point. Pointing, that's your best option.'

Unlike its British counterpart, the French cavalry shunned dismounted action. In 1914 the catalogue of a leading military publisher listed 157 books concerning the cavalry; of these only thirty-seven were devoted to the care of the horse, and just three to combat on foot. At one pre-war staff exercise the colonel commanding the cavalry attached to an army corps was asked for a solution to the problem under discussion:

'I'd charge!' came the reply.

'And your machine-guns? What will do you with them?' enquired the general.

'They'll charge with me!' replied the colonel.

In the event the French cavalry found few opportunities to point and slash. Weakened by poor fodder and long hot marches along paved roads (12th Cuirassiers covering over 670 kilometres during August alone), its performance did not impress. On the French left, Sordet's cavalry corps reportedly lost one-sixth of its personnel without sustaining 'a single wound from a sabre'.

The twelve cuirassier regiments went to war in their heavy metal breastplates – seven kilograms of highly polished steel for the troopers, nickel-plate for the officers. In September Lieutenant Touzet de Vigier (9th Cuirassiers) was on reconnaissance on the Aisne. Approaching his objective, he fell in with some infantry and had a word with their colonel. '"Morsain, you say?" replied the colonel. "But my good friend, it's crammed full of Germans! Our patrols haven't been able to get anywhere near it. We've been trying to gain the ridges since this morning without success ... What the devil do you want to go there for? They'll cut you to pieces for sure ... Now, my dear chap, we'd be awfully grateful if you didn't hang around here with your huge horse and your shiny cuirass. It's a magnet for shells."'

Two days later the lieutenant souvenired a brand-new British waterproof coat, abandoned during the retreat from Mons, and immediately put it on over his cuirass. His men were less fortunate; they had to fashion covers out of their kit bags. Other regiments quickly took similar action – men were ordered to make their own covers, and in some cases to urinate on the cuirass to dull the shine. Nevertheless, the cuirass remained in use until 1916.

But not everyone sought to hide the most visible parts of their uniform. 'Let us swear,' said Sous-lieutenant Jean Allard-Meeus, as he graduated from Saint-Cyr, 'that the first time we go into action we will do so wearing our *casoars* [the distinctive red and white plumes of the cadet's head-dress] and white gloves.' Around a dozen of his fellow cadets swore to do so. On 22 August, clad in casoar and white gloves, Allard-Meeus was killed in action with 162nd Infantry. On the same day, and under heavy fire, his fellow cadet Alain de Fayolle (50th Infantry) calmly reached into his knapsack. Donning his plume and gloves, he rose to his feet, shouting 'Forward, lads! For France!' He too was immediately cut down.

The Saint-Cyr incident received an enormous amount of publicity, especially on the part of journalist and politician Maurice Barrès. Louis Thomas (66th Chasseurs) was also cheered by this 'splendid gesture [which] reunited the youth of France with their predecessors of the Revolution and the Empire'. But the numbers involved were small – by no means the whole of the graduating classes, as sometimes implied. One officer later recalled that, of his 456 classmates, 288 had survived the war; none of them, he maintained, had ever gone into action wearing plume and gloves.

With the battles of the Frontiers, the French offensive ended in complete failure. Much of the inevitable criticism fell on just one element of Second Army, the southerners of XV Corps. This formation had sustained heavy casualties in and around the village of Lagarde (Moselle) on 11 August, bringing the French advance to a complete halt. Eight days later the Germans counter-attacked, catching the French by surprise. XV Corps was forced back, and with them the whole of First and Second Armies. Casualty levels were high: between 10 and 20 August XV Corps (with a fighting strength of around 30,000 men) lost 4,160 killed, including 3,370 during the German counter-attack.

Writing in *Le Matin* just four days later, Paris senator Auguste Gervais placed the blame squarely on the shoulders of XV Corps:

A division of [that corps], made up of contingents from Antibes, Toulon, Marseille and Aix, gave way in the face of the enemy ... Despite the efforts of the other army corps involved in the operation, whose conduct was irreproachable, the shortcomings of part of XV Corps led to a retreat right along the line ... Overwhelmed no doubt by the appalling impact of battle, the troops of gentle Provence were seized by sudden panic. To the rigours of military punishment must be added the public confession of their unpardonable weakness. The soldiers of the Midi, who have so many fine fighting qualities, will ... feel it a matter of honour to erase the affront to French valour so recently perpetrated by some of their comrades.

The prejudice shown by Gervais was shared by many army officers. Southerners were already the object of suspicion – partly the result of pre-war political tensions. In 1907, for example, a local regiment had mutinied rather than put down a demonstration by Languedoc wine-growers. 'Some regiments in XV Corps contain an abnormally large proportion of men weak in appearance, incomplete in their physical development and of well below average height,' claimed a 1912 report. 'XV Corps covers several large towns – Marseille, Nice, Toulon, Nîmes – whose inhabitants show little inclination to bend to military discipline.'

Southern opinion reacted strongly to the Gervais article. The long journey from the Mediterranean had left XV Corps with precious little time to develop into a smoothly functioning whole, and the rush to the frontier had also left the corps one regiment short, the Corsicans of 173rd Infantry being unable to join as planned. 'The Midi has been made the scapegoat for the high number of casualties and the mistakes [of others],' concluded journalist Marcelle Capy. 'The soldiers of Provence, Languedoc and Gascony should not take the blame.'

The shame of XV Corps was certainly used to mask failures in command. Officers were unused to handling large formations in the field, and even ostensibly 'experienced' formations failed to take the most elementary precautions – such as deploying an effective cavalry screen. 'The excellent regiments of the Colonial Corps,' wrote General de Langle de Cary, commander of Fourth Army, 'had insufficient experience of the requirements of continental warfare, especially when faced with the German army. They went forward with great gusto but [also] a complete lack of caution. They were inadequately protected on the right by II Corps ... They weren't able to make proper use of the information provided by the locals or to ensure they had cover from the attached cavalry regiment.'

The French field service regulations of 1913 had placed great emphasis on the importance of the attack, to the exclusion of all else. Charles Péguy was among those who relished the charge. 'What Lieutenant Péguy enjoyed most at the end of every exercise was the bayonet charge ... where his combative nature became apparent,' recalled Victor Boudon. 'He was something to behold ... running ahead of us, sabre drawn, shouting, "Forward! Charge!"'

But, as there had been no chance to undertake manoeuvres under the new regulations, they remained imperfectly understood by many regimental officers:

Once in the presence of the enemy, each unit immediately sought to throw itself forward, more as a reflex action than from any rational thought ... Attacking troops sought speed and energy in forward movement above all else. They conducted the approach quickly, in a fairly dense formation, under fire from the enemy artillery ... The aim was to arrive as quickly as possible, and in good order, at the point where they would launch their attack; then the bugles and drums would sound the charge and the infantry fling themselves on the enemy with bayonets held high.

Lieutenant Marcel Rostin (112th Infantry) was a regular officer who saw action at Dieuze with the ill-fated XV Corps. 'The offensive became mixed up [in our minds] with a crazy, intoxicating speed,' he noted in his diary. 'We looked upon the first engagements as large-scale manoeuvres, forgetting just one thing – the bullets and the shells.'

Reckless speed and tactical naïveté were compounded by a shortage of junior leaders. Poor pay and prospects had made a military career an unattractive option in pre-war France, and as a consequence the army was chronically short of regular officers and NCOs. At full war strength a company numbered 250 men (including 110 reservists), commanded by just three officers and seven NCOs. In an attack the regulations stipulated that men maintain an interval of about a pace. But in the thick of the action leaders permitted their men to close up, compounding a natural tendency to bunch under fire, and the resulting dense formations were an ideal target for German artillery and small arms.

In response to the disasters of the first month of the war, Joffre was ruthless, sacking the commanders of Third and Fifth Armies, almost half the corps and divisional commanders, and some brigadiers. Their replacements included a number of regimental colonels, among them Philippe Pétain and Robert Nivelle.

Joffre had grossly under-estimated his opponent – the German reserves had more than held their own – and had dispersed his offensive strength by sending his armies in three different directions. On the French left the danger was now acute. Despite fierce fighting around the Belgian towns of Charleroi and Mons, the Germans were threatening to envelop the French and the British Expeditionary Force (BEF). To avert potential catastrophe and give his forces time to recover, Joffre ordered a retreat. Along with their British allies, the French turned south, the line pivoting around the fortress city of Verdun. At the same time Joffre called a halt to his abortive invasion of Alsace, hurriedly transferring some of the troops in that theatre across country to reinforce his left. Joined by reservists and other formations from the French right, these men formed the new Sixth and Ninth Armies, which took their place in the French left and centre respectively.

At Guise Fifth Army turned and administered a sharp check to the advancing Germans, as did the BEF at Le Cateau. NCO Olivier Céran (Chasseurs d'Afrique) was buoyed by the success at Guise: 'We are the victors; there's no doubt about it. Such a fillip in the midst of this discouraging and demoralizing retreat.' But the respite was only temporary. Towards midnight the captain gave the order that they were pulling back again. 'In despair,' concluded Céran, 'we set off south once more.'

High above the retreating forces were the aircraft of the French army. General Foch had famously dismissed aircraft as good enough only for sport. Pilots were trained to fly, not to observe, and the reports they produced were disappointingly vague. But with the conspicuous failure of the French cavalry to keep a close eye on the enemy, aircraft played an increasingly important role. Staff officers began to go up as passengers and brought a marked improvement to the quality of aerial reconnaissance reports.

But the task facing the pilot and observer was perilous in the extreme. As Corporal Marcel Brindejonc des Moulinais flew his Dorand DO.1 over Luxembourg, he was 'was seized by a crazy desire to get away, to make a quick turn back towards the airfield. If you've ever had the feeling that thousands of pairs of eyes are following you, thousands of rifles pointing at you, while you hear bullets clattering past, sometimes hitting a wire or a rib, you'll understand what I'm talking about, and why I might have been feeling on edge. Then the artillery joined in.'

On 24 August, with the Germans approaching Arras, volunteer nurse Emmanuelle Colombel was fighting her way through the town: 'Outside the station the crowd was impenetrable ... criss-crossing streets chock-full of pedestrians, cars carried fleeing families who sowed panic as they left.' Georges Bertrand recalled:

> All along the road we passed a pitiful exodus of country folk driven from their villages by the invasion ... All night we passed cars packed in a hurry, each with a large family crammed in, as well as people on foot, carrying their things bundled in a white sheet ... I remember one old grandma in particular. She had dressed up for the occasion

in her Sunday best so she could carry all her valuables on her person and she was struggling to push a little child in a wheelbarrow. Poor lad, he was quite happy, blowing as hard as he could on a penny whistle.

Passing through the Aube, the column of refugees fleeing Belgium, the Ardennes and the Marne was reportedly six kilometres long. The prefect hoped to confine the refugees to a single road on their journey south, 'to limit as far as possible the demoralizing effect of these processions'. Every refugee faced a long march to a railhead, and an even longer journey by train, before finally reaching safety. On 6 September around 1,200 people, mostly women and children, arrived in the Breton town of Lannion. 'Abandoning everything,' reported *Le Lannionnais*, 'these poor souls had been forced to cover 150 to 200 kilometres on foot, walking night and day, to reach a town [Laon] where they could catch a train.'

Local people did what they could to help. One 'person from the north' found refuge in nearby Plestin-les-Grèves. 'My mother used to give him an egg or two, some salad leaves, potatoes, always something or other,' a villager later recalled. 'They were older people, French refugees, for whom the mayor had found a home.' Any householder who took in a refugee received a daily allowance from the government – 1.25 francs for each adult and 50 centimes for each child aged 16 or under.

For the soldiers, the heat and the rigours of the march eventually began to take their toll. Olivier Céran did his best to stay awake: 'I was tired out through lack of sleep. The horses could doze on the march but could we sleep on horseback? You'd have to say yes because I kept having to rouse those in front of me – riders sticking their noses in their saddlebags, or leaning right or left [at a] worrying [angle] ... I figured out what was happening; they knew I was there behind them to wake them up; that I was the last in the line, that I wasn't asleep; they had confidence [in me] and so they slept on.'

Supply lines broke down as troops fell back, forcing them to live off the countryside, contrary to all regulations. The provosts posted warning orders: 'Anyone who disobeys and is caught in the act will be shot on the spot.' But the soldiers had no alternative. 'The supply of rations failed completely and we were marching on empty stomachs,' recalled a sergeant in 122nd Infantry. 'We came across three cows which we milked, collecting three litres of milk for the following day. A quick look in the hen-house brought us eight eggs. A very meagre supper indeed.'

Emile Rocca (24th Chasseurs Alpins) took part in 'the terrible retreat from Dieuze':

Three days and three nights, fighting during the day, beating a rapid retreat at night, with no food and no rest ... Late yesterday afternoon, I'd been marching for so long, my eyes fixed on the heels of the man in front of me and trying to forget the torture inflicted by my heavy pack, when someone shouted, 'Plums, lads, there's plums!' So we all left the column to fling ourselves on these poor trees, breaking the branches to stuff ourselves, even though the plums were still green and we were in danger of getting a nasty case of the shits.

'Let us prevail or let us perish' – the battle of the Marne

Needing a line behind which to halt the invaders, Joffre looked to the river valleys north and east of Paris. A first chance to regroup behind the Somme failed when the Germans outflanked the French before they had a chance to establish themselves. Further south, the Marne provided a second opportunity. French radio intercepts noted a lack of co-ordination on the German right, French air reconnaissance identified a gap in the enemy front, and Joffre decided to seize his chance. But still he was overtaken by events; before he could get all the French forces in position, the two sides clashed on the western end of the French line, north of the town of Meaux, and no more than fifty kilometres from Paris.

American Mildred Aldrich lived some eight kilometres distant, in a village south of the Marne. Her house lay on a low hill and she was able to watch as the action unfolded:

the battle had advanced over the crest of the hill. The sun was shining brilliantly on Mareuil and Chauconin, but Monthyon and Penchard were enveloped in smoke. From the east and west we could see the artillery fire, but owing to the smoke hanging over the crest of the hill on the horizon, it was impossible to get an idea of the positions of the armies ... the Germans were ... to be pushed east, in which case the artillery to the west must either be the French or the English. The hard thing to bear was all that guesswork. There was only noise, belching smoke, and long drifts of white clouds concealing the hill.

Beneath these clouds of smoke lay elements of Joffre's new Sixth Army, a mixture of units transferred from Alsace and local reservists. On the afternoon of 5 September its advanced guards had collided with part of General von Kluck's First Army, on the far right of the German line. The situation threatened the whole of the German advance. If First Army were defeated, the French might go on to roll up the whole of the German line. Von Kluck and his men were forced to a halt and turned around to thwart the French move.

Pressing forward with 276th Infantry at Villeroy, Charles Péguy was soon in the thick of the action: 'Despite our cries of "Get down!" [he] remained on his feet, [possessed by] a glorious, maniacal courage. Most of us had lost our packs, when a pack would have been just what we needed as cover. [Meanwhile] the voice of the lieutenant was still shouting with furious energy, "Fire, for God's sake, fire."' Péguy died almost immediately, shot in the head. He was expecting to meet no other fate, and his poem Eve, written shortly before the outbreak of war, contained the prophetic lines:

Happy are those who die for the carnal earth
But only if it be for a just war.

For three long days the French struggled to drive the Germans back. But the enemy had the advantage of the terrain. They were defending a slight rise, studded with woods and large, well-built, walled farmhouses, whereas the French were advancing over an open plain. On 7 September 216th Infantry attacked the key location of Nogeon Farm: 'The 7 and 8 September were very hard,' recorded the regimental history.

The lines of riflemen that manoeuvred with such precision were driven to the ground by machine-gun fire. Losses were severe. Almost all the senior officers were out of action. Nevertheless, the regiment tried to go forward. But each time they did so an invisible enemy, entrenched alongside a main road, forced them back to the ground with horrific machine-gun fire. Then the 'coalboxes' came into play, their dreadful noise and the huge craters [they made] shredding nerves already stretched to breaking point. Damn beetroot fields! How many brave officers now take their final rest there. Five were killed, sixteen wounded. And to cap it all our 75s had no idea how far our line had progressed and shelled our advanced positions, destroying any appetite for continuing the attack. Fortunately, night fell. What was left of the regiment fell back several hundred metres to the rear, with the whole horizon aglow with burning villages and hayricks. Half the regiment was out of action. The supply officer, Lieutenant Monneyron, brought [us] some pieces of meat, but no-one could be bothered to set to and cook them. Only tobacco was welcome. Worn out by three days of fighting, the regiment slept the sleep of the dead.

Further east, across the Brie plateau, the two sides clashed again. In the face of strong German pressure, the French were attempting to hold a ridgeline between the Petit and Grand Morin rivers, cut by deep valleys and lined with villages and small woods. In Charleville the position occupied by 40 Brigade (20th Division) was hopelessly exposed, so much so that the divisional commander gave his brigadier, General de Cadoudal, permission to withdraw. But the hapless staff officer who brought the message received short shrift. 'How dare I evacuate [a] position that has offered the enemy such resistance, abandoning the bodies of the men who sacrificed themselves to hold it?' replied Cadoudal. 'Tell General Desforges that I'm staying in Charleville, and this is where he'll find me, no matter what happens.'

Further east again, on the border with Champagne, was General Foch's Ninth Army. Several days of enemy pressure had finally forced a gap in the French lines and the Germans saw the opportunity for a decisive strike. On 8 September, in a surprise pre-dawn attack, with no preliminary bombardment, they broke through the tired French ranks. Alexandre Gaudon (32nd Infantry) was hurrying to the front with his regiment:

> The 93rd was falling back in disorder and no little panic. ... The Germans were approaching from three sides, and one of the first shots wounded Captain Baudin. Four of us tried to carry [him] to the right which brought us to a ridge. There we came under fire from both sides and from the rear. Forced to leave the captain in a small pine-wood, but three of his four rescuers were hit and then a bullet went through my greatcoat, just missing my thigh ... Riddled with bullets, my comrades were falling all the time. Sous-lieutenant Daras was wounded by [a bullet] that passed through both cheeks. Joubert took one in the temple. Crossed about 1,500 metres of open ground, under fire from both sides. Got to La Fère; a company formed of men from several regiments. The gendarmes threatened with their revolvers anyone trying to pull back further. Around midday the artillery east of Evry opened fire for three or four hours. When no more than 100 of us were left, we fell back to Gourgançon. ... The regiment lost its colonel, two battalion commanders, the captains and lieutenants from 5th and 6th Companies, many NCOs, and about 1,000 men, either killed, wounded or missing. During the fighting, the Germans waved a white flag and held up their rifles butt first; then, as soon as the French came close, they opened fire on them. The Germans too lost a lot of men, courtesy of our artillery.

Galtier-Boissière was defending the edge of a wood:

> The enemy advances in bounds, gaining ground ... Nervous, deafened, we fire without let-up ... the edge of the wood is nothing but a long jet of flame in the night ... Then suddenly the enemy line bends, eddies, slackens! Up on the parapet, we shoot down those who are running away ... shouting ... 'We've got them! Cease fire!' We can add the joy of victory to that of survival.
>
> 'I don't mind war when it's like this,' said a voice.
>
> 'You're right there,' said the adjutant, something of a philosopher. 'Always better to be the hunter than the rabbit.'

Commanded by Colonel Lamey, 42 Brigade (22nd Division) was in the thick of the fighting. By the night of 8 September Lamey and his men had endured 'a full day under continuous fire without the opportunity to reply', and 137th Infantry had been without water for forty-eight hours. 'I will certainly hold on tonight,' reported Lamey, 'and have no fear of night attacks; but I believe a third such day will be impossible without serious repercussions among the men; we have [already] had to take energetic action to check their tendency to falter. Despite everything, count on us.' Lamey was killed the next day.

Ninth Army managed to hold off the enemy assault with heavy casualties on both sides; then the tide turned. As they ran short of men, the Germans began to move units from one part of the line to act as reinforcements elsewhere, creating a gap that was exploited by the BEF and part of Franchet d'Esperey's Fifth Army. The allied advance unhinged the enemy positions to left and right and, in danger of encirclement, the Germans decided to withdraw.

65th Infantry was part of 41 Brigade, the other half of 22nd Division. The 65th had lost most of its officers in the fighting, leaving it with only a captain, two pre-war lieutenants and four reservist sous-lieutenants. Still the regiment swung back into the line in pursuit of the Germans. Breton François Le Lann was one of the sous-lieutenants: 'The men look tired and dirty. They haven't shaved since 20 August. Some lost their packs on the retreat and have only their rifles and cartridges. No blankets and, for some, no tents. And I'm no different. I'm unshaven, filthy and thinner in the face; my underclothes, dirty; I last saw my baggage on 23 August at Sedan. Nevertheless, we march along merrily in pursuit of the retreating Germans.'

The Germans consistently under-estimated the resilience of the French. Von Kluck later recalled ruefully, 'That men who had retreated for fifteen solid days, and who lay on the ground half-dead with fatigue, yet would pick up their weapons and charge to the sound of the bugle, is the one thing we never thought would happen; it was a possibility that no-one in our military colleges had ever considered.'

Crossing the Aubétin with 10th Cavalry Division, Lieutenant René Chambe (20th Dragoons) reached the village of Courtacon:

> [A] pitiful sight awaited us there. Before pulling back, the Germans had set fire to every house, every single one of them. No more than six or seven remained standing, their walls charred. Amid the smoking ruins and sections of blackened wall, a few things remained which typified the Teutonic horde. The German soldiers had stuffed their faces and got blind drunk. We found them sprawled in every corner [or] in the orchards, plastered. Through the windows we could see beds turned upside down, mattresses stained and torn, cupboards smashed with axes, their contents spilled all over. Everywhere torrents of linen, glass and crockery, all smashed to bits. They had wrecked everything for the sheer pleasure of it. ... I couldn't believe cavalrymen had done this. In every army in the world, the cavalry has a different code of behaviour, a different psyche.

The allies continued on after the Germans. One young officer in Pétain's former regiment, 33rd Infantry, was confident of success. 'We'll be on the Meuse or in Luxembourg before the enemy can halt our pursuit,' wrote Lieutenant Charles de Gaulle. But he was wrong. Exhausted by the battle, and unable to replenish their stocks of ammunition, the French advance was slow. The Germans managed to retreat behind the river Aisne and consolidated their positions by transferring men from Alsace.

'Into the deep night' – the front stabilizes

With the Germans dug in along the steep heights north of the Aisne, Joffre decided to attack again. He launched his assault in poor weather on 13 September, using Fifth and Sixth Armies alongside the BEF. But poor co-ordination allowed the German artillery and well-sited machine-guns to beat it off with ease. Fighting continued in the sector until 27 September, but to little effect other than setting fire to the city of Reims.

In an attempt to relieve the pressure on the Aisne, the Germans attacked the fortress city of Verdun, occupied against Joffre's wishes by elements of General Sarrail's Third Army. The ring of forts surrounding the city held firm against two waves of German attacks. But the enemy advance did achieve one significant success, driving a salient into the heart of the French lines around Saint-Mihiel, cutting off one of the railway lines that supplied Verdun and bringing the other within range of German artillery.

In the hills and forests of the Meuse valley, soldiers easily became disorientated. Lost behind enemy lines, a patrol of 288th Infantry suddenly heard the crackle of gunfire to their rear. 'The ditch at the edge of the wood gave us some protection while we tried to work out what was going on,' recalled Sergeant Baqué.

> How long did we wait? One minute, perhaps two ... The captain shouted, 'Fix bayonets! Charge!' As soon as I got to my feet, I saw the enemy kneeling in a ditch. As I ran forward I noticed pals ... dropping their rifles and crashing to the ground, face first ... Two more came up to the beech tree I was using as cover. Both collapsed – one on my back, the other over my feet. All I could think was, they'll get in my way ... I could no longer hear the sound of Lieutenant Fournier's revolver, firing three metres away. I looked for my commanding officer. He was lying on the ground, quite still.

Lieutenant Fournier was better known as Alain-Fournier, whose only novel, *Le Grand Meaulnes*, remains one of the great works of French literature. Fournier's last resting place was lost in the subsequent fighting, but in 1991 his body was rediscovered in a mass grave among others from 288th Infantry.

The autumn also saw clashes further north as each army tried to outflank the other. Maunoury's Sixth Army launched a major effort on the Oise on 17 September, but the attack failed. In bloody, desperate fighting, the battle moved ever northwards, but neither side was able to gain a decisive advantage. By the third week in October the Germans were at Dixmude in Flanders, held by a mixture of French sailors and territorials. The German attack was repulsed, but the Belgians were forced to open the sluices on the coast at nearby Nieuport, reducing much of the surrounding area to a swamp. Fighting in Flanders continued until November as the French and British held off a number of powerful German attacks around Ypres.

On 25 September Lieutenant Maurice Laurentin (77th Infantry) was in Artois lamenting the failure of another attack by his regiment: 'I thought [at first] that the intense German fire had prevented our infantrymen from leaving their trenches. [Then] I saw an appalling spectacle. The assault companies had been mown down several metres from their objective among the tangled strands of wire in front of the German trenches. Three hundred men of our regiment were lying there.'

Some senior officers had realized the folly of sending infantry into the attack without artillery support. On 26 September, near Wargemoulin-Hurlus (Marne), a battalion of 20th Infantry worked in close co-operation with the guns: '[The battalion] made a bound forward and part of the Bavarian line fell back; a fresh salvo from our 75s, a little longer than the first; another bound, almost simultaneous, from our infantry; leaning on the barrage, advancing with great enthusiasm, they reached the Bavarian infantry almost at the same time as the shells. And so it continued, bounds succeeding salvos until finally the Bavarians ... fell back in disorder.'

Yet close co-operation of this kind was still in its infancy. On 15 October the colonel of 74th Infantry reported from the village of Thil (Marne). 'An artillery officer came to the Les Carrières position to express his regret that no-one had been permanently attached from the artillery to observe the fall of shells and report them to the batteries. Since there is now a telephone link between Les Carrières and the brigade, it seems to me that the moment has arrived to make this link between such an observer and the batteries. I believe,' he added drily, 'that it would prove very profitable to the artillery.'

The two sides were now facing each other from Switzerland to the Channel coast, and gradually they began to dig trenches. At first these were designed simply as shelters to provide cover from artillery fire; then, slowly but surely, those shelters were extended, merged and improved until a continuous line of trenches ran the whole length of the front. 'The engineers came to build shelters for the officers,' grumbled one infantryman (61st Infantry). 'But we soldiers had to dig them out with our entrenching tools ... I learnt to work on my knees, my nose no higher than my pick.'

The men of 5th Foot Artillery were serving in the Argonne. They began by spending their nights in a village close to the battery, while the small group left on guard duty cobbled together a temporary shelter out of branches. But by the end of October a change had taken place. The men had 'begun to build relatively waterproof, deep dug-outs and to excavate gun emplacements. Shelters were also built for the gun crews ... and the whole thing reinforced by gabions.' The regiment was proud of its efforts: 'We became proper woodsmen ... it was a real miniature fort and all our own work.'

Although the battle of the Marne had represented a strategic defeat for the Germans – they had not captured Paris, nor had they forced the French army to surrender – they were still on French soil. They could simply dig in until they had knocked Russia out of the war and then turn their undivided attention to the defeat of France. But Joffre still thought this situation only temporary. This is certainly what Samuel Bourguet (51st Artillery) had been told: 'It's looking more and more as if this is going to be a war of fortresses, but one with a difference ... we have to be ready to move off again at once ... We're even using wooden mangers for the horses to make sure we keep back enough nosebags for the war of movement to follow.'

Back in the Argonne, Marc Bloch had been lucky enough to find accommodation in the evacuated village of Vienne-le-Château (Marne): 'We lay down in the beds of the absent homeowners, we ate off their tables and tablecloths, by the light of their lamps, sometimes we finished off their food. It was an outlaw existence.'

By mid–September confidence in a speedy victory had already started to fade. Marcel Papillon (356th Infantry) was running out of patience: 'We're beginning to get fed up with this. Roll on the end [of the war].' By December, though, Papillon had resigned himself to life on the front line. 'You mustn't think we're worse off [here] than anywhere else,' he reassured his parents. 'It's true there are alerts now and then, but we're starting to get used to them, to accept our lot. That apart, I played hopscotch until ten o'clock yesterday evening. It passes the time. If anything did happen, I had my rifle.'

The enemy was quickly demonized. Major Henri Bénard was a career officer who had retired before the war began. In 1914 he re-enlisted and found himself at the front with 236th Infantry. His wife came from Strasbourg and he took an uncompromising view of the enemy: 'The Kaiser is sick and so is Germany. We must kill them all if we can to stop the vermin from breeding. We've seen off a few these last few days. They were from the Bavarian Guard [sic]. We don't bother taking prisoners any more.' In their letters soldiers describe the enemy soldiers as 'bandits', 'wild men', 'beasts', or 'nasty pieces of work'; the Kaiser as 'mad', 'infamous', a 'bloodthirsty poser'; their country as 'damn Prussia'. 'I can see the Boches in the trench,' wrote one infantryman (343rd Infantry) in September. 'With their grey-green uniform they could be fat rats! They're disgusting.'

The word 'Boche' was not part of common currency in 1914. The enemy were still the 'Alboche' – a slang word dating from the 1860s or 1870s – or the 'Pruscos'. By the following year the prefix had been dropped and the Germans had become simply the Boche (and their allies the 'Austroboche' and the 'Turkoboche').

Meanwhile those who survived the opening battles were slowly becoming 'proper' soldiers. On 24 September Lieutenant Maurice Genevoix (106th Infantry) was impressed by the sight of his men in action: '[They] took full advantage of any bit of cover: they fired on one knee, behind trees, behind piles of logs; they fired lying prone, behind tiny mounds of earth, in holes they'd scraped out with their entrenching tools. That's the way to use your terrain! These are men who know how to fight.' Charged with stitching up the wounded, Dr Faleur had also observed an improvement. 'We are gradually learning how to fight a war,' he wrote in October 1914. 'The men no longer expose themselves to unnecessary danger as they did in the early days when they left the trenches and showed themselves when there was no need to do so.'

Although Paul Lintier had been scared the first time he saw action, he soon found a way to cope:

> At first, danger is an unknown ... you sweat, you shake ... it grows in your imagination. But then you no longer [try to] reason things out ... you use your experience. Smoke is harmless. The whistling of a shell gives you some idea of the direction it's coming from. Fear no longer dominates us, we dominate it. That's all there is to it ... Every day you train yourself to be brave. The danger remains the same but the human spirit rebels less. Your nerves no longer twitch. The effort to achieve self-control becomes a subconscious reflex, and in the end it's enough to do the trick. That's all there is to bravery on the battlefield. You're not born brave: you become brave.

But not every soldier adjusted to army life as well as Lintier. On 7 November General Sarrail reported that during the previous month sixteen men in Third Army alone had been condemned to death for self-inflicted wounds or for abandoning their post.

'Blood, shit and death ... that's war,' concluded Dr Gaston Top (27th Artillery), visiting the Aisne battlefields at the end of September. Casualty lists were long. So long, in fact, that the government banned their publication for fear of their effect on civilian morale. In the Haute Vienne the prefect wanted to isolate the wounded to stop them spreading panic and despondency: 'Ban anyone, medical staff apart, from entering hospitals or medical units. Forbid these staff from discussing outside the walls anything that happens or is said within. There are too many women in the hospitals and medical units. And wounded officers billeted in private homes should also guard their tongues.' But inevitably the news got out. The prefect of the Vaucluse took a more realistic view: 'Every day personal letters arrive in the villages from soldiers telling their correspondents that friends or neighbours have been killed or wounded. These roundabout, unofficial death notices plunge families into despair and they protest vehemently either to the mayor or to other elected representatives or to my office.'

Trains carried the wounded far from the front. On 25 August the *Courrier de Bayonne* published a letter from a curiste describing the casualties passing through Vichy:

> Their pale faces and expressions of suffering made them look even younger ... All the townsfolk had gone to see the convoys pass by. All you could hear were people exclaiming, "Aren't they young? How they must have suffered." Men and women alike did nothing to hide their tears. Most shocking of all was the number of soldiers who had lost their legs: it was as if the machine-guns had simply scythed them down. Smiling sadly, they watched us throwing them flowers, grand ladies and ordinary women, workers and well-to-do, all mixed up together.

Wherever the trains stopped, civilians brought the soldiers food and water. François Carlotti was a 6-year-old boy living on the edge of the Beauce, south-west of Paris. 'Around 15 August,' he later recalled,

> a rumour spread that mysterious trains were passing at night through the big station on the Paris–Tours line. ... We soon learned that they were trains full of the wounded. Then one evening when the little ones were asleep, my mother took my elder brother and me by the shoulders and said, 'Boys, we've got to go down there.' ... We waited a long time on the platform ... Finally the headlights appeared ... I'd never seen a train like it before, wagon after wagon, never-ending, more than sixty [in all] ... Suddenly a huge groan rose up: 'Water! Water!' Our jugs and pitchers didn't last a minute. Then [it was] quickly, run to the station pump, fill them up, turn round and take them back ... Gasping for breath, dripping with sweat, we'd made seven or eight runs by the time the train rumbled off as slowly as it had arrived. And the moans of 'Water! Water!' had grown no less. In fact, they seemed even louder, more insistent, more desperate.

Government censorship was rife. Journalist Alfred Capus, writing in *Le Figaro*, railed at the restrictions: 'As long as this column doesn't discuss the authorities, or the government, or politics ... or finance companies, or the wounded, or German atrocities, or the postal service, we're free to publish anything we like, after two or three censors have checked it through.' And as a result the newspapers contained nothing but facile good cheer. On 17 August *L'Intransigeant* revealed that the hospital trains 'were full of young boys with bullet wounds. Nevertheless they were laughing and joking [and] in reassuringly high spirits.' Two days later *Le Journal* was claiming that 'the German artillery fires badly and fires short; what's more eighty per cent of their shells don't even explode.' On 11 October *Le Petit Parisien* was insisting that, 'Our troops now scoff at machine-guns ... they take no notice of them.'

This sort of nonsense did not fool the troops on the front line. 'Soldiers!' grumbled Dr Paul Fiolle (4th Colonial Infantry), 'what absurdities are written in your name.' Louis Debidour wrote home in November 1914: 'If there's one thing that none of us can abide – it's the rubbish they write about the trenches, the resourcefulness of the soldiers, our seeming enthusiasm, our supposed cheerfulness ... It's all pure fiction. The men are calm, determined, resigned, nothing more, particularly to the cold and the bad weather which are making their lives so miserable.' This 'rubbish' was referred to as 'skull-stuffing' by the French; the British called it 'eyewash'.

Besides those killed and wounded, prisoners were taken on both sides. Wounded in action in Lorraine, Antoine Biesse was unable to regain the French lines and was captured where he lay. Only two weeks previously Ernest Etienne (3rd Zouaves) had been at home in bed. By mid-August he was part of the rearguard covering the retreat from Charleroi:

> At 0730 hours we set off again, coming across wounded men everywhere. Climbing the steep slope which separates Vitrival from Roux, we came under heavy fire from enemy artillery in position at Aisemont. We were ordered to fall back to the wood to take cover, while a deadly hail of shrapnel and shells rained down upon us. Like everyone else, I took advantage of being in the ditch at the side of the road to dump my pack. After that, we tried to get back to the wood in thirty- or forty-metre bounds. It was unnecessary because a shell passed so close that it knocked me senseless amid the potatoes, separating me from my company, my battalion and my regiment.

Etienne came round to find that his regiment had left him behind for dead. He hid in a wood for two days and eventually found shelter at a series of local farms, doing odd jobs in return for food and lodging, and hiding whenever German soldiers appeared. In this way he managed to avoid capture until October 1915, and only turned himself in – along with several compatriots – when the Germans threatened to execute enemy soldiers found hiding in Belgium, along with those who had helped them.

Etienne apparently made no serious attempt to regain his lines. In Lorraine, however, one Captain de Colbert brought together a band of some 300 men who had all become separated from their regiments. They conducted a guerrilla campaign which continued until December 1914, when the last of them was caught.

Etienne continued:

> The German authorities received us well, writing our names down and informing us that we'd be prisoners-of-war. We spent the night at the gendarmerie at Fosses and stayed there throughout Monday morning. When the Vitrival folk heard we were still at Fosses, many of them came to see us, bringing food of all kinds – wine, spice loaf, apples, fruit, jam etc ... We arrived [in Namur] at 1100 hours ... the locals watched with interest as we passed by ... In the [prison] yard they served us coffee, then in the evening they gathered us all together because there were almost 500 of us. They divided us up into two groups and called out almost half. The rest of us were locked up, five to a cell. It was a tight fit. ... The food was badly cooked and there wasn't enough of it. But we gradually got used to it.

Etienne's experience was typical. The Germans first gathered their prisoners together and marched them through captured towns as a propaganda exercise, before putting them on trains and taking them on to Germany. Officers were housed separately from other ranks and were not made to work. As many as 531,000 ordinary soldiers were captured during the war. From June 1915 onwards the Germans repatriated any prisoner who had suffered an amputation, as well as those who were paralysed, blinded, insane or tubercular. The remainder were put to work – on local farms, constructing new railways or labouring in factories or mines.

One native of Epinal (139th Infantry), captured on 26 August, ended up in Fort Orff near Ingolstadt in Bavaria. On 8 October he wrote home to his family in the Vosges, his letters going via neutral Switzerland: 'At last, we have permission to write and send news to our families ... I'm in good health and [have suffered] no wounds.' A week later he wrote again to his wife Jeanne: 'Did you get my letter? Hurry up with your reply and let me have news of Robert, Papa and Georgette, as well as the family in general ... Send me the money I asked you for, i.e. twenty or thirty francs.' By 30 November he was desperate for a reply: 'I honestly don't know how you're doing. I still haven't had your letter, but I did get the money order. Thanks. Marguerite has sent me a small package containing three smoked sausages and two bars of chocolate; please write and give her my thanks. ... Send me the jam I asked you for, two pairs of socks and a shirt as soon as you can because parcels go duty free until 25th December. ...' Prisoners' families spared what they could. Every month Marthe B. sent her husband Benoît a package from their home in the Tarn to the camp at Puchheim near Munich, containing a handful of francs, some chocolate, sugar, tinned food, soap and warm clothes.

A harsher fate awaited some who surrendered to the Germans. Private Chevalier (261st Infantry) was captured on the Aisne on 21 September. The following morning he narrowly escaped with his life:

> The German captain motioned us to lie down on a track leading off through the undergrowth. We all bunched together behind a tree, kneeling, thinking that there was an attack in the offing, but the officer indicated that this wasn't the case and made us lie down one by one, face to the ground, on the side of the tree facing the track. Turning slightly I saw seven or eight German soldiers, their feet about one metre from ours, aiming their guns at us. They fired two volleys on command. The first missed me completely but the second hit me in the thigh and the calf. I pretended to be dead. The first volley hit my neighbour Moulin, originally from Aubenas. It blew his brains out and some landed on me. Then I felt a second body fall across my legs. Another of my comrades, a native of Alissas, was wounded by the volleys. He asked for mercy for the sake of his wife and children; they stabbed him with a bayonet. Once again he begged for mercy, indicating that they should shoot him in the head or the heart, but they stabbed him a second time. Still he managed to beg for mercy but a third bayonet thrust finished him off. The Germans then cut branches to cover us and left about a quarter of an hour later.

Chevalier crawled away and managed to rejoin the French lines. And this was not the only instance of cold-blooded execution. That same week, in the woods near Vaux-lès-Palameix, south-east of Verdun, forty men were found, from three different regiments and two different divisions. All were lying face down, shot in the head.

German prisoners were taken to camps far from the front – in Brittany and the south-west, or even as far away as north Africa. Territorial Louis Barthas and his comrades were given the job of guarding a group of prisoners en route to the Pyrenees. By journey's end, both escort and prisoners were sharing food. On 25 August Joseph Bochet (51st Chasseurs) and his comrades were in the station at St Dié when they heard of a group of wounded German prisoners being held nearby. Eager to see the enemy up close, they hurried over and bundled the sentry out of the way. But they had a disappointment in store: 'They were just ordinary men and we got out of there straight away before that poor territorial's officer could see what a poor job he'd done as a guard.'

Like the Germans, the French put most of their prisoners to work – on public works projects, rebuilding sugar refineries and distilleries, or as farm labourers – replacing those who had been conscripted. Some families, particularly those who had already lost loved ones in action, did not always appreciate the presence of the enemy close at hand; others, however, were grateful for an extra pair of hands. 'The Abbé Olive arrived from Nantes,' reported Father Alfred Baudrillart, Rector of the Institut Catholique de Paris. 'He tells me that employers who use German prisoners find them much easier to manage than French workers, who are so unruly and so demanding.'

On Christmas Day all was quiet on the stretch of the Picardy front occupied by 56 Brigade (30th Infantry plus a detachment of 11th Chasseurs Alpins). At either end of the sector French and German soldiers came out of the trenches and met in the middle of no man's land to exchange newspapers and cigarettes. But the spirit of Christmas did not extend to divisional HQ, where General Berge chose that same day to explode a mine under the German trenches. The engineers laid a charge of 800 kilograms of powder and set it off at a quarter to midnight. An assault group from 30th Infantry tried to seize the crater but was driven back by the Germans.

Towards La Bassée the men of 296th Infantry tried to outsing the Germans opposite, but none appears to have left the trenches. François Guilhem described the scene in a letter to his wife:

I will never forget this Christmas night. Under moonlight as bright as day, and with the frost hard enough to split the stones, we were going up around 10.00 pm in the evening to carry timber into the trenches. You can imagine how astonished we were to hear the Boches singing hymns in their trenches and the French in theirs; then the Boches sang their national anthem and cheered. The French responded with the *Chant du départ*. All this singing from thousands of men right out in the countryside was truly magical.

Close to Verdun, in the trenches occupied by 112th Infantry, Lieutenant

Marcel Rostin was writing a letter to his uncle: 'This time I'm twenty-five metres away from the Boche and shots have rung out from morning to evening. These brigands are bold as brass. As I write to you now in my scrape, they tell me that the wretches are making gestures of friendship to my men, waving cigars and shouting, "Come over here!" I was livid, I was furious, and I gave an order to shoot any Boche head that appeared above the parapet. The scoundrels fired back, but better a few broken skulls than any relaxation in discipline.'

In the Argonne Corporal Louis Bénard (272nd Infantry) had little to celebrate: 'Christmas Day! A beggar's Christmas, more like! We're in the trenches, and Christmas Eve was hardly worth the bother. We had a biscuit and a cup of tea! What a feast! One of my pals sang *Minuit! Chrétien*s for us. It didn't lack a certain grandeur in the midst of intense gunfire. I'm in a hurry to return home. You miss me so much and so do the children. Here we're getting by, cold and wretched. Fortunately, our captain is looking after us well.'

But behind the lines Louis's namesake Major Henri Bénard (236th Infantry) was enjoying a better time of things: 'I spent Christmas at rest in Bray in a nice little house with a fire. The day went well. Presents had come flooding in. There was something for everyone, and I had invited a captain and a lieutenant to be my guests. Someone had given my excellent medical officer a confit of turkey, and the cook had made boeuf à la mode with the ration meat. *Gâteau de riz*, macaroons from Nancy [and] cherries in eau-de-vie. And, to finish, a bottle of Cointreau I'd found in a pile of gifts, to the delight of us all.'

On the final day of the year Adjutant Henri Boulle (76th Infantry), a teacher in civilian life, was also in the Argonne. That evening he took the opportunity to write to his pupils in Bourges:

Cursed be those whose pride, ambition or squalid self-interest have unleashed such a plague upon Europe, plunging us into such terrible suffering, and ruining so many of the towns and villages of our beautiful country, perhaps forever! Cursed be those who bear ... responsibility for so much agony and so much grief ... We the soldiers, defenders of our freedom and our rights, must redouble our efforts to drive forever from this land an enemy who has brought us so much sorrow. We must continue to trust in a victory which will eventually see justice triumph. Each day we must be ready to risk our lives in the most terrible of combats, always prepared to endure a thousand kinds of mental and physical anguish. We gladly consent to these sacrifices for the sake of [that] final victory. We also dedicate ourselves to preserving the memory of those comrades falling in their hundreds alongside us ... But today you too, my dear friends, have your duty laid out before you. Consider this – you are the hope of tomorrow. Yours is the young generation which will have to replace those killed on the field of honour ... Whatever the outcome of the current conflict, the genius of the French people must live on. Those of us who have willingly sacrificed our lives and who tomorrow will perhaps be dead ... confidently leave this task to you.

Boulle was killed the following day.

Chapter 2

'Nibbling at the Enemy'
1915

Chronology

16 Dec–5 Jan	Offensive in Artois: French attempts to capture Notre Dame de Lorette are defeated with heavy losses
20 Dec–12 Jan	The French attack in Flanders, at La Boiselle, in the Argonne, on the Meuse, on the Aisne, and around Reims
16 Feb–15 Mar	First Battle of Champagne: Fourth Army attacks but makes no progress
19 Feb	The French are forced from the dominating position of Hartmannswillerkopf in the Vosges
22 Apr–25 May	Second Battle of Ypres: the Germans release poison gas against French troops
9 May	Second Battle of Artois: Tenth Army fails to capture Vimy Ridge
16–24 June	Second Battle of Artois: the French make another attempt on Vimy
25 Sept–29 Sept	Second Battle of Champagne: despite a three-day bombardment, Second and Fourth Armies are unable to make much ground
25 Sept–14 Oct	Offensive in Artois renewed: some progress made but Vimy remains in German hands
6 Oct	Offensive in Champagne is renewed but halted after only one day

'To arms' – the winter offensives of 1914–15

Although the French had turned back the Germans on the Marne, they had failed to dislodge the invader in the subsequent fighting, and important areas of the country remained under enemy occupation. France's overall strategy embraced all three existing fronts (the western front, Russia and Serbia) and aimed at forcing the Central Powers to spread themselves thinly, thus preventing undue pressure from falling on any single allied power. At the same time Joffre was reluctant to agree to any course of action that reduced the number of divisions in the west. When Prime Minister Ribot suggested sending six divisions to help Serbia in January 1915, Joffre declared, 'It's not Austria we have to beat; it's Germany.'

The French began the year short of matériel, and in dire need of rest and reorganization, but Joffre refused to go on the defensive. In his memoirs he later claimed that 'specialized equipment' was needed to conduct the siege warfare necessary before he could resume the war of movement. But France lacked the heavy artillery, modern rifles, machine-guns, hand grenades, trench mortars and barbed wire it now required, and massive losses of equipment and the unexpectedly high consumption of artillery shells in 1914 only added to the crisis. Yet political imperatives forced Joffre to continue to attack, even without the equipment he needed. Under pressure to remove the invaders from French soil, he was unwilling to surrender the initiative to the Germans, and he also felt obliged to try to bolster the Russians, who were making noises about a separate peace.

Unable to mount any large-scale action, all he could do over the next few months was set in train a number of 'partial' offensives, designed to show 'an aggressive attitude', while 'prevent[ing] the enemy from disengaging and making lateral moves from one part of the front to another'. His subordinate commanders were ordered to demonstrate French 'vigour' and 'will' to fight; they had 'to maintain an offensive spirit amongst [French] troops and not allow them to lapse into inaction on the pretext that the enemy will not attack'. In public Joffre explained that he was 'nibbling' at the enemy. But Louis Barthas remained unimpressed: '"I'm nibbling at them," said that old potbelly Joffre, a phrase the servile press fell upon like a rare pearl.'

A contributor to *Le Crocodile* (63rd Company/3rd Engineers) later recalled one of Joffre's attacks:

It was still only 17 December 1914 ... We had advanced under machine-gun fire and were approaching the lines of wire when we realized they hadn't been destroyed. We had to wait for three hours while dawn crept upon us, without moving, with no cover, each of us hiding his head behind a clump of grass. The German machine-guns fired continuously. Each time the gunners raised them up a notch, the burst drove into the ground at my feet. The rest of the time it fell [just] in front of me and covered my head with liquid mud. I could recommend three hours resting between two steel curtains like this to anyone who fancies trying it.

In Artois the three corps of Tenth Army attempted to capture the heights north-east of Arras – Notre Dame de Lorette and Vimy Ridge – with the intention of breaking through the German line completely. But three days of fighting, from 17 to 19 December, saw German counter-attacks nullify the few French gains, and a renewed attack two days after Christmas was no more successful. The fighting ground to a halt in the winter mud and was finally called off on 15 January.

On the Champagne front Fourth Army launched an attack on 20 December, involving three of its five corps. The assault was directed against the southern edge of the Sayon salient, near Perthes-lès-Hurlus (Marne). Heavy fighting continued without a break until early January, but in poor conditions French gains were minimal. 'It makes you shudder to think,' wrote Dr Gaston Top (27th Artillery), 'that in weather so bad you wouldn't put a dog out, poor souls, brothers in Christ, are trying to rip each other apart with their bayonets.'

A number of other attacks were launched over the winter – Eighth Army in Flanders, Second Army at La Boiselle, First and Third Armies in the Argonne and along the Meuse, and XXXIV Corps in the Vosges. Some of these had proper objectives in terms of valuable terrain features; others offered fewer tactical or operational advantages and appear to have been devised simply to demonstrate a willingness to attack.

Lieutenant Maurice Genevoix (106th Infantry) was wounded during an assault on the ridge of Les Eparges (Meuse) on 25 February 1915:

I fall to the ground on one knee. A sudden jolt goes through my left arm. It's [forced] behind me, bleeding copiously. I want to get up but I can't ... [Now] my arm shudders with the shock of a second bullet and blood starts to flow from another wound. My knee presses into the ground as if my body is made of lead. My head droops; then the dull thud of a third bullet rips off another shred of cloth right before my eyes. Unwisely, I look down at my chest and see a deep furrow of red flesh by my left armpit.

Having applied field dressings to his wounds, Genevoix's men carried him to a first-aid post, where the MO bandaged his arm properly and gave him an injection of caffeine. He then went on to a field ambulance, where he received another injection, this time against tetanus. He was later evacuated into the interior, his arm already 'darkening with gangrene'. Invalided out of the army, he never recovered the use of his left hand.

The fighting in the wooded hills of the Argonne was particularly bloody. Marc Bloch (272nd Infantry) was in the Bois de la Gruerie sector (nicknamed '*Bois de la Tuerie*' or 'Killing Wood' by the troops):

> The characteristic feature of the Argonne was the proximity of the two lines of trenches. At the same time the sightlines (through the woods) were difficult and so was the resulting struggle for observation points. Early on I think that both sides, and sadly ours in particular, attached too much importance to not ceding an inch of ground, to retaking a few lost metres; we put too many men in the front line. We got many of our men killed like that, very foolishly. [It was] a war of trench mortars, grenades [and] mines. To begin with we had too few communication trenches [and] no shelters at all. A lot of men were killed simply moving from place to place (ration parties, runners etc.). This gradually changed during 1915. The fighting in La Gruerie in 1914, insignificant in its strategic impact, was among the bloodiest of the war. The general commanding II Corps [General Augustin Gérard], of which we were part, got his men killed for no reason.

Jean-Marie Carré (4th Division staff) was equally critical of the senior commanders at La Gruerie: 'they confused position and mission. It was our mission to defend [the wood]. It was our job to take up the positions we judged best for that purpose. But the order was given by the Army, and repeated by the Corps: "On no account must you abandon a trench." We obeyed ... Over the last four months we've lost around 800 metres. [And] we also lost 4th Division ... But they say that the energetic attitude adopted by General Gérard in the Argonne will soon earn him the command of an Army!!!' (In fact, Gérard did not receive his promotion until March 1916.)

On 25 February Anatole Castex (288th Infantry) was near Saint-Mihiel, taking part in an attack on the German lines: 'When our infantry arrived at bayonet point all they found were the dead, the wounded and a few stunned survivors: I don't think we gave any quarter.' Two days later it was the same story: 'Wherever we attack now we show no mercy; we kill them all ... we spare no-one.'

The campaign in the Vosges almost constituted a separate war, each side struggling to dominate a number of high peaks and ridges. The terrain imposed itself on both sides, limiting the range of tactical options open to them. One of the principal peaks was the Hartmannswillerkopf, 965m high, which provided extensive views over the lower Rhine valley, towards Mulhouse. The French usually abbreviated the name of the summit to HWK or 'Hartmann'; a journalist mangled the latter into 'Armand', and subsequent newspaper reports claimed the soldiers referred to it as Armand or *Vieil-Armand* – 'Old Armand' – but this was simply one more piece of eyewash.

André Maillet (23rd Infantry) was involved in an attack on the mountain in December 1915:

> The ground is covered with rocks and broken trees, pitted with shell-holes. I run, I climb, I fall, I slip, I scramble, I get up again ... I've fixed my target, I have to get there as quickly as I can. But the sloping ground is slippery. The advance is slow, too slow. Our attack won't be a surprise. The enemy is on the alert, all the Germans are in their positions, fifteen metres away. Shots ring out, gunfire crackles, the men are raked by machine-gun fire. With loud cries, those around me sway, fall, are toppled. ... The whole skirmish line has collapsed. I go to ground and look about me: there's no-one left standing. The attack has come to nothing.

Further north, a feature known as Le Linge commanded views over the Munster valley. The local commander, General de Pouydraguin (47th Division), wanted to move down into the valleys, but GQG (Grand Quartier Général – Joffre's General Headquarters, then located in Chantilly) insisted he take the ridges first. The offensive began on 20 July. After three attacks over a period of six days the French managed to capture part of Le Linge. But the fighting continued until October, with nine major German counter-attacks, and many small features repeatedly changing hands. At the height of the fighting Captain Ferdinand Belmont (11th Chasseurs Alpins) looked out across no man's land: 'the opposing trenches face each other a short distance apart on the rounded hilltop that forms the watershed. Between these two lines the ground has become a charnel house. The bodies of the chasseurs who fell during the attacks [and] the bodies of the Germans killed by our guns in the recent counter-attacks are strewn everywhere amid the rows of twisted wire and felled pines. Every now and then dreadful smells are stirred up by the breeze.'

By the end of 1915 the front here had stabilized, almost by mutual consent, and for the remainder of the war both sides used it largely as a rest sector.

All along the line Joffre's attacks over the winter resulted in only minor territorial gains. Fourth Army made some progress in the hills of eastern

Champagne, but at no point did they penetrate any further than three kilometres – falling far short of his intentions. Although outnumbered, the Germans were well entrenched, and successfully demonstrated the superiority of their defence, especially in their use of the machine-gun. The French experienced particular problems in co-ordinating their infantry and artillery to maximum effect but, where they did achieve success, a full artillery preparation was the key.

The shortfall in equipment, allied to Joffre's decision to continue launching – albeit limited – offensives in its absence, contributed in large part to the heavy casualties the French continued to sustain during 1915. Insufficiently flexible tactics also played a role for, like the other combatants, the French were struggling to develop tactics appropriate to the new situation. Their initial response was to demand that their generals exercise close control over the battle. Waves of infantry were to advance behind a barrage that lifted according to a set schedule. On the first day of the winter offensive in Champagne, for example, the commander of XIV Corps ordered eight batteries to fire for one hour in a preliminary bombardment; the barrage would then lift one hundred metres for a further sixteen rounds per gun, before stopping at precisely 9.30 am, when the infantry would attack. But such a strict timetable gave artillery commanders no discretion to respond to changing conditions. If the infantry encountered unexpected German resistance, the barrage simply carried on without them. The continuing lack of heavy artillery also made it difficult for the French to extend the depth of a barrage. All they could do was cease firing and physically drag the 75s forward – resulting in a pause that the Germans were often able to use to their advantage.

'France calls its children' – mobilizing the country

The French had been expecting a short war. But without a decisive victory in 1914, and faced with serious shortages of shells and equipment, the country quickly had to gear itself up for a longer conflict. With the Germans now occupying the Briey basin in Lorraine, the hub of the nation's iron and steel industry, the French had to create new factories and find the workers to man them. Munitions workers had been called up, along with everyone else, in August 1914. However, their skills were now needed more urgently at home, and many were recalled from the front. Two-thirds of France's 1.5 million male factory workers had been called up by December 1914; by the end of 1915 some 500,000 of them had been returned to their jobs, and the workforce further supplemented by women, colonial subjects and even foreigners.

The arsenal in Tarbes (Hautes-Pyrénées), for example, increased its workforce from around 6,000 in September 1914 to 16,000 by 1917. As many as one-third of its employees were women, including refugees from other areas of France. Its male workers included a good number (around 10 per cent) who were not French nationals — a mixture of Belgian refugees, Indochinese and Malagasies – as well as a contingent of 1,500 soldiers recalled from the front but 'specially detached' from their regiments and remaining under military discipline. Employing foreigners in a munitions factory posed a potential security problem, but the police were on their guard: 'The workers now realize they are the subject of covert surveillance, independent of the management, and are convinced that any attempt to sabotage the smooth working of the factory will be ruthlessly dealt with.' Just two weeks earlier sixteen workers had been sacked for drunkenness or indiscipline, one for biting a fellow worker, and four soldiers were returned to their units as 'bad workers'.

Conscription also produced shortages of skilled labour in other areas of the economy. France's second city, Lyon, threatened to run out of bread when most of its bakers were called up in August 1914. But the needs of the troops took precedence: the local commander refused to release the bakers because he was expecting 25,000 soldiers within a few days time and 'would have to put a large number of mobile ovens into service to feed [them]'. In 1915 the small Pyrenean community of Mauléon also faced a crisis. The town council wrote to the commander of the local Military Region, requesting the return of one Jean-Pierre Etchegoyen, a 41-year-old, blind in one eye since childhood. Etchegoyen single-handedly owned and ran the electricity generating works which provided most of the town with its light and power. Since he had been called up, the works had closed, leaving everyone in the dark.

'Following big government orders at the Tamaris factory, the majority of workers are returning to the plant,' reported a teacher in Alès (Gard). 'They've been mobilized to manufacture steel tubing.' But some in the town found this a little hard to take. As far as they were concerned, men in their twenties belonged at the front, not in a factory. In Le Creusot (Saône-et-Loire) families whose menfolk had returned home were judged to be 'perhaps a little too exuberant in flaunting their happiness while others are learning of the death of men who have remained at the front'.

Faced with a shortage of male workers, the arsenal in Rennes (Ille-et-Vilaine), like its counterpart in Tarbes, also began to employ women. Even at the low wage of 27 centimes an hour, it found it easy to fill the vacancies. With the main breadwinner absent, many families relied on wages from war work, but employing women in heavy industry remained anathema to some traditionalists. 'Women were created for one thing and one thing only, that is bearing children,' argued Dr Adolphe Pinar of the Académie de Médecine. 'The children they bear now and in future will be as vital to our second victory as were munitions to the first.'

In August 1914 the government introduced a separation allowance – worth 1.25 francs per day, plus a further 50 centimes for every child under 16 – for women whose husbands were at the front. By comparison, the average daily wage varied according to region from 3.72 francs in the Vendée to 7.24 francs in Paris. Some alleged that the allowance was excessive and would lead only to idleness on the part of its recipients. But others disagreed. In the village of Berneuil (Charente), for example, 166 people out of a total population of 1,200 were receiving the payment: 'Many have need of it, others could easily do without, but since every man is doing his duty at the front it has been a sensible measure. By ensuring everyone has the basic necessities, it has been the main reason why everything has remained calm on the home front.' The teacher in nearby Bioussac was another supporter of the scheme: 'It's had excellent results because the allowances permit the families of serving soldiers to wait more patiently for the end of hostilities. And the soldier is easier in his mind because he knows that, whatever happens, his family won't be in need.'

With casualty figures of 492,000 in the first five months of the war alone, the government was forced to turn to a number of expedients to keep the army up to strength. Young and old alike were called to the colours. The classes of 1914, 1915 and 1916 were all called up early: the class of 1914 in September 1914; the class of 1915 in December 1914; and the 18- and 19-year-olds of the class of 1916 in April 1915. 'I've had a postcard from Privas telling me they're putting the class of 1916 into uniform,' wrote Charles Auque (7th Chasseurs). 'I'm still hoping the war will be over before they've got to come and be killed. My feeling is that the authorities won't want to send these children to be butchered since they're the only reinforcements we've got left.'

The youngsters were joined by the older men of the classes of 1889, 1890, 1891 and 1892. The class of 1892 was called up in December 1914, and the remaining three in March and April of the following year. At the same time existing territorials deemed fit enough for front-line service were 'combed out' and transferred to the infantry, and each infantry company was reduced in strength to make better use of existing manpower.

New recruits received their basic training at their regimental depot. It was a brief and uncomfortable experience. One soldier joined 112th

Infantry at Toulon in December 1914. Arriving at his barracks, he found 'a few men from the class of 1914, and several who'd already been evacuated once from the front and declared fit to return after a spell in hospital. We kept our civilian clothes until we left for the front and had no weapons other than a Gras rifle [declared obsolete in 1884]. That lasted about two months.'

A report on the training regime of 74th Infantry in 1914 commented: 'Instruction in combat is very rudimentary. No-one at the depot appears to know anything about the present conflict. The men claim they only fire their rifles once a week. The volunteers from Alsace have no idea how to shoot.' Faced with the shock of adjusting to military life, the soldiers had to turn to one another for help. In 53rd Infantry a young agricultural worker from the class of 1916 came to the aid of a post-office clerk from Lyon. This city-dweller 'had no more idea how to handle a pick than a shovel. I took hold of his pick and showed him how to use it while remaining crouched down. He stayed with me until May or June 1915 and I made a proper digger out of him.' In return, the clerk helped the farm labourer with an application form for his wife's separation allowance.

After their basic training, recruits were sent to camps in the nearby countryside for field exercises. Conditions in these camps were often poor, as a member of 161st Infantry, also called up in December 1914, quickly found out: 'It was a shocking camp. We slept in stables. Some men caught typhoid. They trained us quickly, but in the worst possible conditions of hygiene.' Trained recruits would then continue on to their regiments in the field. As the front stabilized, they went first to a divisional depot, sometimes for further specialist training, and were then dispatched in drafts to whichever regiment within the division was most urgently in need of reinforcements.

'We are all martyred' – the summer offensives

Joffre planned two major offensives for the summer of 1915, one in Artois, the other in Champagne. He aimed first to fix the enemy in place, then to make a breach in his lines which could be exploited, forcing the Germans to retreat. Joffre sent a message to his troops: 'The hour of attack has sounded; we have contained the German assault; now we have to smash them and completely liberate all occupied French territory.' One German unit promptly put up a sign above their trench. When was the offensive going to start? it asked. 'We're waiting.'

But before Joffre could put his plans into effect, the French fell victim to a brutal new weapon. On 22 April 1915 the Germans released clouds of chlorine gas over the French lines north of Ypres. The full impact of the gas, and the accompanying barrage, fell on the north African regiments of 45th Division, and with no form of protection the men were forced to withdraw in some disorder. Colonel Jean Mordacq, commanding 3rd bis Zouaves, described its lethal effects: 'Everywhere men were trying to escape – territorials, African light infantry, tirailleurs, zouaves, artillerymen – unarmed, distraught, their greatcoats torn off or thrown wide open, neckcloths pulled off, running like madmen in all directions, crying out for water, spitting up blood, some even rolling on the ground in their desperate efforts to draw breath.'

Yet the newspapers could still make light of the danger. 'Take heart,' wrote André Lefebvre, correspondent of *Le Matin*, 'it's nothing to worry about ... [gas] poses no threat ... comparing the total number of victims with [those produced] by other [weapons], we really don't need to pay it any further attention.' Nor did the Germans anticipate the impact of the new weapon, failing to position fresh reserves close enough to take advantage of French disarray. Lieutenant Louis Botti (1st Zouaves) was euphoric at surviving the attack: 'We're alive! Forgive us, o spirits of [our] fallen comrades! We're alive; the steel shackles which have been strangling us for days have now been lifted. We want to make the most of the moment, to savour the joy of life. ... Look at us! Look at all these men! Their eyes sparkle, their faces aren't pale any more ... they're standing up, they're breathing. They're overjoyed.'

In his main Artois offensive Joffre planned to make a new attempt on Vimy Ridge and Notre Dame de Lorette, aiming to capture both before advancing south-east, in the direction of Cambrai. The artillery preparation began on 4 May, and five days later the attack was launched by five corps from Tenth Army. The ridges at Vimy were significant because they offered excellent views over the German positions. From his observation post at the Ferme de Chanteclair, wrote Pierre Veurpillot (4th Foot Artillery), 'the view plunged down to the German front lines stretching north–south across the Farbus plain. Powerful view-finders allowed you to search the smallest fold of ground. Yet the same terrifying sight continued to haunt our vision: in front of the two army corps overlooked by our position appeared unbroken lines of chalk barely touched by the shells, an endless thin red line indicating a tangled network of rusted wire.'

Many of those who took part in the assault on Vimy had little confidence in its outcome. For the first time Henri Bouvereau and his comrades in 276th Infantry exchanged addresses before going into action, promising to write to the family of a dead or injured comrade if the worst should happen. But the attack met with some success, despite determined resistance in the villages of Neuville-Saint-Vaast, Souchez and Carency. Notre Dame de Lorette was captured and elements of Pétain's XXXIII Corps managed to penetrate four kilometres into the German position. However, the French were unable to capture Vimy Ridge itself and, despite a series of bitterly contested attacks and counter-attacks, the offensive was eventually closed down on 25 June. Just over 100,000 casualties (a third of them killed) and lavish artillery expenditure (over two million rounds were fired) produced a final gain of just three kilometres along an eight-kilometre front.

Fernand Le Bailly (36th Infantry) and his company went into action on 1 June around Neuville-Saint-Vaast, in an attack which got under way without any kind of artillery preparation: 'Ninety-seven men set off, and I remember that after we'd taken the German trench – it was my good fortune to jump in first – there were only eleven of us left. The attack had lasted fifteen to twenty seconds.'

Stretcher-bearer André Kahn (37th Infantry) witnessed one of the German counter-attacks:

> We gave them a warm welcome! Their corpses are heaped up in front of our lines. They were advancing in columns of four. Our machine-guns and 75s made mincemeat of them. Alas! They bombarded our trenches heavily. We patched up our gallant lads all night. ... Some officers were killed. Amongst them was Captain Dunant ... torn to pieces by a shell. ... He'd been wounded twice and received the Légion d'Honneur. After six months of hardship and suffering he died senselessly in a hole! Think about this instead. Thousands of strong, alert, eager Germans were mown down by men certainly fewer in number ... but fortified by a thirst for victory and hatred of the enemy.

The French tried once again at Vimy, on 25 September, but only as a diversion from the main offensive in Champagne, and in conjunction with a British attack at Loos. They managed to capture the stronghold-village of Souchez but made no impression on the defences of the ridge itself and called off the attack four days later. A third attempt was made on 11 October. Let down by poor artillery preparation, it was closed down after three days.

In Champagne the Germans had made several attacks during March and April against the outer defences of Reims. The fighting, particularly around Ferme d'Alger and Beauséjour Redoubt, went on until the end of May. In September it was the turn of Joffre to go on the offensive, ordering Fourth Army to attack towards Rethel and continue on towards Mézières. Optimistically, the regiments in the assault waves had been given locations for their next bivouac some fifteen kilometres behind the German lines – 69th Chasseurs were to be billeted in Vouziers (Ardennes) that night – and even had local men attached to the battalion to act as guides. A preliminary three-day bombardment opened in fine weather on 22 September. But the weather changed and, with insufficient ammunition to extend the barrage, the attack was forced to go ahead in poor conditions.

Taking part in the preliminary bombardment, Paul Toinet (2nd Artillery) remembered

> a tremendous, unremitting thunder, reaching its peak when all the batteries fired at once, sometimes diminishing in intensity, but never letting up. From high in our observation post it was a magnificent, tragic show: lined up before us were the German trenches, mounds of earth, like huge molehills, giving a feeling of chaos and death [even] when things were quiet. But now the trenches pulsed with satanic life; they were crowned with a series of plumes continuously rising and falling. Occasionally a mine exploded; huge columns of black smoke formed a dense veil only slowly dispersed by the wind.

As zero hour approached, Sergeant Emile Morin (60th Infantry) was counting off the minutes on his watch:

> 0911 ... 12 ... 13 ... 14 ... 15 ... 'Forward!' The command was passed crisply along the line. No-one faltered, no-one cried out. We threw ourselves over the parapet. Men were hit as soon as they left the trench and fell back heavily into it. Straining every sinew, the survivors threw themselves forward, screaming at the enemy. The firing doubled in intensity: it was a hell of rifle and machine-gun fire, a fire whose like I would not see again for the rest of the campaign!

As they ran on, leaning on the bombardment, Morin was passed by the wounded Adjutant Manche. 'Bastards!' shouted Manche. 'They've holed my water bottle. And it was full of spirits! Forward! Forward!'

Opposite Mesnil-lès-Hurlus the men of 65th Infantry had brought their colour into the trenches with them. When one of the colour party was killed crossing the parapet, the regimental CO, Colonel Desgrées de Loü, immediately picked up the flag. Along with a handful of men, the colonel 'stood motionless on the parapet, holding the colour ... for five minutes, five long minutes', trying to encourage his men as they advanced into heavy German small-arms fire. But, despite the preparatory bombardment, the German wire remained uncut, and the regiment was unable to make any progress. In all, the 65th incurred 791 casualties – the colonel and the rest of the colour party were among those killed.

L'Echo de Tranchéesville (258 Brigade) described another of the attacks:

At the appointed hour, the officers gave us the usual pep talk, a few final instructions, then asked if we were ready. A moment's silent contemplation followed our positive reply; then suddenly someone shouted 'Advance'. We were in the second departure trench. Officers and men jumped onto the parapet without hesitation and ran to the front line to take the place of those already closing in on the Boche lines. Scarcely had we stopped before we heard the cry again, 'Advance!' We scrambled over the next parapet and ran towards the first wave, shouting whatever came into our heads: '*Vive la France!*' 'Death to the Boches!' 'Come on boys!' The guns were rattling away ahead of us. ... We caught up with our friends but – to our horror – met a barbed wire barrier that was still intact and more than thirty metres deep. And all this time the enemy machine-guns carried on, rat-tat-tat, while to right and left we could see our comrades falling, strewing the ground with their blue uniforms, red with blood where they'd been hit. Then the third and fourth waves arrived in their turn. Up ahead a handful of men had managed to slip under the wire and reach the Tranchée des Empoisonneuses. In they jumped but alas we never saw them again. ... There just weren't enough of them. But neither was it possible to get across the wire en masse and our position became ever more precarious. Up went the shout, 'Tools!' We scrabbled like fury and had soon dug ourselves in right up against the Boche wire. Shots whistled overhead and we clung on to the ground we'd gained. This is what we achieved that day but ... if the wire had been cut ... And if we [hadn't also lost] our commanding officer, our captain, my lieutenant and so many pals killed or wounded.

The French did their best to supplement their inadequate artillery by improvising extra weapons under the control of the infantry. Placed in command of a section of mortars, Aspirant Paul Vaillant-Couturier was struggling. His new weapon consisted of a shell case from a 75 fixed onto a wooden base. ... In the breech, a fuse. We loaded the weapon any old how, using a spoon and powder lying around in a rusty metal cap. We put a bomb made of tin in the case. We lit the fuse, and then ran as far away as possible from this dreadful weapon which, just when it seemed to have failed, suddenly exploded amid noise, fire and heavy black smoke, immediately bringing down upon our heads a deadly cloud of ... German bombs.

Where the German front line was destroyed, the French were able to occupy the enemy positions with some ease – in places almost four kilometres of ground were captured, and nearly 12,000 prisoners taken. But always there seemed to be machine-gun posts which remained untouched, and all along the line, from Souain to Tahure, Beauséjour and the Main de Massiges, the Germans first drove the attacking troops to ground and then forced them back. The German second line remained largely intact, with its wire uncut. But over the next three days the French continued to launch attack after futile attack against solid enemy positions. On 6 October the French made yet another attempt, but once again in vain.

On 27 September Captain Edouard Junod (2nd Régiment de Marche/1st Foreign Legion Regiment) was trying to write a letter in his dug-out: 'I'm writing in the dark. This has been a dreadful day. We're advancing slowly. Our opponent is tough, his well-served artillery is continually bombarding us with 140mm gas shells. There's no respite, day or night. It's raining. Watery sun; we're shivering. Morale excellent. I don't know how I'm keeping going.'

The following day two Foreign Legion regiments (2nd Régiments de Marche/1st and 2nd Legion Regiments) attacked the Ferme Navarin position. Advancing to the foot of a ridge, American legionnaire Edward Morlae and his comrades 'left the cover of the trench formed in Indian file; fifty metres between sections, and, at the signal, moved forward swiftly and in order. It was a pretty bit of tactics and executed with a dispatch and neatness hardly equalled on the drill-ground. The first files of the sections were abreast, while the men fell in, one close behind the other; and so we crossed the ridge, offering the smallest possible target to the enemy's guns.' They captured the German first line and consolidated there, but were unable to make any further progress against the enemy's second line. Fortunately, the German position was turned, and the French took possession of the farm. Almost a third of the legionnaires became casualties, among them Captain Junod.

At 3.00 pm on 8 October 249th Infantry attacked further east, near Souain. 'Magnificent attack,' commented Aspirant Laby.

We captured three lines of trenches (Tranchée des Satyres) with almost no casualties. But 51st Division's artillery, which should have been bombarding a trench to our right, stopped firing, and the Boche machine-guns caught us in the flank. We were forced to fall back to our start line ... Huge losses. We were bandaging constantly from 4.00 pm to 1.00 am, under a monstrous bombardment. It's absolutely crazy. We lost about 800 men, and all but four company officers. ... There's only one left in the 5th Battalion. In 17th Company, Lieutenant Sibille, seeing us forced to pull back, rushed forward on his own with his pistol and grenades and was killed in the midst of the Boches.

The September offensive in Champagne also saw the last hurrah of the French cavalry in its traditional mounted role. On 25 September a charge by two squadrons of 5th Hussars at Beauséjour captured 800 prisoners at a cost of 17 men killed and 42 wounded (but 140 horses killed). Even here, while the charge began on horseback, it ended on foot. On 29 September the experience endured by 11th Chasseurs à cheval was perhaps more typical: 'A detachment of cavalry trotted forward into action. ... You could say the battle was hanging on this handful of men, offered up as a target for the enemy.' The German artillery quickly found its range: 'Men disappeared, their horses panicked and fled ... The charge ended in tragedy under machine-gun fire which mowed down the animals, and bursts of gunfire which killed the men.' The regiment lost half of its horses and a quarter of its men in the action.

Other cavalrymen were now fighting on foot. In the spring of 1915 Robert Desaubliaux (11th Cuirassiers), unhappy at the lack of action, had obtained a transfer to 129th Infantry: 'At the moment, we're rather ashamed to be cavalrymen when we've played such a minor role compared with the infantry. What have *we* done?' His comment may well have found an echo among disgruntled infantrymen. Later in the year maintaining full mounted regiments in the rear was finally deemed a wasteful and unacceptable use of manpower, and all cavalry regiments were compelled to create dismounted squadrons to serve on foot in the trenches. Lucien Cocordan (22nd Dragoons) was part of one such squadron. In September Cocordan was behind the French lines at Suippes (Marne). On 27 September the regiment moved up to Souain, where it remained for four long days: 'We were waiting to charge at any moment, but under what kind of conditions? [And] against what? A line of machine-guns or a redoubt.' When the attack eventually took place, Cocordan's brigade was in the van.

'It'll be us who are sacrificed,' he thought. And he was right; just 40 of the 220 men in his squadron returned to the start line.

In conjunction with his two major summer offensives in Artois and Champagne, Joffre also planned a number of supporting actions right along the front line: Eighth Army south of Ypres, with British assistance if they were willing to take the offensive; Second Army on the Somme, north of Péronne; Third Army between the Argonne Forest and the Meuse; and First Army east of the Saint-Mihiel salient.

In May 1915 Roland Dorgelès (39th Infantry), later the author of *Le croix de bois,* one of the great novels of the war, took part in another of Joffre's supporting attacks, around Le Choléra, near Berry-au-Bac, on the Aisne: 'Yesterday, you could hear the wounded shouting all night, "It's so-and-so from such-and-such a regiment. ... Don't leave me out here ... I've been hit ... I'm going to die ..." And there were others groaning "Mum". Horrible! And we couldn't go out there under the glare of the flares and the searchlights, and with bullets whistling by thick and fast. Much to our relief we were finally able to bring them back yesterday evening!! They'd been out there for forty hours, amid the corpses and the shelling.'

The series of attacks mounted in the Argonne during 1915 were particularly bloody. The infantry were thrown against uncut barbed wire on a narrow front with little or no artillery preparation, and the French suffered 65,000 casualties for negligible gains. Despite making extensive use of both gas and mining, particularly around Le Vauquois, they were unable to make deep inroads into the German positions. The mining war was unpopular with the men on both sides, and many contests were rendered formulaic by their participants. By the end of 1916 mines at Le Vauquois were only exploded in the morning, allowing time for the forward posts to be evacuated. One day a mine went off unexpectedly at midday. 'Accident' read a placard which appeared over the German lines; 'Yes. Many dead,' came the French response. 'Here too,' replied the Germans. By the end of the war the crest of the Vauquois ridge lay almost eighteen metres lower as a result of the mining and counter-mining operations which took place beneath.

Captain Marcel Rostin (112th Infantry) had been in command of his regiment's machine-guns since January 1915 and his early zest for the war had long since disappeared: 'It's true that men were killed in the opening battles, but they died a noble death; they were out in the open air, they could see ahead of themselves; whereas now, on a restricted front, in a tangle of wire and traps, thousands of men separated by [just] twenty to fifty metres hurl themselves against each other under a scarcely conceivable hail of bullets: it's just slaughter.'

For civilians, too, the enthusiasm which marked the beginning of the war was beginning to ebb away. In the spring of 1915 a draft of 200 men set off for the front from the depot at Béziers. But they left in the dead of night – no ceremony, no cheering crowds, no band to speed them on their way. Charles Auque (7th Chasseurs) was amazed by the passivity of his fellow countrymen. How was it, he wondered, that 'civilians had not risen up *en masse* to protest against this scourge?'

'One day France will bless us' – life in the trenches

By February 1915 men were spending three or four days in the front line, another three or four days in the reserve trenches, and then a similar period in rest – but that would include one night's guard duty and one night serving in work parties. As Emile Tanty (129th Infantry) soon discovered, 'In the front-line trenches you only sleep during the day. From 4.00 pm to 7.00 am you've got to stay on your feet, wide awake. You've no idea how long these nights are. So come daybreak you've just one thing on your mind: lie down, huddle under your blankets and go to sleep.' One soldier wrote to his family from Champagne: 'Yesterday evening I was still working as part of a covering party, protecting the men burying the horses killed since the war began. It's brave of them to do this work. When we got back I went on watch. From 1.00 am until 3.00 am I was on sentry-go before the barbed wire in front of the trenches. Then I returned to the trenches and was relieved at 6.00 am. We slept until 9.00 am and then we were hard at work again.'

For Blaise Cendrars (2nd Foreign Legion) the war soon took on an industrial aspect:

> You spent four days in the front line, then four days in the rear, then it was back up to the front for four days and so on until the end, if there was ever going be an end to this sad tale. The soldiers were disheartened. This coming and going was the lousiest trick in that war, and the most demoralizing; all that was missing to remind the poor buggers of their factory jobs was a hooter at the entrance to the trenches – a hooter, a clock and a time-card machine ... with an automatic iron gate.

Henri Desagneaux (359th Infantry) thought his life consisted of nothing but waiting: 'We wait to get out [of the trenches] and once we've left, we wait to go back in again. Back in the lines we wait for nightfall, then for daylight, and most of all we wait to be relieved. We wait for orders, we wait for the counter-orders. We wait and wait for the shell that's coming to wipe us out.'

The French, like the British, had initially conceived of trenches as a short-term measure, a temporary shelter before the war of movement could begin again. 'French soldiers knew nothing about trenches,' thought one anonymous commentator. 'They'd never been taught how to dig them, at least not systematically. Whenever you wanted them to [dig], you could rely on their disgust.' One soldier reported despairingly on the state of the Bapaume sector: 'The trenches are falling in. Here it's a boulevard 2.5m wide which wouldn't be deep enough even if you were up to your knees in muck. There it's a narrow track filled with stagnant water, with shelters built out of tree stumps sawn into four and laid across the narrowest parts of the trench, topped off occasionally by a bit of steel plate.' On 20 August 1915 GQG sent out a note remarking that 'certain formations consider that digging is beneath them. A good infantryman should be able to handle his tools as well his gun.'

Captain Marcel Rostin (112th Infantry) had been an officer in the pre-war army and hated the trenches. His life, he thought, had become '[that] of a mole ... because any excursion into the light and open air is hazardous and therefore forbidden ... This trench warfare is taking us back centuries. We throw melinite charges [and] hand grenades at each other. Soon we'll be pouring boiling oil over each other's heads and throwing stones.'

Yet men gradually became used to the idea of living in holes in the ground. Marcel Papillon (356th Infantry) wrote to his parents in March 1915: 'We've been in the trenches since October and we've got so used to life there that it all seems quite normal.' Some took pride in their efforts to make their new life more bearable. On 5 June Lieutenant Colonel Victor Bourguet (116th Infantry) boasted: 'At one and the same time, I'm a front-line soldier, a pioneer (with no assistant) and a chief engineer. Bit by bit I'm transforming my sector into a proper fort with [bomb]proof shelters. ... I'm trying to keep my men and their officers in good spirits by showing them all what we're aiming towards. They happily admit I've got the knack, and if it wasn't for the bullets and the shells it's really interesting work.'

Just before daybreak on 2 June Gaston Lefebvre (73rd Infantry) and his company took over a stretch of trenches on the Aisne, in a wood about one kilometre behind the front line.

The shelters in our sector were foul so the lieutenant made each section build a new one. We dug a hole about 1.4m deep, long enough for a dozen men to lie down in. We were right in the middle of a

wood so the roots made it hard work. ... When the holes were deep
enough we covered them with logs, each about fifteen to twenty
centimetres in diameter, then with branches and earth. We wouldn't
be bothered by the rain any more but it still looked as if a single
Boche 77 would go straight through the roof. We'd no straw, so we
made our beds with green leaves instead.

Territorial regiments were often employed at the front as work battalions.
Maurice Faget (129th Territorials) and his chums were 'busy with different
tasks from dawn 'til dusk, always something to do with improving or
rebuilding the trenches'. Nor did they get any chance to relax during their
rest periods: 'Tomorrow evening we'll be going back to camp for five days,
but we don't welcome the break quite so much any more because they drill
us like new recruits from morning until night.'

In the mountainous Vosges units often constructed their shelters above
ground rather than excavate into the rock. Naming one of their shelters
'Modern Villa', 343rd Infantry promised potential residents 'comfortable
rooms with all mod cons, central heating, magnificent view, wireless, a
terrace protected from the shells, Boche-shooting galleries, Teuton
Dancers, and tea and tango in front of the trenches'. Over the winter of
1914/15 the Artois billets of 142nd Territorials included an Avenue de
Bayonne, to remind the men of home, but also a Boulevard des Pieds
Humides ('Wet Foot Boulevard'). 'Mud up to your knees – it's pitiful,'
complained Lieutenant Capdevielle. Florent Fels quickly learned 'to sleep
with sodden boots on – since it would be a waste of time to try putting
them on again once you'd taken them off — [and] to sleep for four hours
in a wet greatcoat, amid the din ... and the foul smells'.

Behind the Aisne front many civilians had refused to be evacuated and
provided accommodation in their houses and barns, supplying a welcome
touch of home for Jacques Roujon (352nd Infantry) and his comrades from
the Vosges: '"Ours is a poor house," said the woman, black shawl framing
her round face, "but we'll look after you well." Poor, here! Certainly not.
The windows have glass in them, the roof is intact, the doors close, the
stove is lit! In a small room there are two beds and a mattress on the floor
for us to use.'

In the trenches and dug-outs soldiers soon discovered they were not
alone: rats were everywhere. In front of Les Eparges, Jacques Vandebeuque
(56th Chasseurs) found that:

Rats, too many to count, are the masters of the position. Hundreds
of them swarm around every ruined house, every dug-out ... the

nights are terrible. Completely covered by my galoshes and greatcoat, I can still feel these vile creatures gnawing at me. Sometimes there are fifteen to twenty of them to every one of us, and after they've eaten everything, bread, butter, chocolate, they start on our clothes. Impossible to sleep in such conditions. I struggle under the covers a hundred times a night [but can] only give them a temporary fright with a sudden burst of electric light. Almost immediately they're back, in even greater numbers.

GQG suggested rat hunts, with a bounty of five centimes for every animal destroyed, but financial wrangling soon made the proposal a dead letter.

And rats were not the only problem. 'You rarely lose a bet that your neighbour has fleas,' ventured gunner Paul Lintier. Flea hunts were a regular occupation for all soldiers. 'Can't you send me something to get rid of fleas,' Julien D. wrote home in desperation. 'You might be running short of lots of things behind the lines, but there's no shortage of these filthy insects here. Obviously I'm not asking for the powder you sent me before, try and find some sort of liquid that I can put down my shirt. That's where all the trouble is.' Two weeks later a crestfallen Julien picked up his pen again. 'Gomerol has no effect on fleas,' he reported sadly.

When their men went into action, officers and NCOs were encouraged to lead them from the front, not to push from the rear. Sergeant Marc Bloch (272nd Infantry) immediately tried to put this advice into practice: 'At first my men fired too high ... and too rapidly because above all else they wanted to expose themselves as little as possible ... I set an example by determinedly sticking my head up. These good men quickly learned the habit of courage.' But Colonel Campagne (107th Infantry) thought it easy to take this attitude too far: 'In 1915, it was quite the fashion among officers ... to go into battle weapon in hand. ... For all the respect I extend to those killed [in this way] I cannot agree with that view. An excellent captain can be no more than a mediocre bomber, and one cannot fight and lead at the same time.'

Maurice Genevoix believed it was impossible for officers to drive men on by threatening them. However, the soldiers themselves sometimes took a very different view. 'Some of the buggers would have been quite capable of shooting us,' commented a member of 81st Infantry. And, in fact, some of them did. After the failure of an attack on the Aisne in September 1914, General Blanc, commanding 73 Brigade (37th Division) wrote to his divisional commander, General Comby, regarding the performance of his brigade in general and 2nd Battalion/5th Algerian Tirailleurs in particular:

'In my opinion 73 Brigade isn't in any fit state to resume serious action tomorrow. As a former tirailleur colonel, I was distressed by the behaviour of the tirailleur units today ... I myself killed a dozen men who were running away but their example wasn't sufficient to prevent the tirailleurs from abandoning the field.'

But other officers were more conscious of their responsibility to look after their men. After a bloody reverse in his sector in the Vosges, Captain Ferdinand Belmont (11th Chasseurs Alpins) refused to send his soldiers back into action: 'Angry phone calls. I received the order to attack again. To prevent further pointless killing, I decided not to do so. I haven't regretted it for one second.' Clément Massignac (11th Infantry) recalled another officer who took a similar stance: 'He refused to leave [the trench] when the major gave the order, telling him the company wouldn't be setting off until the artillery had wiped out all the Boche machine-guns opposite, and that he had no intention of leading us to the slaughter.'

In the opinion of Jean Azan (414th Infantry), the best kind of commander was one 'who knows his trade and is a good father [to his men]' – a phrase which occurs again and again in soldiers' letters and memoirs. In Azan's experience these men were 'very rare', but André Bridoux (2nd Zouaves) had met one such paragon: 'My captain exercised absolute authority over his men, not only on account of his rank and rigour, but because of the respect that we had for him. [He was] the bravest and most intelligent man in the company. Everyone thought highly of him, including, perhaps especially, the hard cases, even though he made their lives very difficult. After he was killed on 16 April the men kept his memory alive for several months, which says a lot in wartime.'

Marcel Rostin (112th Infantry) knew it was up to him to motivate his men. 'I try hard to drill [some] comforting thought[s] into the minds of all the brave men around me who believe their captain's word is gospel,' he wrote to his uncle in January 1915. 'But sometimes their confidence flags out of [sheer] physical exhaustion ... For a moment I'm afraid. But I ... quickly get over it. Using my knowledge of the soldier's psyche, I buck them up and give them as much practical help as I possibly can.'

Julien D., who served in a regiment from the Midi, had a low opinion of his platoon commander, 'a Corsican who shouts a lot. He's completely useless. He's scarcely able to read and write.' And his successor was little better: 'a total incompetent ... he can't even read a map and when he wants to know where he is he has to ask an NCO. It's disgraceful to see officers as useless as this in the French army.'

Even worse were officers who thought only in terms of their next promotion. 'The real trouble is that many regular officers see only the extra stripe, not the result of an action,' thought Sous-lieutenant Paul Tuffrau (246th Infantry). 'And what's monstrous is that they're making use of human lives. Two colonels whispered something ... about a partial attack that "would allow them to give [someone] his star" [i.e. promotion from the rank of colonel to brigadier]!' On 6 April 1915 Henry Duché (28th Infantry) took part in a raid near Berry-au-Bac:

> Nine assault groups were formed to launch a surprise attack against the cemetery ... The regular lieutenant commanded a reserve which didn't take part. The captain stayed in his dug-out and waited to see what happened. [The raid] itself was a total failure with heavy losses, including one officer and several NCOs killed. We ended up in exactly the same position we started out from. But officially everything went swimmingly. The captain [was praised] for his ability "to galvanize his men and lead them into the attack with admirable elan and cohesion", and [was] recommended for mention in despatches.'

Louis Barthas, one of those territorials combed out earlier in the year, was now part of 280th Infantry. The socialist Barthas remained an anti-militarist at heart. 'We could've have been led by officers in the Kaiser's pay, sold out to the enemy,' he wrote after one attack. 'They couldn't have done any more to lead us into an ambush and get us killed.'

Most officers were drawn from the moneyed or the professional classes, although a certain proportion had always been raised from the ranks. Promotion from sergeant was more common in the French army than in its British and German counterparts, particularly in the 'technical' arms: in 1910, for example, three-quarters of artillery officers had once been NCOs. Yet whatever the individual variations in background, character or temperament, officers as a group remained distinct from their men. Pierre Chaine made this wistful observation: 'In the officers' dug-outs, they talk of women; in those of the NCOs, of pay and promotion; the corporals and the privates discuss wine. But love is rare, wine expensive, and promotions rarely given.' The railway station at Creil made the distinctions abundantly clear. Signs there pointed to 'WCs for officers/Toilets for NCOs/Latrines for soldiers.'

'Let the officers do the fighting, that's their job after all,' grumbled one of Sergeant Paul Cazin's men. But Cazin (29th Infantry) thought differently. 'It may be their job to conduct an offensive war, to support a warrior prince,' he replied. 'But defending one's country? That's my job, and it's yours too.' For Adjutant Jean-Marie Carré (4th Division staff), everything depended on the Other Ranks. 'What would become of the army without its sergeants and corporals?' he wondered. 'This is a war of platoon leaders and [ordinary] soldiers. You must have confidence in the private soldier. He alone is master here. He's only a few metres away from the enemy, in a fire zone, separated from his commanding officer by night and by death. What can a general do? The occasional piece of paper tells him what's happening, but who provides the information?'

Joffre's repeated attacks were beginning to sap morale among the men, and some had already had enough. 'It's true there's nothing sweeter than one's country,' thought Paul Cazin, as he waited to go into action in the Argonne. 'But it's not true to say that the finest of destinies is death. The finest of destinies is to live a long and happy life. Why lie?' Elsewhere on that front 131st Infantry refused point-blank to launch yet another attack. 'Not a man moved when the order was given to scale the parapet,' recalled Captain Pierre de Saint-Jouan. 'Eventually some decided [to do so] and none of them returned. Having ordered the attack, the officers were left powerless when the men refused to move off. In exasperation, the [officers] abruptly left the trench and got themselves killed. It was suicide.'

The men of the 131st were not the first to flout a direct order of this kind. During 1914 alone 509 men were found guilty of refusing to obey orders, and in 1915 the number rose to 2,433. On 12 November 1914 a number of men from 305th Infantry had refused to leave their trenches, and on 24 May 1915 twenty-three men from 56th Infantry were sentenced to death for refusing to attack.

On 1 September 1914 Joffre had obtained permission to set up special military tribunals (*cours martiales*) to replace the pre-war system of courts martial (*conseils de guerre*), which he thought too slow. All sentences were henceforth to be carried out within twenty-four hours. On 6 September these measures were extended down to unit level. Desertion or disobedience in the face of the enemy carried a sentence of death. Shocked by the indiscipline apparent in the first month of the war, Joffre felt strong action was required. Adolphe Messimy, the minister of war, thought desperate times required desperate measures, drawing a parallel with the Revolutionary Wars: 'In my opinion, just as in 1793, there can be no other punishment but cashiering or death. You want victory. Then take the necessary measures – swift, brutal, energetic and decisive.'

The first man to fall foul of the system was Major Henri Wolff. Commanding 4th Battalion/36th Colonial Infantry, Wolff was accused of trying to surrender his battalion without sufficient reason during the battles of the Frontiers in August 1914. He was found guilty and shot on 1 September.

This summary procedure was quickly extended to all manner of offences. The case of Lucien Bersot (60th Infantry) was typical. In February 1915 Bersot's regiment had lost 25 officers and 1,800 men near Soissons, reducing it to five weak companies instead of the usual complement of twelve. On 11 February he requested a pair of regulation red trousers – none had been available in his size in August 1914 and all he had were his white canvas working trousers – but the quartermaster sergeant could offer him nothing but a pair taken from a dead soldier, still covered in blood. Bersot turned them down and was given eight days' confinement by his company commander. But the colonel, fresh in post and anxious to impress new replacements, decided to make an example of Bersot. Brought before one of the new-style courts martial, he was charged with disobeying orders, convicted and sentenced to death. Two of his comrades who tried to speak in his defence went unheard and were punished in their turn. Bersot was shot the following day.

The men of 56th Infantry who refused to attack on 24 May were reprieved; not so four corporals from 336th Infantry who, after a legally dubious trial, were shot on 17 March for refusing to leave their trenches at Souain – an incident that later served as the basis for Stanley Kubrick's film *Paths of Glory*, nor Corporal Henri Floch (298th Infantry) and five of his men, shot 'for the sake of example' at Vingré (near Soissons) on 4 December 1914. After a vigorous post-war campaign, Bersot, the 'corporals of Souain' and the 'martyrs of Vingré' all received posthumous pardons.

On the eve of his execution Floch wrote to his wife:

By the time this letter reaches you, I will be dead. Here's why. On 27 November, around five in the evening, after a violent two-hour barrage over our front line, and just as we were finishing our meal, the Germans got into our trenches and took me prisoner, along with two of my comrades. I took advantage of a bit of confusion to escape German hands. I followed my comrades and was then accused of abandoning my post in the presence of the enemy. Twenty-four of us appeared yesterday evening in front of a court martial. Six, including me, were condemned to death. I am no more guilty than the rest, but they have to make an example of someone. My wallet and its contents will be sent to you. I'm going to confession in a few moments time and hope to see you again in a better world than this. I die innocent of the crime ... I stand accused of. If I hadn't escaped from the Germans and had remained a prisoner, I'd be safe and sound. That's fate. To the very end my final thoughts will be of you.

A total of 871 men were condemned to death during the war, and 236 executions were actually carried out (from 15 January 1915 onwards any death sentence had to be confirmed by the president). The new judicial regime was at its most stringent in the first two years, with one hundred men shot in 1914 and seventy-three in 1915. In subsequent years the numbers fell sharply – twenty-nine in 1916, thirty-three in 1917 and only one in 1918.

Convicted of abandoning his post in the Bois de la Gruerie, Michel D. (147th Infantry) was executed on 19 September 1914. Paul Ricadat served in the same regiment:

We were all distraught at the verdict of the court martial. And particularly this morning ... when the regiment gathered in a clearing for the execution. How would they choose the firing squad? Each platoon leader refused, giving all sorts of excuses. [D] was part of my section in the barracks at Sedan. With all the hesitation, it was decided that his section pals would form the squad. That really frightened me. Would I have to perform this task I so dreaded? I searched my conscience. What would I do? Fire into the air or aim straight for the heart? I could find no answer to this dilemma. However, after further reflection, I made up my mind. Nothing could save this poor soul now. If he wasn't killed instantly, the coup de grace would finish him off. He'd know what was happening, only increasing his physical and mental anguish. For the sake of humanity I had to aim at the heart. I was still arguing with myself when the men were chosen. They only wanted ordinary soldiers and I was a junior NCO ... What a relief. With the regiment drawn up, [D] was led out by an escort with bayonets fixed. They covered his eyes ... The poor man cried out, begging for mercy: "I'm sorry, I'm sorry. I don't want to die!" A command. The squad takes aim. "Fire!" It's over. [D] was struck down. A sergeant gave him the coup de grace and the companies filed in turn past the body. Few could hold back their tears and feelings were running high. Clearly, his dereliction of duty had cost us seven dead [and] an example was needed. But all the same! His crime: fear. Any one of us could have done the same thing. As I entered the Bois de la Gruerie for the first time two days ago, I was so afraid that I might well have been driven to it. Those who have no experience of the conflict between fear and duty cannot understand. We who do ... have forgiven [him]. After all, who knows? He might be the Unknown Soldier.

Within each infantry section soldiers depended on each other for help and information. Captain Julien La Chaussée (39th Infantry), an officer who had come up through the ranks, thought it easy to explain wartime camaraderie: 'particularly in trench warfare because it lasted so long ... like-minded men ended up sticking together. So they formed small communities, where you often saw each man contributing what he could – food, drink, tobacco etc. – and sometimes money. Those who sought solitude were few, and they were misguided, because everything about war proves that no-one can go it alone.' For Joseph Varenne (414th Infantry) this mutual solidarity was everything: 'If ours wasn't a camaraderie borne of mutual suffering, the wealthiest would spend good gold to get hold of it. But gold has no value here and, even if it did, it couldn't debase the brotherhood which unites us regardless of fortune or religion.'

Once they had settled in, many soldiers were reluctant to leave their comrades behind. Germain Cuzacq 'gave up a post of orderly because it meant following an officer to a different platoon; I didn't want to leave my chums.' Abbé Jean Dervilly was another who was reluctant to move: 'Here I am in the 120th. I'm joining my new regiment with some apprehension. I'm not familiar with [the regiment] or its character.' Dervilly retained the badges of his old regiment, 47th Infantry, for as long as possible: 'It was my regiment and, I could say, I felt closer to home there.'

But some could hardly wait to get away. 'At last, that's it,' crowed Marc Boasson. 'I've got my transfer to HQ Company. It's the pinnacle of my ambitions. The crowning of my hopes. ... Top notch.' Louis Krémer (231st Infantry) was of the same mind. Krémer moved within his regiment to become a telephonist in HQ Company. There he found a 'much more intelligent environment, better treatment, better care. Constant communication with the officers, the colonel, the admin section. No more tedious fatigues, or guard duty, and even, for the moment, no more trenches.'

In their off-duty moments soldiers did what they could to occupy themselves. Making souvenirs was a popular occupation. 'We always take advantage of any lull in the fighting and there hasn't been much happening for several days now,' wrote Germain Cuzacq. 'Everyone is busy making aluminium rings from German shell caps; it's turned us into boys again, so much so that we all want one as a souvenir.' In his rest camp Jean C. (173rd Infantry) was also hard at work: 'I've got something to keep me busy when we're at rest; I've brought out a whole knapsack full of aluminium. I'm also going to make some pen-holders out of German cartridge cases. I've got nine clips, each with five rounds per clip, with my tools I'll send home something nice, you'll see.'

But in the Vosges Georges Roumiguières (343rd Infantry) had no time for relaxation. He was kept busy on less agreeable tasks: 'Following orders given by the captain in my absence, I dug latrines in the field. Cleanliness is important, otherwise epidemics will take hold!'

Letters from home, often passed around or read aloud, were vital in keeping up morale. During a spell of 104 days at the front in 1915, one soldier sent no fewer than 390 letters and received 256 in return. 'What a let-down when I arrived in the trench yesterday evening,' Louis Vieu (280th Infantry) wrote to his wife. 'Not a single letter, then on another day they all arrive at once. But I'm writing to you all the same. I'll send you a word whenever I can ... if I don't write it can only be because I'm really tired.' Artilleryman Firmin Bouille (Moroccan Division) also encouraged his correspondents to keep in touch regularly: 'once again it's the old refrain: write, always write, it's the only way to exchange news.' If no letters came, men soon began to worry: 'Four days without news is a long time, my everything,' complained Jean Xatard to his wife Marie in 1917.

Those at home were just as anxious for news. Georges Roumiguières had scarcely left the regimental depot at Carcassonne on 4 August 1914 before he received a letter from his wife: 'I'll be happy with a line, a word, an envelope with nothing in it, but write to me often.' 'The more letters you send, the more I want,' confessed another woman. During 1915 alone the army handled four million letters, all routed through a single sorting office in Paris; it took two or three days for a letter from the front to reach a southern town, plus a further day to reach one of the outlying villages.

Farmers and smallholders were always worried about the state of their crops and animals. 'Peasant soldiers had one foot in the trenches and one foot in the farmyard,' observed Breton Benjamin Cariou, and their letters were often full of advice for their wives back home. 'Have you sold the potatoes?' Jean Dron asked his wife Lucie. 'If it were me, I'd plant plenty of Blacks. They crop better than the others and are easy to dig ... You haven't said how things are doing in the Petite Chaîntre [field], and if the oats are coming on well.' 'Throughout the war,' recalled Ephraïm Grenadou (27th Artillery), 'I dreamed I was in Saint-Loup [Eure-et-Loir].

I dreamed I was harvesting, I dreamed I was ploughing.' In the dug-outs, recalled Daniel Mornet (231st Infantry), 'The farmer talks about his fields, his coppices and his fallow; the shopkeeper about his customers and his profits; the worker, his skills and his pay.'

Men returning from a spell of leave also brought news back with them. The practice of giving leave to front-line soldiers began in July 1915. In theory, every man was entitled to six days' leave every four months, providing that no more than 4 per cent of the unit was away at any one time, and wounded men were allowed fifteen days' convalescent leave. Leave was always cancelled before major attacks so its reinstatement indicated the prospect of a quiet period. In certain circumstances, men were also given leave to help with agricultural work on local farms. The mayor's office acted as a clearing house for farms in need of workers, but the system was open to a certain amount of abuse. When a soldier turned up in Sablé (Sarthe) in late 1915 bearing a chit confirming that he was absent from his unit to help with the sowing, the mayor decided to investigate further. The man did not in fact have permission and was hauled back to his regimental depot for sixty days' confinement.

Leave periods were counted from the day the soldier arrived at his destination, a benefit to the men when wartime disruption to the transport network meant journeys were subject to enormous delays. But it also meant the regiment could never be quite certain when a soldier might return. Dominique Paoletti (163rd Infantry) was an extreme case. Paoletti set off for Corsica on leave for the first time on 11 November 1915. After a 25-kilometre walk from his billet at Jury (Hauts-de-Meuse) to the railhead, and a wait in an unheated hall, he finally left at half past midnight. The train then trundled slowly south: 'they're not trains, they're wheelbarrows,' he grumbled. A full day later he arrived in Marseilles, found a hotel for the night, and whiled away most of the following day touring the city. But bad weather meant Paoletti was unable to sail for home until 19 November, making his way to Ajaccio at a stately seven knots – a twenty-three hour crossing. After a night in Ajaccio, he travelled on to Propriano, and from there to his home village, arriving at 4.00 pm on 21 November. His leave passed all too quickly and then it was back to the front. In kinder weather conditions the return journey was somewhat quicker and he arrived back with his regiment at 8.45 am on 1 December. His 'six-day leave' had thus cost his regiment an overall absence of twenty days.

Les Boyaux du 95 (95th Infantry) described the journey back to the front:

Imagine your departure from one of the big Paris stations, where naturally you always arrive at the last minute! Crushed, shaken, jolted, there you are at the barrier holding out your scrap of paper to an employee who stamps it abruptly, almost angrily. The critical moment of parting has come ... a few last kisses and then a sudden leap, no looking back, into the open compartment. ... Your leave has ended, the illusion of happiness has vanished, you're already flying towards terrible reality. After a night spent half-asleep you've arrived at your destination. A territorial tears off the return coupon. What can you do in the town at this time in the morning? An orderly is waiting for you and gives you a straw mattress. Then an NCO orders you to fall in, and all the leave-men assemble by regiment to be driven to their destinations. You're allowed to do some shopping and after a frugal meal you head for the right jalopy. The lorries with benches are taken by storm ... on your arrival you jump in a 'British ambulance', then a truck and finally a cart which puts you down in the little village where your regiment is billeted ... the dapper and cheerful leave-men have once again became serious soldiers in muddy blue uniforms.

Letters and leave were the only means by which ordinary soldiers could keep in touch with their families. Wives were barred from the forward areas, although many an officer used his money or connections to arrange a rendezvous with his wife in a local town. 'The whore is a necessary distraction,' explained one general, 'while the wife, who represents home, weakens the soldier's resolve.' But not every man had a family to correspond with, and in early 1915 Marguerite de Lens founded La Famille du Soldat (The Soldier's Family), an association which encouraged its members to become a soldier's pen-pal. The organization was designed to appeal to women in rich, Catholic and conservative families. Its ethos was not to provide a romantic relationship – the woman became a *marraine* or godmother, the soldier her *filleul* or godson – but a 'replacement family', effectively a personification of everything the soldier was fighting for.

But many soldiers were looking for something more than this, and the popular magazine *Fantasio* launched a promotion entitled *Le Flirt du front* to put soldiers in touch with the girl of their dreams. The response from eager would-be Romeos was overwhelming and in November 1915 *Fantasio* was forced to call a halt to the whole campaign. But by then other magazines had taken up the idea and lonely hearts columns filled their small ads pages throughout the war. On 6 January 1917, for example, *La Vie parisienne* included no fewer than 216 announcements. Sergeant Heufel promised 'a gentleman's discretion': 'The war is never-ending and I too would like a kind and affectionate little godmother to make me forget how slowly the days roll by.' Lieutenant Raoul Denys (155th Infantry) added a note of urgency to his appeal: 'It's raining! Our shelters are flooded. Quickly, little godmothers, one word from you is all we need to see us home and dry.' Trench newspapers reported gleefully that one (un-named) sergeant had supposedly collected over 200 'godmothers' (but failed to explain how he found time to write to them all!). Some convalescents wrote to six or seven *marraines* and received food parcels from them all.

For *La Saucisse* (205th Infantry) the word *marraine* quickly became 'unbelievably flexible'. A contributor to *L'Echo des marmites* recognized two main varieties: 'the romantic *marraine*, a regular reader of *Fantasio* or *La Vie parisienne*, and the motherly figure, provider of money and food.' The author favoured the second type, but many preferred the first. For some the term eventually concealed a darker reality. 'People now hide their hypocritical pimping behind a word which once implied so much in terms of piety and patriotic charity,' warned the newspaper *L'Œuvre de Paris* in 1917. The British army provided a long list of 'undesirable' *marraine*s it considered no better than prostitutes. But the French apparently took no action, feeling perhaps that the list said more about British attitudes than their own. Others thought the danger lay not in prostitution but in espionage – Army Intelligence received a report making the solemn claim that the letters purportedly written by *marraine*s were in fact produced by a group of moustachio-ed Prussians in a secret base in Switzerland, with the sole purpose of wheedling military secrets from lonely, innocent Frenchmen.

Not every soldier was in search of a permanent relationship, even with a *marraine*. According to Henry Poulaille, sex was 'the main preoccupation of most soldiers. They thought about it from Monday morning to Sunday night and their conversations often revolved around it.' But Drs Louis Huot and Paul Voivenel disagreed: 'a man who's completely exhausted from fighting finds it easier to remain chaste than you might think. You hardly think of love when you're out on your feet.' And how could a soldier straight from the trenches expect to cut a dash amongst the opposite sex? 'At present the gentleman who introduces himself in his trench uniform hears nothing but "Pooh! How filthy you are!"' complained *L'Argonnaute*. 'Sadly, not everyone can be an [air] ace.'

At Raumont (Vosges) Georges Roumiguières visited the local café: '[it]

was crammed full of men singing and drinking beer. Others were chasing after the two or three girls of the house. The oldest of them couldn't have been more than eighteen; they were all tiny little things, but they still seemed to be flirting with the soldiers. I don't know what it's like round here in peacetime. But the war will quite certainly be fatal to the virtue of many women and girls in the frontier zones.'

And, of course, many soldiers were forced to turn to relationships of a more commercial nature. 'A soldier's too common ... too hard to understand, too coarse, too rough, always has a few fleas in the folds of his tunic, always the risk that he won't come back,' observed René Naegelen. 'Say goodbye to any female affection; if your heart runs over, bad luck ... and if your senses speak too insistently, congratulate yourself that you've a twenty-franc piece in your pocket; foot-sloggers are the clients of whores.'

As early as October 1914 the police in Amiens were already complaining of a large floating population in the town, most of them 'sporting women', while in Paris arrests for prostitution offences numbered around 50,000 a year throughout the war. Of the 10,000 people remaining in Reims – from a pre-war population of 140,000 – 9,000 were women. Civilians needed a pass to enter the area immediately behind the lines, but prostitutes found these easy to obtain. 'We turn these women away as soon as we uncover them,' complained a police inspector in Langres (Haute-Marne), 'but a fortnight later they're back with another safe-conduct.'

Railway stations were a magnet for the sex trade. In a street close to Bordeaux's Saint-Jean station, a man spotted 'about thirty soldiers taking turns to satisfy their animal passions with one or two women'. Dr Léon Bizard, a Paris police doctor, noted the same phenomenon: 'As soon as they arrived [in the city], some soldiers went straight from the station to the brothel, like animals in heat, and threw themselves on the first woman offered to them.'

By the end of the war sex too had been industrialized. In March 1918 the government opened officially controlled brothels, allowing the authorities to impose health checks on the women who worked in them. Prostitutes could earn some 400–500 francs per day, working up to eighteen hours and dealing with between fifty and sixty clients. René Naegelen described a routine encounter between a soldier and a prostitute in Châlons-sur-Marne's 'Public House No. 12' (elsewhere in the town, the more expensive and upmarket No. 16 catered for officers):

> Upstairs, in a bedroom with a damp floor, reeking of cheap perfume, the woman sits on a sagging bed and tries to get as much money out of him as she can. She rifles his pockets, totting up the contents.

'You could still give me a hundred sous. ... Let yourself go, dear. I'll be nice and let you stay a bit longer, you'll see.' Jacques has a fight on his hands just to salvage a few francs from the wreckage. There's no more reason for the prostitute to hang around with this man, a poor bugger who's gone without booze and cigarettes for weeks on end just to possess her for a few minutes. She's not sentimental, there's no more 'dear' or 'darling', and no more kisses. She's got other customers waiting so she gets rid of him quickly.

To prevent the front-line soldier from unwittingly betraying secrets – to family, *marraine*, or friend – postal censorship was introduced in January 1915. Each army henceforth included three sections, two or three men strong, which read every letter posted from the front to a foreign address, plus another 500 letters per regiment per month. One sergeant in 57th Artillery simply stopped writing home in protest. Anxious at the lack of news, his parents went so far as to contact Joffre himself to enquire after their son's well-being. Although reprimanded by his battery commander, the sergeant refused to change his ways, never sending more than a postcard bearing his signature. If soldiers had something important or controversial to say, many wrote simply, 'I'll tell you when I next see you.'

In August 1915 Edouard Coeurdevey (167th Infantry) was another angry man: 'Three days ago we received an order from GQG prohibiting us from sealing our letters, which from now on will be censored by one of our own officers! So now your most intimate secrets will be fed to a man who knows you, who hands out your orders, who can offer no guarantee other than his gold braid that he'll behave properly. And we know only too well that stripes are often sewn onto the sleeves of scoundrels. I can hardly believe such an intrusive inquisition.'

The number of letters examined might increase whenever GQG had a particular interest in finding out what soldiers were thinking – for example, during the unrest of the summer of 1917. But censorship, coupled with a natural wish to reassure friends and relatives, made many letters bland affairs, most soldiers confining themselves to matters of personal health and other uncontroversial topics. 'Nine-tenths of the letters say nothing at all and represent the obedient, loyal, stoical, uncomplaining mass,' reported one censor in October 1916. 'What's difficult to decide is how far pacifist comments represent more widespread sentiments. For a censor who finds the odd one or two among 100 or 200 inconsequential letters, they remain the exception.'

Like Maurice Genevoix, many soldiers found it impossible to describe what was really happening to them: 'I carefully sharpened my pencil and quickly scribbled a few short lines, using my notebook as a desk. Just a single phrase: "In good health and good spirits". I don't want to ... say what's really on my mind ... to repeat time after time, "Write to me. I haven't heard anything from you since the day I joined up. I'm feeling lonely and I'm finding things very tough." I know they write to me every day. Why disillusion them, why hurt them?' A soldier at Verdun later noted in his diary: '12 July. Ravin de la Mort. Lots of green flies on bodies which are drenching the soil with their stench ... rations limited to bread and spirits ... They handed out some pre-printed postcards. I just sent one to my parents, telling them that things aren't too bad, that I like the sector I'm in, and that I hope to be here for some time.'

But there were still some soldiers who preferred to tell it straight. 'My dearest Jeanine,' one man wrote to his wife in April 1915. 'Back from the trenches where we were on the receiving end of seventy-six bombs and were covered with earth four or five times. Return to the trenches tomorrow morning. Lots of kisses.' And on 21 November 1914 Baptiste Cantalou (171st Infantry) sent his family a picture postcard apparently showing an artificial lake. 'The crater you see on the card was made by a shell which went straight through my pack and grazed my head,' he wrote calmly on the reverse.

Photographs were always welcomed, by soldiers and by their loved ones. Taking snaps in the front line was officially frowned upon, but some officers and men had got hold of compact Vest Pocket Kodak cameras and used them to photograph themselves, their comrades and their surroundings. 'Have a shot of yourself taken in full dress,' one mother wrote to her son, 'and send it off to us as soon as you can.' 'You're always asking me for a photo,' wrote another soldier, with some exasperation. 'I've sent three to Berlou [including] one for you ... Take good care of the[m] because I mean to have them enlarged eventually.' But photos could be as much of a worry as a comfort: 'You're looking skinny and one of your cheeks is white and one dark. You look better in a frame than you do on a postcard, but please send me another card all the same so I can put [your picture] in a locket.'

Photos of his wife and children meant a great deal to prisoner-of-war Benoît B. 'I got your photo yesterday,' he wrote to his wife Marthe. 'I think you're looking well and you can imagine how pleased I was to see your face.' Marthe was worried that Benoît would no longer recognize his elder son in a class photo: 'You asked me in your letter if I'd have spotted him if you hadn't put a cross on his chest. I can tell you, dearest Marthe, that I'd have had no trouble [at all].'

For soldiers and public alike, official information on the progress of the war was provided by communiqués and the *Bulletin des armées de la République*. 'I never felt I needed it,' recalled one infantryman (53rd Infantry). 'I was actually taking part.' Trooper Honoré Coudray (9th Hussars, attached to a chasseur battalion) was equally dismissive, describing the *Bulletin* as a 'toy for soldiers to play with', full of errors and hot air, 'a vainglorious bag of wind'.

Many combatants expressed views in their letters which were strongly at odds with the official line. Emile Bègue, from the Indian Ocean island of Réunion, found himself quite unprepared for his experience in the front line: 'When I was at school I learned about French history [and] ... about war; but this is something quite different; it's just men being slaughtered.' 'Don't be hankering after joining us here,' a soldier told his cousin in February 1915. 'There's plenty that's bad here and not much good.' And Louis Herbin (106th Infantry) wrote to his sister on 14 April, shortly after seeing his best friend killed by his side in front of Les Eparges: 'In your letters, you're always telling me to take heart, that it won't go on like this for ever. But it's never-ending, and right now I'm all out of courage. I'd rather be dead than see what I see every day and suffer as we do. It's obscene!' Louis died of his wounds during a German counter-attack twelve days later.

Some units took to producing their own newspapers to bolster esprit de corps, proclaiming themselves the 'true' voice of the soldier. Some regiments sold their paper in their home town, allowing relatives to keep in touch, albeit indirectly, with their loved ones, while *Le Coin-coin* was distributed to men from the same Gascon towns (Jau, Dignac and Loirac) whatever their regiment. Some issues included articles on regimental history or recalled specific incidents of the war. But most adopted a humorous tone, poking gentle fun at regimental or battalion personalities (the cooks were the butt of many a joke). 'You can't spend all your time killing the Boche,' opined *Poil ... et plume* (81st Infantry); 'you've also got to kill time – hence this paper.'

Other trench newspapers turned their attention to the rear areas. On 30 May 1915 *La Marmita* (267th Infantry; 69th Division) was scathing about a rival publication, while poking fun at the credulity of a Paris newspaper:

> An amusing mistake. In *Le Journal*, Gustave Téry wrote recently about our humorous sister publication *La Tête à queue*, published at divisional headquarters, and sang the praises of its contributors, 'those proud poilus who manage to retain their good humour under the shrapnel at the bottom of their damp trenches!!!' This is a good

joke, and we should congratulate those in charge of *La Tête à queue* on this witty tease! We must hope with all our hearts that the editors of that paper stay put in their comfortable offices and never reach the trenches, for they would deprive the quiet little town where they reside of unaccustomed bustle, smart uniforms in dazzling colours, and elegant cavalrymen dressed with the greatest attention to style. Above all, they would deprive the handful of bourgeois salons which receive them each week of tasteful musical entertainments, given by genuine virtuoso performers, and would put an end to an artistic rivalry hitherto totally unknown in B[ar-le-Duc].

Food played an important role in maintaining a soldier's morale. At the beginning of the war each infantry section did its own cooking and carried its own pots, divided up between the men and strapped on top of their packs. From 1915 mobile cookers were gradually introduced, centralizing operations and reducing the burden on the individual soldier. But food still had to be bought locally and every company received a small sum of money to do so. Lieutenant Paul Tuffrau (246th Infantry) remembered one of his men marching along a road with a piece of salt cod peeping out of his pack, between his spare boots, while another pushed a baby's pram filled with macaroni. Whenever possible the cookers were placed relatively close to the front line so that meals would at least be warm when they arrived. But the smoke from their fires was all too visible from the German trenches, and they quickly became targets for mortars and artillery. Only when a unit was out of touch with the supply echelons for several days, or if the cookers were silenced by the enemy, could it broach its reserve of dried and preserved food – tinned, stringy meat preserved in oil, universally known as 'monkey', or sardines in oil.

The food freely handed out to the soldiers in the first weeks of the war was a thing of the past. In October 1915 Germain Cuzacq was horrified at the way civilians tried to make money out of the soldiers: 'Here [in Bouxières (Meurthe-et-Moselle)] you're paying double the peacetime price for everything. They're all shopkeepers and they're all really greedy; the bigger traders quite close to the lines are making a huge amount of money because the front isn't moving.' Raoul Battarel thought things were much worse at the front than in the rear: 'You talk about high prices,' he wrote to his mother. 'I can scarcely imagine [how] you['d go on] here. It's an absolute disgrace. The farmers and shopkeepers are just a bunch of pigs. One egg, five sous; sausages, eight francs a kilo; a goose, sixteen francs; a tin of boot polish, five sous etc. etc.' Georges Bertrand (6th Chasseurs Alpins) came across a farm where he tried to buy some chickens: 'We'd had nothing to eat for two days. ... I quarrelled with [the farmer] because he was asking way over the odds for them. As if to excuse his greed he kept on repeating: "I'm a good Frenchman, I'm a good Frenchman!" ... [But] just as our men were happily plucking the birds, we got the order to pull out. ... 'Twas ever thus!'

According to Raymond Escholier (59th Infantry), salt cod could be a mixed blessing: 'the brine never completely masked the rot and the men were tortured with thirst at a time when they'd been reduced to a quarter [of a litre] of wine [a day] and had no drinking water.' Thankfully, meals in the trenches rarely contained fish; according to Jacques Meyer (329th Infantry), the main meal of the day was normally stew. Called 'soup' – whatever its ingredients or consistency – it contained 'poor quality meat, forming a rubbery magma with pasta or rice, or perhaps beans, more or less cooked, or potatoes, more or less peeled, [all] in a sort of thin gruel, so justifying its name, even though it was covered with a thick layer of solidified fat. There was no question then of vitamins or green vegetables.' Another common dish was '*rata*' (short for ratatouille), a vegetable stew, usually consisting of potatoes and beans. These stews would be accompanied by loaves from the field bakeries, 'considered fresh as long as the date of baking, stamped on the crust, was within the past week'.

'During the most recent meeting of the cooks' union,' reported *Le Bulletin désarmé* (44th Chasseurs), 'they decided to wash at least once a month. That's progress.' On 25 April 1915 Pierre Baulard (39th Artillery) wrote to his parents telling them how much he'd enjoyed a new variety of fresh meat: 'The other day I ate rat, it's more delicate than rabbit. I'd just killed [a rat] and two other men made a bet with us that they'd eat it. We began by skinning it, then someone else cooked it, and [I decided] to have a taste as well. If the war's a long one I think I'll end up trying everything.' Tongue firmly in cheek, *Boum! Voilà!* (401st Infantry) offered a recipe for this new delicacy: simmer for three days, then serve over ice with finely chopped orange rind and strawberries. 'Better than "monkey",' it claimed.

Although often poor in quality and indifferently prepared, the food supplied as part of the rations, with its regular supply of meat (400g per day) and bread (750g per day), represented a distinct improvement on the diet of many men from poor agricultural backgrounds, where meat was a rarity and bread baked only once every three or four weeks. 'At ten o'clock,' wrote Simon Hastoy (6th Infantry), 'the cooks arrive ... they're carrying the stew, a bit of meat and bread. You can guess what the stew's like – always cold, because the poor chaps have had to carry it for three or four kilometres.' In normal circumstances the men ate at 10.00 am, the NCOs at 10.30, the officers between 11.00 and 11.30, and the colonel at midday. But this timetable was not always closely observed. 'We adopted the old habit of eating whenever we were able in case we couldn't eat when we wanted to,' commented André Pézard (46th Infantry). Once the food arrived in the trenches, it was shared out between the fifteen men of each section. 'The art of the perfect corporal,' thought Gabriel Franconi (272nd Infantry), 'is the ability to divide a tin of sardines into fifteen equal portions and still have some left over. Left-overs from left-overs ... make it seem as if there's a limitless amount; an army needs it to keep up morale.' The cooks always sent up enough food for fifteen men and any surplus was shared out between those present.

Regular parcels from home also helped to vary the soldiers' diet and bolster their spirits. Parcels represented the affection of their loved ones, as well as the soldier's peaceful pre-war home life. 'Your parcels are providing me with some of the most emotional moments in my life,' Paul Cazin (29th Infantry) wrote to his wife. 'Affection, curiosity, surprise, admiration, regret, so many feelings pass through my mind when I unwrap the paper and untie the string.' Cazin also thanked her for some pots of mustard, 'the last word in progress'. Local produce – sausages, pâté, cheese, even rabbit stew – was sent from home; one soldier from the Cévennes (81st Infantry) asked his wife to send him five kilos of the region's famous chestnuts. Meanwhile Maurice Faget (129th Territorials) was receiving gourmet parcels from his home in Agen (Lot-et-Garonne). According to Faget's son, they were 'a real inventory of Gascon cuisine, foie gras, *confits*, *civets*, rice and brains, poultry cooked in several different ways, *gateaux pastis*, *crêpes*, *merveilles* etc.' Treats like these helped to keep 'dark thoughts' at bay, believed Faget.

Crack shots could also use their skills to supplement the menu. Lieutenant Capdevielle (142nd Territorials) recalled one such feast: 'a soldier in 8th Company killed a hare in front of the trenches with his Lebel [rifle], but he daren't go beyond the wire [and one of our] machine-gunners pounced. Albert Lamaignerie made it into an excellent civet with summer herbs from the trench itself. Fried eggs, pancakes, the saddle beautifully cooked. Delicious. Meanwhile, the machine-gunners ate an old cockerel they'd christened "Von Kluk" before condemning it to death. The men used to make it crow every morning by feeding it eau-de-vie.'

Meals were washed down with wine or sweet, milky coffee – 'hot when it left, but always cold when it arrived', according to Jacques Meyer. The wine, *pinard*, was simple *vin ordinaire*, but it did lift the spirits, despite constant suspicions that the company cooks watered it down to disguise their pilfering. In the rest areas many battalions would find a pretext for sending a party to visit a nearby village, complete with twenty or thirty water bottles to fill up with wine. The canny soldier remembered to fire a blank round into his aluminium water bottle for just such an occasion, since the gases from the discharge expanded its capacity beyond the standard two litres. Each man was allotted a daily ration of a quarter-litre of wine in 1914, increased to half a litre in 1915 and three-quarters of a litre in November 1916. In the words of *La Femme à barbe* (227th Infantry): 'Water, the ordinary drink of the soldier; wine, the extraordinary drink of the soldier'.

Wine was a relatively new pleasure for all who did not come from wine-growing areas. Only the expansion of the railway network in the 1890s had brought prices down and put the drink within the reach of most of the country. By 1904 annual consumption per head averaged 194 litres – man, woman and child – and 250 litres in bibulous Paris. Then in 1907 the price of cheap wine collapsed, leading to widespread unrest in the south, and the army was encouraged to issue wine with meals to provide a market for the growers of the region. Ironically, when the daily ration was increased in 1916, the home market was unable to produce enough, and France had to import wine from Spain and Portugal to make up the shortfall. In parts of northern and western France cider or beer was the preferred alcoholic drink, but soldiers from these areas still had to get used to drinking wine instead.

Spirits in the form of eau-de-vie, *gnôle*, were sometimes distributed before an attack or in extremely cold weather, at the rate of one-eighth of a litre for each section. *La Femme à barbe* defined *gnôle* as 'a corrosive liquid obtained by distilling beets, pieces of wood, leather and other organic matter'. One infantryman (90th Infantry) thought it tasted of ether, while the best one chasseur could find to say was that 'it scours out your guts'.

But Lucien Auvray (87th, later 119th Infantry) thought a tot of *gnôle* played a useful role:

Eau-de-vie was welcome [especially when] distributed with a free hand at times of great trial, superhuman effort, attack and counter-attack, [or] particularly bad weather (driving rain, snow or extreme cold) when the ground seemed to suck you down. Some killjoys have tried to spread the lie that ... it was a way of drugging men, of getting them drunk just as they were thrown into the assault. Personally, I never saw spirits distributed just before we jumped over the parapet; in fact, with the enemy counter-bombardment, it would have been impossible.

Nevertheless, three and a half hours before they went into an attack scheduled for 5.00 am, Sergeant Louis Larché and his men received a warm meal and half a litre of wine per man. This was followed at 3.00 am by coffee, cheese, chocolate, tobacco, rum and a quarter-litre of spirits each.

Tobacco was another comfort. 'I've got the pipe,' stretcher-bearer (and future author) Henri Barbusse (231st Infantry) wrote to his *marraine* in September 1915. 'It arrived in its little box right next to the tobacco ... The pipe seems quite perfect to me. So much so that it stops me from saying too much about it.' Tobacco was supplied as part of the rations, but soldiers had to buy their own cigarettes. Both were normally kept in the waterproof pouch intended for the gas mask. 'Smokers formed a kind of community,' thought Charles Chenu. It was a religion with its own rites ... bring[ing] the officer and the soldier closer together.' Indeed, smoking received official medical encouragement. '[The MO] ... gave us a bit of health advice,' wrote Julien D. early in 1916. 'In particular he told us that we ought to smoke because it was good for us.' Artilleryman Firmin Bouille was another true believer: 'You mustn't forget that tobacco is the soldier's one inseparable companion. Smoking, even though it's a vice, is his only distraction in the front line, and the only remedy he has for the blues. Tobacco and wine are the Terror of the Boche.'

The winter of 1914/15 was bitterly cold and wet and soldiers had to do what they could to counter its debilitating effects. For Drs Huot and Voivenel, 'The social animal of times past was no longer recognizable in this hairy, bearded fighter, covered in mud and dirt, ridden with lice, wrapped in a sheepskin, wearing trench boots.' Charles Chenu recalled that during 'the terrible winter nights of early 1915, exhausted figures hauled themselves ... onto the firing step. An army of hooded ghosts, wrapped in blankets, tent sections and oilcloth.' Soldiers from the sunny Midi were particularly susceptible to bad weather. In November 1914 one (81st Infantry) wrote to his mother: 'It looks like I'll need a pair of long johns, a woolly vest, a big square handkerchief [and] a muffler.' Likewise, in October 1916 another wrote home urgently: 'Send me a thick sweater, a pair of woollen socks and a pair of gloves ... [and] if you're knitting another sweater, make the neck as high as possible.' The following day he wrote again with an extra reminder: 'Send all this winter clothing as soon you can. It's not warm [here].' And in February he needed yet another layer: 'It's still very cold. Make me a balaclava. Send it as quickly as possible.' Barbusse, happy with his pipe, was also in need of warmer gear. 'Please send me a thick sweater,' he wrote to his *marraine*, 'but only if you happen to have one. I can claim one from stores if need be. So there's no need to go to any expense ... Especially since it's a garment I wouldn't dream of wearing in civilian life.'

The peacetime uniform was plainly inadequate: not only did it lack cold-weather elements, but its very colour was unsuitable. Alone among the Great Powers, the French had not adopted a camouflage uniform in the years before 1914, and went to war in patterns first introduced in the 1850s. Pre-war attempts to introduce a camouflage uniform, initially delayed on grounds of cost, had foundered in a morass of misplaced sentimentality and political point-scoring, as the 'uniform question' become embroiled in the wider struggle between left and right. For the left, the red trousers were too visible on the battlefield and symbolized an unwelcome differentiation between the military and the ordinary citizen. The right opposed this view on principle, turning the trousers into an article of faith as much as a functional garment.

One deputy claimed that red trousers were the 'uniform of legends', another that their abolition ran counter to all of France's military traditions. *L'Echo de Paris* went further, denouncing any attempt to introduce a camouflage uniform as the work of a Masonic plot! The army itself had no say in the matter – the inherent weakness of French governments of the period (there were forty-two ministers of war between 1871 and 1914), and the anti-militaristic attitudes of the left, deterred serving soldiers from venturing any opinion in public. Radical Adolphe Messimy, minister of war from July 1911 to January 1912, was moved to predict that, 'This stupid blind attachment to the most visible of colours will have cruel consequences.' Yet, even in 1913, one of his successors, right-winger Eugène Etienne thundered, 'Abolish red trousers? Never! Red trousers are France!'

The magazine *L'Illustration* was sceptical about the search for a new uniform: 'In reality, it is absolutely impossible to find a colour which harmonizes with every aspect of the changing and diverse faces of nature; one must take into account the different seasons and crops, and if you were to take these obsessions to extreme lengths you would have to devise some sort of chameleon uniform for soldiers.' But in the end common sense prevailed. By July 1914, after the failure of four previous attempts to produce a uniform in different shades of grey or green, and with Messimy once again in charge, the government finally settled on a pattern in 'tricolour' cloth, made up of blue, red and white threads.

The red was quickly omitted when it became apparent that it could be produced only by using a dye manufactured in Germany, and the resulting shade was officially named light blue (*bleu clair*), although it was popularly christened horizon blue (*blue horizon*) when the uniforms first appeared. In January 1915 *L'Illustration* mourned the passing of war in the grand style, complaining that 'the war of panache, gleaming uniforms, gold buttons and silver helmets was about to get bogged down in the trenches, covered in mud, its colours fading'. But elsewhere the heavy defeats suffered by the French in the opening month of the war had served to bolster support for the new uniform. The sight of so many men lying dead on the battlefield triggered an emotional public response which took up the old mantra of the left – the disaster had happened because their red trousers made the soldiers too visible to the enemy.

Yet blaming the uniform was always an over-simplification. During the battles of the Frontiers, German artillery had opened fire at ranges of 3,300 metres, at which distance the colour of a soldier's trousers was immaterial. 'The colour red only becomes visible,' observed Pierre Bringuier (358th Infantry), 'when you've already spotted other things about the man, particularly his dark greatcoat standing out on the horizon.' Far more significant were the dense formations employed by the French and the lack of artillery support.

Production of the new camouflage uniforms began at the end of August 1914, but it proved impossible to turn out the huge numbers required quickly enough, and in the meantime a number of temporary expedients were adopted. These included an issue of royal-blue cotton overtrousers, which 240th Infantry began wearing in November: 'the men ... put [them] on over their red ones, which hampered them even more, especially when they were coming back from the trenches; the thick layer of mud which covered them turned them into blocks of clay, out of which poked a rifle barrel and pack full of the most disparate objects.'

The first deliveries of the new uniform were made over the winter and spring, and in April orders were given that it would be worn by all regiments serving at the front. In the Vosges the men of 343rd Infantry began to receive their new kit in January 1915, although Sergeant Georges Roumiguières took some time to get used to it. 'I've seen the new light-blue uniform,' he noted in January. 'It would be easy to mistake soldiers dressed like that for Boches.' By the following month his attitude was softening a little: 'We look peculiar in our new uniforms, everyone seems younger. However, the greatcoat doesn't have enough pockets.' And by March he was a convert: 'I can see the advantage of the light-blue uniform. We can pick out the soldiers in front of us by the black of their packs. In the dark the new greatcoat is almost invisible.'

But in action the new uniform still had its drawbacks. 'A wet, muddy greatcoat weighs you down,' grumbled Lieutenant Colonel Auvergnon (72nd Infantry). 'Its skirts tangle round your legs. There's good reason to wonder if during attacks the tunic shouldn't replace the greatcoat which hampers your movements and provides little real protection from the rain. The Germans normally attack in their tunics.'

The number of head wounds sustained during the opening weeks of the war also forced changes to the peacetime uniform. Over the winter of 1914/15 soldiers received an iron skull-cap to wear under the kepi, after Joffre had turned down a proposal to start manufacturing steel helmets: 'We won't have any need to [do so]. We'll have sorted out the Boche within a couple of months.' The steel helmet was eventually introduced in September 1915. Captain Jules Henches (46th Artillery), although a pre-war regular, approved of the new uniforms 'without lots of braid', and especially of the new helmet, identical for soldier and officer alike. But Roland Dorgelès was not impressed. 'Unfortunately, they're going to give us a helmet! We already have a mask and goggles. ... I'm certainly not cut out for this kind of war. I can easily see myself as a cavalryman, a Guardsman [or] a King's Musketeer [though].'

The mask and goggles were there to combat gas. Not only did the French have to adapt their uniforms, they were also forced to respond to unexpected new weapons – poison gas and flame-throwers – introduced by the Germans. 'I've seen war in all its horror [and] I'm sickened by it,' wrote a stretcher-bearer from 81st Infantry. 'Our enemies are barbarians; they've thought up some terrible weapons to burn our men.'

After attacking with chlorine gas at Ypres in April, the Germans went on to experiment with a number of different chemicals – both tear gas and poisonous gas. The first French gas-mask was an improvised affair, a simple pad, treated with chemicals and placed over the mouth, with accompanying goggles. René Naegelen (172nd Infantry) received both helmet and gas mask before the start of the Champagne offensive: 'One morning a lorry full of helmets arrived. It took all day to try them on. The next day, they handed out cotton pads, reeking of chemicals. You put them over your mouth and under your nose, securing them with tapes, the first gas masks.'

A new mask with built-in eyepieces was devised in December 1915, only to be replaced four months later by an improved pattern which was carried for the remainder of the war. And the French also learned to retaliate in kind. 'The war still continues, guns and rifles are no longer sufficient,' wrote a member of the Colonial Infantry to his sister in June. 'Now there are other weapons, even more terrible. We'll be using poison gas, and petrol to burn the woods where the troops have their camps. Just how far will things go?'

Carlos Diez, who served with a Basque regiment, was caught in a gas attack in September 1915:

> The Germans used gas, [causing] panic in the trenches. Despite our masks, which greatly impeded our view, we continued to move forward by walking over the dead and wounded ... I couldn't breathe and I thought my end had come ... Dreadful panic reigned in the trench, some wanted to fall back, and we had to fight to stop them, punching and kicking. It was horrible. Everyone was screaming [and] all around the earth was exploding, burying us. We got up again, some men clutching their throats. The whole trench contains nothing but the dead, the wounded and fragments of human flesh.

The front-line soldier increasingly felt himself isolated not only from those at home but also from his comrades in the rear. Louis Chirossel (261st Infantry) was especially scornful of a general and his entourage:

> When the chasseur buglers sounded the *Aux champs*, and their band struck up the *Marseillaise*, the general appeared through a gateway in front of us. [He was] riding a beautiful horse and followed by a magnificent suite – a dozen staff officers, plus an orderly carrying [his] distinguishing flag – their black or brown boots polished to a high shine. We were at the Present Arms and ... it was all I could do not to burst out laughing. How absurd! I could've been at Pinder's Circus. The longer this war goes on, the crazier things will be. There's too much emphasis on matters which have nothing to do with real war.

Particular dislike was reserved for 'shirkers' – soldiers who avoided front-line service. 'The front stops at the first gendarme,' ran a saying popular with the front-line soldier, and everyone beyond that demarcation line was considered beyond the pale. But Georges Demonchy (4th Zouaves) extended that definition somewhat: 'Corporals and soldiers weren't shirkers: they manned the trenches and suffered there; they occupied advanced posts and went on patrols ... But sergeants were shirkers, as were machine-gunners, artillerymen, officers, the regimental transport, and staffs at regimental, brigade and divisional level. Heavy artillery, engineers, aviators, drivers and all the services at the rear were also thought of as shirkers by the division, and even more so by those at the front.'

According to Honoré Coudray, the spa town of Gérardmer, a major supply centre for the French in the Vosges sector, 'was a rendezvous for all the dandified shirkers, from the secretary's secretary to the nursing staff, via all the rarefied grades of the army staff, male and female. And all these people were having a fine old time, living it up in the lap of luxury.' Not only did shirkers avoid all the dangers of the front line, they also had the pick of the girls: 'ugly or handsome, young or old, the winner will be the man who's always on the spot.'

'I can understand when men wearied and weakened by several months of fighting succumb for a time to apathy and pessimism, because I've had the same feelings myself,' admitted André Kahn (37th Infantry). 'I can understand at a pinch that a veteran who's been kept back at the depot waiting for a wound to heal might have negative thoughts about the outcome of the war and some misgivings about returning to the front. But I could never accept that a real man would boast of staying in the rear – something he should be ashamed of – making fun of those being killed in his place.'

Yet Quartermaster Corporal Henri Fauconnier (273rd Infantry) had no qualms about seeking a posting out of the front line, even after returning home from distant Malaya to join up. Fauconnier spoke good English and was keen to become an interpreter: 'All the Englishmen I've talked to complain about [their interpreters] ... As far as I'm concerned it wouldn't be shirking if I were to become [one]. I'd even accept a winter leave in Malaya if it were offered to me.' But, when he received his orders to report to the rear just as a German attack was looming, he found it hard to face comrades who were staying behind: 'I was horribly torn between joy at leaving and a desire to stay ... I came back here feeling almost like a deserter.'

It was public outrage at the idea of shirkers that lay behind the measures taken by the government to comb out men fit for front-line service from territorial regiments and regimental depots. So great was the hysteria produced by the 'hunt for shirkers' that any man in uniform away from the front immediately became suspect. Léon Vuillermoz (44th Infantry), responsible for training recruits at his regimental depot, was on leave in January 1916: 'I noticed some people were surprised to see me so often in barracks dress. This is the third time I've been home since I came out of the front line. While others remain in the trenches, I'm seen as some kind of shirker.'

Padres generally escaped this kind of censure. Approximately 28,000 clerics served with the army, conscription making no exception for men of the cloth, who were called up alongside everyone else. But in 1905, after a rancorous debate, the French republic had separated church from state, so officially there were no regimental padres, and the republic was determined to avoid showing any hint of preference for one religion over another. In 1914, when the colonel of 1st Hussars officially requested a blessing for his men, then assembling in Lourdes, he was reprimanded for his pains. And in 1917, when members of a group connected with the Catholic cult of the Sacred Heart of Jesus suggested presenting their flag to all front-line units, it brought this stern rejoinder from General Pétain:

> Soldiers (officers and men) who receive flags or banners bearing religious emblems, whatever their source, will turn them over immediately to their commanding officer, who will ensure they are returned to the sender. Generals commanding armies will remind their officers that any act of a sectarian nature constitutes a flagrant violation of the freedom of conscience of their men, and of the neutrality of the French state, and they must refrain [from such acts] while in uniform.

Unlike the British army, there were also no compulsory church parades. But only a colonel very careless of the welfare of his men would prevent a priest from conducting his ministry while serving in the ranks, particularly in regiments recruited in the deeply Catholic areas of Brittany and the Vendée. Most priests found a place among the stretcher-bearers, either unofficially at regimental level or officially with a division. 'I've just received some really good news,' wrote the Jesuit Paul Doncoeur, serving with 28 Brigade. 'I've managed to bring three priests into one of my regiments (42nd Infantry) as stretcher-bearers. So now there'll be [a priest] for each battalion. I'm still looking for one for the 35th.' Nevertheless Jacques Meyer's padre trod a careful path: 'Just as we were about to attack, in the chaos of the trench, wearing soutane and helmet, he approached me with all due propriety to ask permission to provide absolution for everyone who wanted it before the perilous journey.'

Corporal Abel Ferry (166th Infantry), who also served as a parliamentary deputy, expressed a deep mistrust of clergymen shared by many on the left. 'Clericalism dons a soldier's uniform the better to go to war ... against the republic,' he confided in December 1914. Pierre Roullet

(277th Infantry) was another sceptic, giving short shrift to one of his officers in 1914: '"Can you think of anything greater than the glory of God?" [he asked me.] "Human stupidity," I replied. "If people weren't stupid, we wouldn't be here trying to kill total strangers." He just shrugged his shoulders and walked off.' Philippe Barrès (12th Cuirassiers) noted that there were few takers when his padre wanted to hold a mass.

The experience of stretcher-bearer Ernest Brec, ordained just before the war, was rather different: 'The lads of 77th Infantry are good Christians for the most part [and] prepare for combat through drill and through prayer. In the days preceding the attack they crowded into the small village church every evening to pray.' But not all those who wished to practise their religion were able to do so. Joseph Bousquet (55th Infantry) was one who gave vent to his frustrations: '15 August today [the Feast of the Assumption], no mass, no service, [our] barbarous life continues. Even more fed up because the day conjures up [such] memories: [my wife] Marie's name day, start of the hunting season, pilgrimages etc. When [will we see] an end to this sad existence and a return to family life?'

Sergeant Georges Roumiguières (343rd Infantry) thought the experience of war sufficient in itself to produce converts. 'Many soldiers who weren't regular church-goers before the war abruptly joined the faithful when they made the acquaintance of danger,' he observed at Easter 1915. 'It's this kind of sudden piety that the clerics exploit. And clericalism is the rule among the officer class.' But a columnist in *La Saucisse* (205th Infantry), writing in 1917, disagreed: 'The war won't have created any new believers or any new atheists because each man in this calamity finds a weapon with which to support his own convictions.'

Many looked to their beliefs to keep them safe from harm. 'Let's hope it's the will of Almighty God that we should be together again,' Germain Cuzacq wrote to his wife on 24 December 1914. Simon Hastoy (6th Infantry) had a fortunate escape when a shell burst close by, wounding two of his colleagues but leaving him unharmed. Hastoy attributed his good luck to St Joseph and a pre-war pilgrimage made to a chapel dedicated to the saint. Others wore medals and tokens of one sort or another. 'The supernatural isn't out of place [here],' observed the Breton Augustin Bervet (135th Infantry). 'Few men pretend to be brave. A handful wear medallions on their chest or on their kepi.' Antoine Redier (338th Infantry) knew one sergeant who wore eleven medallions of various kinds pinned to a sweater under his greatcoat.

Those back home also sought comfort in religion, and tokens of this kind were often sent by relatives to their menfolk in the trenches, accompanied by a suitable message: 'Take this and keep it safe in your pocket.' The men hung on to them, sometimes for religious reasons and sometimes simply as a reminder of home and loved ones. Marthe B. sent her husband Benoît a St Christopher's medal, telling him that if he was unwilling to ask the saint to look after him, she would do it for him. 'Either way my dear husband keep it close by you,' she concluded. 'It'll make me happy and I'll pray night and day for your safe return.' The Sacred Heart of Jesus was not the only Catholic cult which gained new adherents during the war. Another was that of the distinctively French warrior saint, Joan of Arc. 'Joan of Arc is with us, she will lead us, she will be the first into the fight,' one woman wrote to a friend in 1916. Meanwhile General Hellot, commander of 56th Division, called on the saint to bring comfort to the mother of one of his officers, killed in the Woëvre: 'You can be sure that your son is already in a better place, at the side of the God of Clovis and of Joan of Arc.'

Believers were easy prey for the many charlatans ready to take advantage of them.

> Last August figures were published regarding the hypnotists, fortune-tellers, mediums, seers ... who live by exploiting a gullible public,' wrote the parish priest of Mauléon. 'There isn't enough evidence to provide [something similar] for th[is] parish, but I know of one popular clairvoyante who for fifteen or twenty sous – it's not expensive – will promise a young woman the return of her soldier, or girls in distress that they will find a husband. A little less frivolity, a little more faith, and you can be sure a dozen [rosaries and] a communion will do more good for your absent loved ones.

Dislike of the outpourings of Parisian newspapers showed no sign of abating, soldiers reserving a particular dislike for the nickname 'poilu', literally meaning 'hairy one'. The newspapers had used the term almost from the first weeks of the war, especially in regard to soldiers from Africa, the colonies and Paris, but by the summer of 1915 it had come to mean any soldier. Water was always scarce in the front line and men returning to the rear were consequently dirty and unshaven. 'I'm sending you a photo taken in the front line six weeks ago,' wrote one soldier. 'At the moment my hair is 20cm long. I'm disgustingly filthy. It's nearly three weeks since I changed my underwear. Fortunately, the muck doesn't show up on the photo!' But they had no wish to be reminded of this, particularly by journalists who never went anywhere near the front. The traditional nickname for the infantry was '*la biffe*', and that of the individual infantryman '*le biffin*', both derived from a word meaning 'rag-and-bone man'. The front-line soldiers preferred '*bonhomme*' – lad, but this did not stop them from appropriating 'poilu' to describe anything considered particularly good or strong. As the war went on, they also began to refer to themselves as the PCDF – the *pauvres cons du front*, 'the poor sods at the front'.

It was a similar story with another epithet – 'Rosalie', the infantryman's alleged nickname for his bayonet. Popular on the outbreak of war, the original Rosalie was a song, a hymn of praise to the bayonet – the 'sister' of Roland's sword Durandal, drinking the blood of Bavarian and Saxon alike. But the song was too bloodthirsty for the soldiers. In the words of *Le Poilu:* '[The soldier] does not call [his bayonet] Rosalie. The bayonet is called Rosalie only in a song by Théodore Botrel, which nobody sings, and in the *Bulletin des armées de la République,* which nobody reads.' Emile Morin (60th Infantry) had no time for Botrel, a prolific composer of patriotic ditties. Maurice Barrès had written a preface to Botrel's *Songs of the Bivouacs,* noting that the composer had been asked to visit all the camps, barracks, field ambulances and hospitals to perform his songs and poems. 'In fact,' admitted Morin, 'everyone ordered on "Botrel fatigues" did their level best to get out of them.'

Nor was there any such thing as the kind of bayonet attack immortalized in the song. 'Bayonets were routinely fixed before action,' argued Jean Norton Cru (250th Infantry), 'but that was no reason to refer to it as a "bayonet attack" – you might as well call it a "puttees attack".' 'Devil take the bayonet,' grumbled Guillaume Gaulène. 'It's had its time, like the paddle steamer.' Soldiers did, however, manage to find some use for the weapon – opening tins or driving it into the wall of a dug-out to use as a hook for their equipment.

Gabriel Chevallier (163rd Infantry) is now best known as the creator of the fictional town of Clochemerle. In his largely autobiographical novel *La peur,* he wrote of the kinship between ordinary soldiers on either side of the front line:

The man in the slit trench is caught between two [opposing] forces. Opposite, the enemy. Behind him, a line of gendarmes, a series of hierarchies and ambitions, sustained by the psyche of a country which continues to live off a century-old idea of war, and screams 'On to the bitter end!'. On the other side, the [enemy] rear replies: 'Nach Paris!' [Trapped] between these two forces, the soldier, French or German, can neither advance or retreat. So the cry sometimes heard from the German trenches, 'Kamerad Franzose!', is probably genuine. Fritz is closer to the poilu than he is to his Feldmarschal. And, by reason of their shared suffering, the poilu is closer to Fritz than he is to the people of Compiègne.

On 10 January 1915 *La Marmita* reported that: 'for some time now short conversations have been starting up between the lads in the German and the French front lines ... they exchange a few choice phrases, almost going so far as to express sympathy.' Such incidents met with official disapproval, but the generals were far from the front line and unofficially they continued to take place. In October Clément Massignac (11th Infantry) was in the trenches in front of Arras, where the neighbouring 9th Infantry had been swapping bread with the enemy (even though 'it's not as white as ours'). Their officers had even chatted with their German counterparts in front of the trenches. 'It ought to be like that everywhere on the front,' thought Massignac. 'Perhaps that would bring the war to an end.' But things were about to change – the regiment had been told that the next man caught fraternizing with the Boche would be shot on the spot.

Much depended on the attitude of regimental officers. Unlike his predecessor, Major (later Colonel) Campagne (107th Infantry) refused to tolerate fraternization of any kind. However, he did his best to remain civilized about it: 'Two enemy officers appeared above the trench ... I had a rifle shot ostentatiously into the air in front of them. They understood and disappeared. Next day, after the rain had stopped, I made everyone go down into the mire, and the enemy did the same. Conversations had not yet resumed when at a barricade one morning the Germans asked why our attitude had changed and if there'd been a relief. They were answered by a bomber and his sergeant.'

Commanders undoubtedly feared that fraternization would make it more difficult for a soldier to kill his opponent. But one infantryman (58th Infantry) found it easy enough: 'It was kill or be killed. In combat, the man is no longer important, the man opposite is an enemy you have to defeat.' Others found more personal reasons. A member of 112th Infantry stated simply, 'There was always a pal to avenge.' A cavalryman (4th Chasseurs à cheval) had a similar motivation: 'It was my duty to avenge my brother ... killed on 8 May 1915 at Fosse Calonne, east of Notre-Dame-de-Lorette ... I kept the letter he wrote on the eve of the attack; he said he was counting on me if things turned out badly.'

By the end of 1915, with no sign of the promised breakthrough, morale was beginning to flag. 'It's maddening the way people think,' commented

Alfred Joubert (124th Infantry) on 8 December. They've gone off the idea of war and many talk about surrendering. ... Happily they don't suit action to the word.' Meanwhile Sous-lieutenant Pierre Masson (261st Infantry) wrote with considerable prescience: 'an immense weariness seems to be weighing on everyone and neither side can feel triumphant. We wondered if perhaps we were heading for a worse catastrophe: one of morale.' Masson did not live to see his prediction come true; he would be killed near Flirey in April 1916.

Chapter 3

'They Shall Not Pass'
1916

Chronology

21–26 Feb	Battle of Verdun: German attacks capture much of the French forward line, including the key position of Fort Douaumont on the right bank of the Meuse
6 Mar	Battle of Verdun: the Germans switch the point of attack to the left bank of the river; French counter-attacks halt the initial advance
9 Apr	Battle of Verdun: the Germans renew their attacks all along the front; west of the Meuse these peter out by 29 May
22 May	Battle of Verdun: the French fail in an attempt to recapture Fort Douaumont
7 June	Battle of Verdun: the Germans capture Fort Vaux
23 June	Battle of Verdun: the Germans capture Thiaumont and Fleury
24 June	Battle of the Somme: the preliminary bombardment begins
1 July	Battle of the Somme: the first day of the offensive
11 July	Battle of Verdun: the French halt a new German offensive in front of Fort Souville
1–6 Aug	Battle of Verdun: the Germans launch their final assault on the east bank of the river
4 Sept	Battle of the Somme: Tenth Army relaunches its offensive
12 Sept	Battle of the Somme: Sixth Army relaunches its offensive
24 Oct	Battle of Verdun: the French counter-attack and recapture Fort Douaumont
2 Nov	Battle of Verdun: the French recapture Fort Vaux
15–18 Dec	Battle of Verdun: renewed French offensives recover much of the ground lost since February

'A shock like a thunderbolt' – the battle of Verdun begins

Verdun had been a stronghold since Gallo-Roman times. Its fortifications had been extended and modernized in the aftermath of the Franco–German war and by July 1914 its 'fortified region' was defended by a network of some nineteen powerful forts, garrisoned by around 65,000 men. Despite these elaborate defences, the Germans had come close to encircling the city in September 1914, brought to a halt only seven kilometres from its northern approaches. Verdun was now the hub of a salient, lying open to attack from three sides. But in 1915 this was a quiet sector, a number of local actions failing to shift the front line.

Joffre held no particular attachment to Verdun. In the mobile campaign he had initially envisaged, clinging on to fortress cities would only hamper his manoeuvres. And sixteen months of warfare had shown that fortresses were rather more vulnerable than the engineers claimed: German super-heavy artillery had quickly reduced the Belgian city of Liège in the opening weeks of the war, and Austria had lost the Polish fortress of Przemyl in March 1915, only to recapture it in June. In the opinion of the commander-in-chief, defending Verdun would simply tie up men and weapons better employed elsewhere – and liable to be lost if the stronghold fell.

Desperately short of artillery in late 1914, Joffre had stripped many of the heavy weapons from the forts surrounding Verdun to supply his field armies. However, his strategy still had its critics, among them Colonel Emile Driant – in civilian life a parliamentary deputy, but in 1915 commander of a chasseur brigade at Verdun. By autumn Driant thought the number of men and guns at Verdun and nearby Toul had fallen dangerously low, and he took his concerns directly to the war minister, Gallieni. Ever-sensitive to political interference in the running of his campaign, Joffre was vehement in rejecting all criticism: Driant should not have by-passed the chain of command, he argued, and Gallieni himself was wrong to intervene.

When Driant voiced his opinions, Verdun was not yet in the enemy's sights. The city became a target only at the end of December, as part of a wider strategy unrelated to the condition of its defences. Abandoning the 'uncertain method of a mass breakthrough', the Germans turned instead to a strategy of bleeding France dry, designed to 'knock England's best sword out of her hand'. General von Falkenhayn, chief of the German General Staff, outlined their thinking: 'There are objectives within our reach behind the French sector of the western front, which the French ... could only retain by throwing in every man they have. If they do so, the forces of

France will bleed to death – as there can be no question of voluntary withdrawal – whether we reach our objective or not.'

Falkenhayn identified two potential objectives – Belfort and Verdun – and geography determined his final choice. At the hub of a salient projecting into German lines, Verdun lay only twenty kilometres from a German railway line, and might in future form a springboard for a French offensive. The Germans successfully masked their intentions from French Intelligence for some time. German counter-intelligence had broken up a French spy ring in the autumn of 1915, temporarily halting the flow of information, and French aerial reconnaissance was poor – hampered by a combination of bad weather, timid patrolling, lack of photo interpreters and effective German camouflage.

By early 1916 accurate intelligence was becoming available, and material obtained from deserters pointed increasingly towards an imminent attack in the Verdun sector, but Joffre once again failed to act on the information he received. Unable to see any strategic purpose in a German attack on Verdun, he assumed that any offensive in that sector would be little more than a diversion. Even had he wished to reinforce the city, he had few troops available to do so; and besides his attention was focused elsewhere – on the forthcoming allied offensive on the Somme planned for that summer. Joffre and President Poincaré both visited Verdun early in the year, but to little effect. Joffre simply ordered General Herr, the commander in the sector, to continue strengthening the existing defences, and gave him two territorial divisions as reinforcements. Then, at the last minute, he added two more army corps to the garrison.

Events proved these measures hopelessly inadequate. The initial bombardment began at 4.00 am on 21 February and was the heaviest and most intense of the war to date, reaching a rate of forty shells a minute. The barrage concentrated on the French positions, destroying trenches and machine-gun posts, cutting telephone cables and the railway lines into the city. General Nayral de Bourgon, commanding 3rd Division, described the effect of heavy shelling on those beneath: 'The feelings inevitable when under fire put many men into a daze; their wits desert them, their vision becomes blurred as their pupils enlarge; the face tightens up, the eyes turn wild. Men act by reflex alone amid a mental, and even physical, fog in which they lose all self-awareness.'

Cowering under the bombardment was NCO Henri Robert (123rd Infantry), a Protestant pastor from Pons. Robert drew what comfort he could from his religion: 'It's absolute hell. You think every second might be your last; the earth is shaking, stones are falling, you're in a daze; with every fibre of your being you're asking, begging, for just a moment's respite, a moment's grace! ... I'm in the hands of God ... for over two hours it was most the dreadful experience imaginable.'

At 5.15 am on 21 February stretcher-bearer Robert Pillon (24th Infantry) was on the receiving end of a gas attack. 'They're a gang of murderous barbarians!' he wrote to his parents the following day.

> Luckily for us, two comrades who were keeping a vigil for a dead soldier warned us when the gas arrived. We grabbed hold of our masks and goggles straight away so we didn't suffer. At 7.00 am we set off through the trenches to look for the poor souls who'd been gassed ... Three companies from 1st Battalion had suffered so badly that they were relieved by three companies from 2nd Battalion that evening. What savages these Boches are! There was complete panic in the trenches when the gas arrived, men were dropping like flies. But the German attack has failed. Our machine-guns and artillery never stopped firing and prevented them from leaving their trenches. What a dreadful racket in the middle of the night!

The positions occupied by the French artillery were specifically targeted by the Germans, and the survivors were unable to muster in sufficient strength to mount an effective counter-bombardment. Ivan Cassagnau (57th Artillery) described the guns in his battery as 'literally devouring shells' in an effort to support the front-line trenches. The brunt of the initial assault fell on the 1,300 men of Driant's chasseur brigade. The death toll was high – no more than 120 survived – and Driant was not among them; he was killed fighting outside his HQ. The Germans made few gains that first day. But by 23 February they had virtually eliminated three divisions, and French resistance was waning. Lucien Gissinger (174th Infantry) took part in one counter-attack around the village of Douaumont: 'The Germans in the front line threw down their weapons and raised their arms with shouts of "Kameraden". Our men showed no mercy and shot them on the spot because we had orders to take no prisoners.'

Garrisoned by only sixty territorials instead of its full complement of five hundred men, the key fort of Douaumont fell easily to a German coup de main – a major blow, both tactically and to French morale. Douaumont was the highest point of the Verdun position, commanding an excellent field of fire, and the French considered withdrawing completely from the right bank of the Meuse. But the Germans were tiring and, helped by artillery fire from the opposite bank, the French held the enemy in check.

Aspirant Bourdillat was among the few survivors of 2nd Chasseurs, a battalion torn apart in the fighting around the village and fort. He described the scene as Captain de Rohan took temporary command of those who were left. Arranging the men in a square, Rohan did his best to rally them: 'We are going to wait for the Boches without flinching and we will fight to the last man, just as we did at Waterloo!'

Five minutes later Bourdillat heard a voice from the rear: 'Is that you, Rohan?' It was Major Fouchard of 4th Chasseurs, the other battalion in the half-brigade.

'Yes, sir,' replied de Rohan.

'What on earth are you doing?'

'As you can see sir, I'm waiting for the Boches.'

'You most certainly are not! Dying like that is all well and good, but saving the lives of these brave men is more important. We've done what we had to do. Right now the Boches will be banging their heads against a defensive line behind Fort Douaumont. Come on! Single file, move out.'

Two days after the fighting began, Joffre's chief of staff, General de Castelnau, arrived at Verdun to see for himself what was happening. Castelnau persuaded Joffre of the gravity of the situation, and of the need to hold on to the city and bring in reinforcements – more for reasons of prestige and morale than military necessity. Joffre gave orders to defend the right bank of the Meuse and, at Castelnau's urging, appointed a new commander of the Verdun sector. General Pétain replaced General Herr, bringing with him his Second Army, withdrawn from Champagne in early January.

Pétain had enjoyed a swift rise to prominence. In August 1914 he was on the point of retirement, but the performance of his well-trained 4 Infantry Brigade brought him promotion instead. By early September he was commanding 6th Division; by October, XXXIII Corps. He further enhanced his reputation in 1915, when his infantry attacks – well co-ordinated with the supporting artillery – had achieved some of the few French successes in Artois and Champagne. Pétain arrived in Verdun on 25 February 1916 and immediately set to work reorganizing the defences and improving infantry/artillery co-ordination. In response to his requests for men, extra divisions were sent to join him, including some previously ear-marked for the proposed Somme offensive. But within a couple of months his incessant demands for reinforcements had become too much for the commander-in-chief. On 30 April Joffre kicked Pétain upstairs – to command Central Army Group – with General Robert Nivelle taking over Second Army.

Supplying the sector immediately became a critical issue. The Germans had already cut the main railway line east to Nancy when they captured Saint-Mihiel in 1914. To make matters worse, the only other standard-gauge line – to Sainte Ménehould – had been cut on the first day of the offensive and was now under constant bombardment. That left *Le Meusien*, a single narrow-gauge railway line linking Verdun with Bar-le-Duc, and, more importantly, a narrow country road running by its side. Pétain and his transport officers quickly devised a system to move men and equipment along this artery. Some 3,500 lorries were involved. Each night they came in an endless stream, carrying in men and supplies, then filling up again with the wounded and with units coming out of the line. Other units moving in or out of town marched along the roadside. At peak periods vehicles passed, nose to tail, every ten seconds – any lorry that broke down was simply pushed aside. In all, some 90,000 men and 50,000 tons of supplies were carried along that road each week. After the war Maurice Barrès would baptise it '*la voie sacrée* [the sacred way]'.

This huge operation placed tremendous demands on transport units and their drivers. On 25 February, for example, transport unit TM388 set off on a four-day, 685-kilometre marathon in freezing conditions. Leaving their billets at Stainville at 12.15 am, they travelled for over five hours in the snow to reach Chaumont, fifty kilometres distant. There they picked up 146th Infantry and took them to Fort Regret, south-west of Verdun, arriving at 8.00 am. Then it was on to Vitry-le-François to collect 127th Infantry, arriving at midnight. After a few hours' sleep they were on the road again, depositing the men at Fort Regret at 2.00 pm. It was 8.50 pm by the time they returned to their billets. The following day they brought up the men of 206th Infantry from Ligny to Longueville. It was midnight when they got back to Stainville, but less than five hours later they were off once more, this time taking 257th Infantry and 3rd Algerian Tirailleurs up to the line. They returned to their billets at 11.00 pm. 'I've never been so cold or so hungry,' confessed one driver.

'Our driver,' recalled Sous-lieutenant René Arnaud (337th Infantry), 'had not let go of his steering wheel for twenty-four hours. Exhausted, haggard [and] sleepy, he nibbled at a grubby piece of bread while he waited for us. In 1915, we spoke of "shirkers" with a capital A – the A sewn onto the collars of the Automobile Service. Today we discovered that ... their life isn't always a bed of roses.' The newspaper caricaturist Sem also described the drivers: 'night after night they were riveted to the wheel, tired out, stiff through lack of movement, snacking when they could from a hand swollen with frostbite [and] covered with frozen vaseline ...

struggling against the cold, struggling in particular against the relentless, cruel tyranny of sleep ... the ceaseless thrum of the engine lulling them into a trance.'

The movement of traffic was strictly maintained by the local provost unit, which placed detachments at every crossroads. Georges Lélu (43rd Divisional Provost Squadron) described their lot: 'the police posts were above ground and unprotected; they were open to the skies, and the provosts who manned them had to stay outside to keep up their surveillance and fulfil their mission, without trench or shelter, nowhere to take cover if their particular crossroads was shelled. Come ice or rain, they had to remain stoically at their post, with nothing more than a tent section for cover or protection.' But the provosts had few friends among the passing infantrymen, and their hardships are unlikely to have won them much sympathy from that particular quarter.

Ten battalions of territorials, approximately 10,000 men, were assigned the task of keeping the road in good repair. Before the war the role of the territorial regiments was limited to home defence. But at Verdun they had much more to do: they were 'earth-movers ... expert navvies ... improvised carpenters, temporary joiners, chance roofers, skilled in all kinds of services and trades; with their patience and good humour, they personified French resourcefulness'.

The soldiers travelling by lorry were the lucky ones. Those who marched in and out on foot carried all their equipment on their backs. Daniel Mornet (276th Infantry) complained bitterly about the soldier's *barda* (a slang word for personal equipment drawn originally from service in north Africa):

> First of all you put on your equipment. Divers getting ready to plunge beneath the waves move with roughly the same amount of grace as an infantryman going into the line. Let's list the average equipment of a bomber or rifleman in a sector which isn't absolutely quiet: one or two blankets (not excessive when it's cold) rolled in a tent section; a change of footwear (if you're wise); a sheepskin or quilted jerkin; a shovel or pick, or a pair of strong shears; a mess-tin; a cooking-pot for carrying food; two litres of wine, coffee or water in a water-bottle; four days' worth of emergency rations (bread, tinned food, biscuits, chocolate etc.); two hundred rounds; six hand-grenades; personal effects like writing paper, tobacco, underwear, good-quality tinned food, mint spirit etc. ... Not forgetting the rifle, bayonet and gas mask. All squeezed, for better or worse, into three knapsacks.

René Naegelen marched up to the line, passing lorries full of men returning from the front:

> The companies seemed to be all skin and bone. The men in their greatcoats were ashen-faced, staring like those who have come back from the brink. Watching me go by, one of these ghosts ... stood up on his seat, mouth pinched, eyes glittering in their sockets, and waved a bony arm towards the horizon. And you knew this silent gesture signified unspeakable horror. From time to time, a soldier stood up, muddy, haggard, terrifying ... and shouted hoarsely at his comrades heading into battle. 'Don't go down there' was the ominous cry. We were on the road to Verdun and our imaginations were working overtime.

'Don't go down there, it's dangerous' was a catch-phrase of the front-line soldier, imbued with as much – or as little – humour as the occasion demanded.

Pierre Chaine (351st Infantry), a lieutenant with one of the machine-gun companies, entered the line to relieve another unit:

> The guide who was leading us picked up the pace. This was the final trip of his tour, and the thought that relief was imminent spurred him on. He was our only safeguard; without him we were [just] a band of blind men. Our fate depended on his memory and coolness. ... It wasn't unusual for units to spend the entire night roaming around the shell-holes without finding the correct position. Come morning ... these stray companies sometimes fetched up in the Boche lines, where they were surrounded and killed.

'The relief. About time too,' thought Private Branchen (405th Infantry). 'A fortnight ago, you'd have found ten volunteers for every task in this elite regiment, [but now it] was beginning to run low on pluck. As we came out of Bevaux Barracks [in Verdun], we bumped into a regiment going up to the line. The men stared at us, wide-eyed with fright. "Which company of the 405th are you?" they asked. "We *are* the 405th!" we replied.'

For units remaining within range of the German guns, a period spent out of the line was no guarantee of a proper rest. Verdun itself was well within range; almost all the civilians had been evacuated – only three stayed behind to run a canteen for the troops. Empty too was the village of Dombasle-en-Argonne. 'Before we went up to the line, we spent six days in reserve at Dombasle-en-Argonne,' recalled one soldier. 'We looted the place. Wine, spirits, groceries, we ransacked everything ... the village had been evacuated the evening before we arrived and it was under bombardment all the time we were there. We could never relax ... and many were killed.'

But regimental officers still wanted their men to get as much 'rest' as possible, unhindered by the military police. When a battalion of chasseurs alpins arrived at their rest area, their commander went straight to the local provost detachment: 'I hope your men will leave my chasseurs alone. They've been risking their necks in the front line for weeks, so it's only right for them to be the masters here and do whatever they like.'

The Germans relaunched their offensive on 6 March with attacks on both sides of the Meuse. On the left bank their objective was the twin hills of Mort Homme ('Dead Man') and Cote 304; on the right, Fort Vaux. French counter-attacks moved quickly to limit German gains. 'I've never seen such an avalanche of shells,' commented Lieutenant Armeilla (17th Division staff); 'the smoke rose to an incredible height, forming a curtain so thick not even the sun could pierce through.'

A fresh attack against Mort Homme and Cote 304 began on 14 March, but made little headway in a landscape which no longer contained linear positions, only holes in the ground. The Germans renewed their attack on 9 April, preceding it with an intensive bombardment that included the use of phosgene gas. Pétain's order of the day was optimistic: '*Courage, on les aura* [we will get them].' But back on the Aisne Clément Massignac (11th Infantry) had his doubts. Writing home to the Gers, west of Toulouse, he asked his family to send him a copy of the socialist newspaper *La République des travailleurs*: 'The newspapers round here are forever telling us that "we'll get them". I say "we'll get them" as well – empty water bottles or fleas – but the Germans, never.'

The German assault took Captain Augustin Cochin (146th Infantry) close to the limit: 'My poor second lieutenant was completely raving for an hour or two yesterday evening ... I admit that I'd just about had it [too] ... [and] I prayed that my poor swaddies and I wouldn't die so senselessly; half of them were crazy, eyes staring, no longer replying when I spoke to them.' André Pézard (46th Infantry) was caught in a gas attack: 'I can't breathe in this mask any more; my chest is on fire, a taste of hot oil and rotting pear fouls my throat, making me feel sick. Without thinking I peel back my mask. But now I'm drowning, the gas is making my nose bleed; my eyes are starting out of my head, I'm coughing fit to burst. Quickly I lower my mask again.'

Enduring an enemy bombardment was terror enough, but the French were also shelled by their own artillery. 'The glorious 75,' commented

Charles Delvert sarcastically, 'Bravo!' The front-line trenches were equipped with red rockets to request an emergency barrage and green rockets to halt firing, but these signals were often missed in the thick layer of smoke and fumes which covered the battleground. In René Arnaud's 335th Infantry several men were seriously wounded by a French battery firing short: 'The following day an artillery officer came to explain to us that the influence of sunlight shortens the trajectory of the shells. This episode gave us an overwhelming distrust of the artillery. A distrust common to all infantrymen.' Captain Tabourot (142nd Infantry) would surely have agreed with that sentiment, having appealed in vain for a supporting barrage from his own artillery during the desperate struggle around Fort Vaux. Mortally wounded, Tabourot reportedly shouted to his men: 'You there. Pay close attention. This is my final order! If any of you manage to get out of this, go and beat up the gunners!'

But, after watching a battery in action, Private Rousseau (87th Infantry) took a more charitable view of the artilleryman: 'At Vaux, under fire. To get our courage up, we watch an artillery battery in the trees next to us; [they've] no cover and are firing at full tilt; the men can't move around like we can; they can only do their duty and wait to die where they stand.'

During the three weeks between 5 and 25 April 43rd Artillery was positioned south-west of the village of Fleury. Over this period the regiment fired 150,000 rounds and lost ninety guns to enemy action or breech explosions. Twenty men were killed, fifty wounded and fifty-one horses lost. In the same period 34th Artillery lost seventy guns to enemy fire: 'that is to say,' commented the regimental history, 'each gun was replaced twice.'

Jean-Paul Vaillant was part of a 75 gun-crew. Despite all the hectic activity, he felt remote from the action: 'There's a singular pleasure in firing a gun. At the end of it all ... you know there are dead men. But here there's only duty, a desire to defend yourself, to overcome. And on the German side the dead are anonymous, you can't see them. You don't kill, you destroy targets. The gun-layer sets the bubble between its marks, sets the direction and elevation to the figures he's been given. All you're aware of is the science [of it] ... I fired all day.'

Bad weather and mud brought the Germans to a halt until 3 May. Corporal Malecot and his comrades in 152nd Infantry were enduring heavy shelling in their position on the flank of Cote 304:

We've eaten nothing but 'monkey' for the past five days; our stomachs are growling. We're hungry, weary and feverish. One company, predominantly made up of young soldiers, is starting to lose heart after sustaining [heavy] losses to shell-fire. Physically and mentally exhausted, some of these young men tried to escape this damned spot by leaving their trenches. As soon as Lieutenant Colonel Oudry heard about this, he rushed out from his HQ and set himself in front of them. He stood unarmed amid the shell-fire, spoke without threats, calmed them down, and led them back to their front-line trench, as meek as sheep following their shepherd.

But Oudry's work was not yet done. Shorn of its CO and three of its four company commanders, 3rd Battalion was falling back, with men taken prisoner en route. Oudry once again sallied forth, pistol and sword in hand. Gathering up men from 1st Battalion, he put in a counter-attack that not only restored the front but also liberated those who had fallen into German hands – and took some enemy prisoners for good measure. Despite Oudry's heroics, Mort Homme and Cote 304 had both fallen to the enemy by the end of May. The Germans had pushed some seven kilometres into the French lines and now had a field of fire for their artillery across the rear of the French right-bank positions.

Yet Nivelle remained characteristically confident. Convinced that the Germans were finally running out of steam, he decided on a counter-attack; but an attempt to recapture Fort Douaumont in late May ended in costly failure. Then on 1 June the Germans attacked again, making a final effort to take Verdun before the start of the Somme offensive. The blow fell primarily on Fort Vaux, isolated from any reinforcements or replacements by the German artillery.

Captain Charles Delvert (101st Infantry) and his men were part of the covering force trying to maintain contact with the fort. 'Are we going to be caught here [like rats] in a trap?' he wondered.

Two machine-guns cover the ravine. In front of the beaten zone you can see groups of grey bodies on the ground. The trench looks awful. Everywhere little spots of red spatter the stones. In places [there are] pools of blood. On the parados in the communications trench, a tent section covers the stiffening bodies. A wound is opening up in Aumont's thigh. The flesh is already rotting under the fierce sun. It's swelling beyond the fabric and a swarm of big blue flies is crowding round. The ground to right and left is strewn with unidentifiable bits of debris, empty ration tins, packs ripped open, helmets holed, rifles shattered and splattered with blood. An unbearable stench fouls the air. To cap it all the Boches send over a few tear-gas shells, making it absolutely impossible to breathe. And all the time the heavy hammer-blows of the shells continue to strike around us.

Sergeant Vincent Martin (119th Infantry) was in a similar position:

We ... are taking an incessant pounding – 210s, 305s and 420s fall with mathematical regularity ... Complete immobility is the rule of day. Enemy observers at Douaumont call down a bombardment if we show the slightest sign of life. We can only move at night, but woe betide the ration or water party that lets itself get caught in a barrage. We will never recognize sufficiently the heroism of the ration parties whose bodies line the tracks ... The most terrible bombardment on 1 May between 3.45 am and 1.00 pm: the 380s and 420s fell on the fort fifty yards behind us, and other smaller-calibre rounds also headed our way: two 420 rounds every six minutes, followed by four rounds of 380s every four minutes, whose explosions make us flip like pancakes when they hit the fort ... We don't think we'll ever get out of this hell on earth.

Inside the fort, the garrison was exhausted and running dangerously short of water: the reservoir had cracked under the bombardment and men were reduced to licking the condensation from the walls. Lieutenant Albert Chêrel was one of those trapped inside: 'Fort Vaux, built to house one company, now contained six. It had become difficult to move. You could hardly breathe, all the more so since an endless stream of shells, bursting close to the windows and entrances, blew clouds of smoke into the corridors, or dust from the earth and rock they threw up. The dust had another drawback; it increased your thirst until it was almost unendurable.'

On 6 June Commandant Sylvain Raynal set out to inspect what remained of his command in the fort: 'I toured our posts: exhaustion shows on every face, my words are no longer enough to rally the men. ... The[y] ... no longer react to my entreaties, those who look at me have a dazed expression. They are suffering and in my opinion can take no more.' Raynal surrendered the next day; he and his men were received by the Germans with full military honours.

On 23 June the Germans launched a gas attack, directing it principally against the French artillery. The French defence wavered and Pétain once again considered withdrawing from the right bank. Falling back here would uncover the mouth of the Tavannes tunnel, whose capture would give the Germans a route straight into the heart of the French lines. But the line held and crucially the French clung on.

The Tavannes tunnel carried railway lines east from Verdun under the ridges on the right bank of the Meuse. With the Germans occupying the ground beyond the Verdun salient, trains were no longer running, and the tunnel itself was now a storage dump and first-aid post. Louis Hourticq described the scene there in July:

> There's heavy traffic all day and especially all night: water parties, ammunition parties, ration parties; troops going up, others coming down, stretcher-cases brought back from the battle and then evacuated. This underground existence and the alternating periods of sleeping and waking which punctuate our lives obliterate any difference between day and night. The [amount of] activity, movement and noise is always the same, continuous, non-stop, without pause from midday to midnight, from midnight to midday. Too many people and too many things have come to seek shelter within this indestructible vault: stores of water, grenades, flares, small-arms ammunition, explosives; under lamps black with flies, surgeons sew torn flesh back together. Any noise is drowned out by the rapid chugging of the electric generator.

Charles Delvert was sent to Tavannes to get some attention for a wound. He found the tunnel full of 'latrines, [and] vile puddles of urine. The air is foul, so heavy with the smell of sweat and excrement it makes you ill. One night spent there and the men are pale, their faces drawn, they can hardly stand up. The cry you hear most often is a gleeful "Watch out, shit!"'

'Too many people and too many things,' were Hourticq's prophetic words. On 4 September a stray spark would set off some pyrotechnics, and they in turn set off ammunition. The ensuing blast and fire exacted a heavy toll, although the exact number of deaths remains uncertain: some sources claim around 500 men, others give a figure closer to 1,000. The casualties included the commander and staff of 164 Brigade; officers and men of 8th and 10th Engineers, and 22nd, 24th and 98th Territorials; and the medical officers and orderlies of 346th, 347th, 368th and 369th Infantry. It was impossible to identify most of the bodies: Colonel Marc Florentin, commander of 164 Brigade, was not formally declared dead until February 1918.

On 11 July the Germans launched another attack around Souville, but this was their last throw of the dice. Protected by their new-pattern gas-masks, the French artillery remained unaffected by the bombardment and drove off the enemy. Germany now had to turn its attention, and its ammunition reserves, elsewhere – to the Somme and, with the opening of Brusilov's offensive, to the eastern front.

Resuming the counter-attacks they had originally planned for early June, Nivelle and his main subordinate General Mangin continued them on into August, nibbling away at vulnerable German positions. But those in the front line did not always find it easy – or advisable – to comply with the orders sent out by HQ. Henry Morel-Journel (74th Division staff) knew just how much the army depended on the instincts of the ordinary soldier:

> General Mangin told General de Lardemelle [the divisional GOC] that the Boches seemed to be in total confusion, and that we needed to take advantage of this to extend the front during the night. 'Tally ho!' Fortunately, after more than two years of fighting, the troops now have the experience and judgement ... to assess the orders given by those who command from afar; they only follow those which have a chance of success; as for the rest, they claim to have tried and failed.

On 26 September 1916 Vincent Martin (119th Infantry) was picked to accompany a party of volunteers in a trench raid – its objective, a troublesome machine-gun:

> After two barrages from field and trench artillery, broken by a ten-minute interval, we crossed the parapet. [Apart from me] there was Sous-lieutenant Winter, another sergeant, a corporal, and about twenty men in two equal columns about 100 to 150 metres apart. I took one man to cover the left-hand column; we had two bags of grenades each – his were all fragmentation grenades, while I had one bag of fragmentation grenades and one of incendiaries. I reached a position close to two dug-outs which I thought were linked to each other. I threw all my incendiaries into the four entrances ... thinking that their occupants – forty men at least, I reckoned – would have a hot time of it. Don't worry, we'd no problems on the way back because they'd cleaned up completely behind us. A machine-gun had been trained on us from a position in front of the two dug-outs, [and] Sous-lieutenant Winter ordered us to take it with us when we left. So it was a good job I'd killed the gunners as soon as we left our trenches, otherwise they'd have nailed us. Once we got back to our front line, the Germans started sending one or two minnies over; one

made a huge crater when it burst and perforated my left ear-drum, but that apart we took no casualties. We also brought back two unlucky prisoners; one of them had come to say goodbye to a friend before going home on leave to Germany.

Shortly afterwards Martin himself went home on leave and so missed the counter-attack. The Germans sent a whole battalion to raid the French lines in retaliation, but succeeded 'only in leaving another prisoner in our hands'.

In late October the French launched their heaviest preparatory barrage yet. Involving two 400mm railway guns and a battery of 370mm mortars, it opened on the German lines over a five-kilometre front. The infantry attack began five days later and met with complete success. Covered approach routes disguised French intentions, and their air superiority over the front prevented German observation balloons and air reconnaissance from directing countering fire. Fort Douaumont was recaptured, as was, a few days later, Fort Vaux. Stretcher-bearer Abbé Gustave Vartan (107th Chasseurs) watched from the French trenches as the final act of the drama at Fort Douaumont unfolded: 'Towards 2.30 pm the wind blew the fog away and first through broken cloud, then right to the skyline, a miraculous sight appeared to the watchers: our soldiers silhouetted on the Douaumont ridge, approaching the fort from every side, reaching [their destination] and then establishing themselves there. Through binoculars, you could follow them as they came and went, then columns of prisoners emerging from the fort.'

Raoul X. (perhaps a junior officer of chasseurs) took part in the action at Douaumont:

> On the morning of the attack the fog was very thick. All the better for us! At 10.00 am we received our orders. The battalion would attack in four waves ... At 11.40 am the signal was given. 'Attention, men,' I shouted. Then I blew the whistle and sang 'Forward, brave battalion' from *Sidi Brahim*. The manoeuvre was first-rate. All the waves set off with equal energy and a fierce enthusiasm. The first Boche lines were overcome. They were almost completely empty ... We carried on. There were no longer any waves, just a crowd of men moving forward behind our barrage! ... The advance continued and at 1.00 pm we'd reached our objective with not a single man killed or wounded. Isn't that splendid? We settled in. To our left, Douaumont had fallen. Everything was going well and we passed a peaceful night.

The French success at Verdun in the second half of the year was due in part to their hard-won air superiority. Pétain knew that control of the air would confer a dual advantage – preventing German observers from targeting French positions, and in turn allowing French aircraft to act as spotters for their own artillery. So Major Charles de Rose, commander of Fifth Army's aviation component, was given carte blanche to clear the skies of enemy planes. De Rose took immediate action, concentrating as many squadrons as possible at Verdun, ensuring they had the best pilots, and equipping them with new Nieuport 11 scouts.

The Nieuport was far easier to manoeuvre than its German counterpart, the Fokker EIII, and the new units, formed into a *groupement de chasse*, proved an immediate success. The French now crossed the line in patrols of four or five: 'Sizeable patrols operated over the enemy lines between the front and the line of German observation balloons, attacking every enemy plane they met. This strategy gave [us] the upper hand, forcing the enemy to withdraw his scouts to cover his own aircraft, so leaving our observation planes unhindered.' From midsummer onwards the 11s were replaced by the more powerful and better-equipped Nieuport 16, whose machine-guns were synchronized with the propeller, and which carried Le Prieur rockets for anti-balloon work. Pétain later referred to Verdun as 'the crucible from which the French air force emerged'.

Lieutenant Arnaud de P. rated his service highly, particularly de Rose's own squadron, C66: '[Its] pilots are the best in the world, and the squadron is renowned from one end of the front to the other. It holds all the records for knocking over the Boches, and its members are called the Sparrowhawks.' Pilots were judged by the number of planes they brought down, but strict rules applied to the recording of kills. Arnaud was anxious to ensure he received due credit for one success: 'I attacked and brought down a Boche, but unfortunately he was able to make it home and set himself down about 100 metres beyond his own lines. I'm hoping someone from our side ... saw him land, two kilometres less and it would have been the Croix de Guerre [for me]. I'm hoping for a citation if one of our balloons managed to spot it, but did they? I'm going to find out. You have to have two witnesses.' Sadly, Arnaud seems to have searched in vain for he registered no claim at this time.

But it seemed to the soldier on the ground that French aircraft were never around when they were most needed. 'The German air force has been very active since daybreak,' wrote Sergeant Edmond André (61st Artillery) in February 1916. 'Their aircraft flew over our positions for long spells absolutely untroubled – neither by our air force, of which we've seen not a single representative, nor by the AA, whose battery on Cote 344 is now in German hands.' Colonel Rohan (358th Infantry) added his voice to the criticism:

> The shortcomings of our air force at Verdun weighed very heavily on the spirits of our men. There was a complete lack of organization and discipline; the aces could do more or less what they liked and naturally chose the dashing, dangerous jobs in preference to th[os]e thankless tasks which were nevertheless so vital. And at that time no-one had organized continuous cover over our lines, if only to give our infantrymen, who felt very much forsaken, the sense that their winged brothers were fighting alongside them.

High above the battlefield was American volunteer pilot James McConnell (N124, Escadrille Lafayette):

> The battle passes in silence, the noise of the motor deadening all other sounds. In the green patches behind the brown belt, myriads of tiny flashes tell where the guns are hidden; and those flashes, and the smoke of bursting shells, are all we see of the fighting. It is a weird combination of stillness and havoc, the Verdun conflict viewed from the sky ... Our knowledge about the military operations is scant. We haven't the remotest idea as to what has taken place on the battlefield – even though we've been flying over it during an attack – until we read the papers; and they don't tell us much.

By autumn the enemy too had introduced new types, the Fokker D1 and the Albatros D1, both superior to the Nieuports. But by then the Germans had been forced to withdraw many of their squadrons to the Somme, leaving a free hand to their opponents in the Verdun sector. The year closed with the French on the offensive. On 15 December they launched a final eight-division attack and succeeded in pushing the Germans back even further.

'A living impassable wall' – under the bombardment

The devastating scale of the bombardment conducted by both sides completely changed the character of the battleground; lines of trenches became nothing but a series of overlapping shell craters. Arriving in Verdun for the first time, Marcel Dupont (7th Chasseurs) had 'an impression of desert and wide-open spaces. Where are they? Where are we? Nothing, you can't see a living thing. Might everyone be dead, swept away by the hurricane swirling around them over the past four months? In this dead and deserted landscape only one thing shows any sign of life, the gun.'

Even during large set-piece attacks, the fighting at Verdun took place between small, isolated groups, moving from shell-hole to shell-hole. According to Jolinon, holes with 'groups huddled in the bottom ... invisible to each other, and often closer to the holes occupied by enemy infantrymen than to those of their own section, formed the front line. Overlapping holes of grey and blue, imperceptible to the shells. ... Further away were other groups, from other regiments.'

La Saucisse (205th Infantry) commented:

There's nothing in war more terrifying than being caught in a barrage. A man is out there in his hole. He's not in the midst of an attack. He's alone. He analyzes. His judgement is extraordinarily sharp. First he chats with his neighbour in the hole next door; he likes to feel there's another human being close by, a comrade running the same risks as him. It's only natural. He shows off, he forces himself to crack a joke or two: 'Let me know if everything goes west'; 'I'd rather they were twenty-franc pieces!'; 'They'll stop when they get bored'.

But he realizes that his laughter rings false, and suddenly he'd rather be honest with himself. There's no doubt about it, it's a proper barrage, one of those artillery preparations which precedes an attack, where the ground to be gained must first be chewed up completely, where not a single living being remains in the devastated trenches. He isn't afraid of air bursts because the thirty to forty centimetres of soil above his head are more than enough to stop fragments. [But] shells hitting the ground won't spare him; it's certain death if the earth falls in.

The shells follow one after another with no let-up. His skull feels like it will burst, he thinks he's going mad. The agony is interminable.

Suddenly he's afraid he'll be buried alive. He sees himself, back broken, suffocating, digging at the earth with clenched hands. He pictures the excruciating agony, wishing with all his might that the shelling would stop, that the attack would begin, that he could choose where to wait for the enemy. But what's happened to his comrades? Have they gone? Are they dead? Is he the only one left alive in his hole?

Then suddenly he can see his loved ones: his wife, his mother, his child ... there they are smiling at him in the familiar surroundings of home.

He wants his final thoughts to be of those he loves ... He speaks their names out loud, quietly, reverently. ...

Then he rebels; he has a lunatic desire to jump up. It's daft to sit here waiting for death! Anything's better than that! Oh, to look danger in the face! To fight! To do something!

The shells continue to rain down. A blind force has been unleashed ... and the man stays in his hole, helpless, waiting, hoping.

Communication failures compounded the isolation of the battlefield. It was impossible to maintain land-lines under the shelling, and attempts to repair them simply invited needless casualties. Nor was it feasible to string air-lines in the crater field created by the bombardment. Ground buzzers were open to interception by the enemy. Carrier-pigeons were used in the forts, but their cages were too bulky for them to be employed regularly in the field. Runners provided the only practical alternative. In this otherwise most modern of wars, the speed of communications was reduced to that of a man running over broken ground, usually under fire, 'covered with mud and sweat, sometimes barefoot so as to escape the grip of the clay'. Casualties were high, but there was no shortage of volunteers. 'I liked my job as a runner,' claimed Louis Foucault (120th Chasseurs). 'The confidence placed in us and the sort of exultation we sometimes felt in overcoming the dangers we faced provided ample reward for my efforts.'

Lucien Durosoir (129th Infantry) was another runner:

Apart from the incredible bombardment, the worst thing back there is the state of the ground, all chewed up, craters everywhere. You go down into one crater, then up and out and back down into another. Again and again. So you can see you need to be some kind of acrobat to survive with wounded on your back. Heavy shelling means the roads to the rear are often impassable, so you may well have to stay where you are for two or three days with nothing to eat or drink but 'monkey' or water taken from a shell-hole at night. If you're lucky no-one sees what you're doing, otherwise there'd be nothing to drink.

Food and water all had to be carried up to the lines. A ration party from 18th Chasseurs 'spent a whole night fetching meat, bread, wine, chocolate, tinned rations. ... They returned exhausted at dawn, covering the last hundred metres under machine-gun fire. They declared they would rather die of hunger than go back to the rear to fetch food again, [but] in the evening they set off once more on their chaotic journey across the fields and craters.' And the quality of the food was poor. 'GQG apparently didn't have the leisure to take as much care over the supply of rations as they did about the supply of ammunition,' thought one anonymous combatant. 'They could perhaps have found something more appetizing for the men in the front line than boiled rice, which goes sour after a few hours. They could perhaps have taken the time to taste the issue beans. Then we wouldn't have wondered why they so often tasted of wet dog. They could perhaps have spared us heavily spiced meat and salted herrings when men were already dying of thirst.'

Although normally positioned away from the front-line trenches, the regimental cooks were never completely immune from the action. Up at the front, Jean Thiais (64th Infantry) and his comrades had been complaining that they weren't getting their rations: 'At the relief we understood why ... the shelters had collapsed, beneath them were bodies with limbs sticking out; mobile cookers, drivers, horses, wagons, cars were lying any which way ... everything was in pieces, ripped apart.' Some men found themselves in desperate straits. Jean Castelnau (95th Infantry) remembered that 'a horse lying dead by the roadside was quickly carved up and the meat cooked over spirit lamps or blocks of solid alcohol, and eaten half raw'.

Timothée Méléra was an NCO serving with the hard-fighting Régiment d'Infanterie Coloniale du Maroc – the regiment which stormed and recaptured Fort Douaumont. Méléra had just one thing on his mind – the relief: 'My nerves were strained and my body ached ... [I had to] get out, get out of this hell.' And, once he got out of the lines, his thoughts turned to 'coffee, coffee and more coffee, followed by hot coffee'. No wonder he was anxious to escape the trench equivalent. One trench newspaper defined it as follows: 'a liquid, normally blackish [in colour], more or less clear depending on the water used. No sugar for a long time now, as punishment, without us ever really knowing why ... Conscience sometimes impels the cooks to throw in a few grains of real coffee, although they regard this almost as cheating.'

Most men in the front-line trenches would have settled for a drink of water. 'We soon got through the two litres we carried in our water bottles,' reported Daniel Mornet. 'We toiled hard and were almost always thirsty. We were often in dire need of water. There was no water on the left bank of the Meuse. On the right bank ... there were lots of springs. But the Germans ... knew that as well as we did. Day and night they rained so many shells upon them that you ran the risk of being killed whenever you went for a drink of water.'

Water parties were also prey to the shelling. In June a soldier on water fatigues arrived back at Charles Delvert's HQ. He was carrying three two-litre water bottles, one of them empty; the contents were to be shared between sixty men, eight sergeants and three officers. 'We've been racked by thirst for the past two days,' wrote Louis Vion (370th Infantry). 'We suck pebbles, buttons off long johns, we burn our throats with what's left of the mint spirit.' Sous-lieutenant Roger Campana (151st Infantry) saw a man reduced to 'taking big gulps from a pond covered in green scum. It contained a body floating on its stomach, swollen as if it had been filling up with water for days.'

On his way up to the line, Pierre Amond (19th Chasseurs) regretted how selfish he had become: 'A little further on we passed a large number of casualties begging for water ... it was cruel of us to let them die of thirst, but we marched past all the same, not daring to look, because we too were heading into the line. Our canteens were pretty small and soon enough we'd be needing the water ourselves. "Swine, bastards!" shouted the wounded men when they saw us turning a deaf ear to their cries.'

When every drop of water had to be brought up by hand, washing and shaving came low on the list of priorities, and many men were happy to see a clean chin once they reached the rear areas. Among them was 4th Group/107th Heavy Artillery: '"Do I look better with the beard or without?" That was the question some agonized over. Today we have the proof: "You look better without." On the arm of that young lady yesterday, you looked like her grand-dad; today you're Don Juan. Young, handsome – many's the heart you've captured already and in future you'll conquer even more! Watch out, here comes trouble!'

L'Echo des marmites (309th Infantry) summed up some of the 'highlights' of a spell in the trenches at Verdun: 'Not washing at all for a fortnight, not changing your clothes or shaving for thirty-five days ... spending a night on sentry duty next to a cow which died ten or fifteen days ago ... being grazed by a shell which lands at your feet but doesn't explode ... sleeping in the snow for eighteen days with only branches for cover ... [and] seeing your best friends get killed around you.' Franciscque Vial (112th Territorials) and his comrades went into one trench to find it full of corpses: 'What are they thinking about? What are they feeling? Suddenly, there's a voice, raw with tension, "If only our poor wives could see us now!" Sorrowful words, but also compassionate ones. They summed up the territorial spirit.'

Visitors saw a very different, and unrealistic, slice of trench life. Georges Ripoull (81st Infantry) reported on a sudden flurry of activity:

'sprayed the trenches and communications trenches with sulphur, and cleaned the latrines with lime, trenches swept, the main communications trench in a state of perfect cleanliness – the reason, General Grossetti [the corps commander] must be visiting the front line.' Novelist René Boylesve, reporting for *Le Journal*, was another sightseer: 'We turned into a communications trench; another surprise, it was perfectly clean. No mud, no rubbish, not a single scrap of paper ... In the shadows, a rations party, all in a line, reminded me of bas-reliefs from the golden age of ancient Greece.'

Léon Florentin (44th Territorials) was scathing about an officer who tried to maintain these standards in real life: 'What can you say ... about an officer, in command of two sectors, who ordered us to sweep up the dead leaves which had fallen into the communications trenches.' Yet cleanliness was not completely despised. 'It leaves us cold if they're talking about moving us to a new sector,' reckoned *Le Pépère* (359th Infantry), '[or] if someone says the Boche are twenty metres away. But there's outrage if they say the dug-outs are full of lice.'

Dug-outs offered shelter – and comfort of a sort. Much depended on the quality of the original construction. Technical competence was sometimes at a premium, as Florentin soon found out: 'Our *major des tranchées* was a Parisian upholsterer, a sous-lieutenant in the 351st, who knew absolutely nothing about digging and still less about "the strength of materials" ... [And] what can you say about [another] captain who ordered his HQ dug-out to be covered so deeply that it collapsed beneath the weight of the earth above.' But Florentin had struck lucky: 'Fortunately the regimental pioneers were all miners from the Nord and the Pas-de-Calais.'

Lieutenant Louis Hourticq (330th Territorials) found his dug-out 'a source of unexpected pleasure ... a sudden breath of fresh air ... peace, silence, the serenity sought by the desert fathers ... the isolation is wonderful ... I'm truly alone with myself.' In contrast, Daniel Mornet (276th Infantry) treasured the companionship he found there: 'There's a lot of chatting in the shelters, often even during bombardments. Talking makes the time pass more quickly and the waiting less trying. We hardly ever talk nonsense though. The shell-blasts seem to see off the trivialities. But we like to chat about our lives, past and future, and anything but the war.'

Louis Mairet (127th Infantry) thought,

The soldier of 1916 doesn't fight for Alsace, or to destroy Germany, or for his country. He fights out of honesty, habit and duty. He fights because he has no alternative. He continues to fight because, after the initial burst of enthusiasm, and the despair of the first winter, the second brought acceptance. What we hoped would be only temporary ... has become a situation stable only in its instability. We have swapped our homes for a dug-out, our families for our fellow soldiers. We now cut our lives from the cloth of sorrow, rather than well-being. We have tailored our feelings to the daily grind and found our balance in imbalance. We no longer believe this will ever change. We no longer see ourselves going home. We carry on hoping it will happen, but we're not counting on it.

Mairet was killed before Craonne the following spring.

The threat of disbandment horrified Charles Delvert's infantry company: 'Dinner was on the way when the news was broken to my men. No one could eat. Many wept. The bonds uniting the soldiers were very strong.' But Paul Lintier thought the bonds between fellow soldiers were closest in the artillery:

> Our unit is the gun. The seven men who serve it are closely connected, interdependent, a single being which springs into life: the gun in action. The links between these seven men, and between each of them and the gun, makes any weakness more obvious, more laden with consequence, the resulting shame heavier ... [But] the infantryman normally finds himself alone in combat. Under fire, a man lying four metres from another is on his own. All his energy goes into worrying about himself. That's when he's liable to succumb to the temptation to stop, to hide, to slip away, and then to flee.

However, fear of appearing a coward kept many a soldier at his post. 'It wasn't a blaze of patriotism that inspired this spirit of sacrifice,' claimed Louis Barthas (296th Infantry). 'It was just bravado, a reluctance to seem more faint-hearted than the next man, [or] a foolhardy trust in one's luck; for some [it was] the secret, forlorn hope of a medal or a stripe, [and] finally for most the futility of railing against implacable fate.' Even Barthas, a committed pacifist, could mock a soldier for being a 'weakling.'

Old hands scorned the naïveté of newcomers: '[they] duck their heads ... unsure what to do when they see the shells coming over ... while the veterans remain unmoved.' Nor were the rank and file necessarily intimidated by rank. Maurice Genevoix (106th Infantry) recalled another occasion when the bullets were flying: 'A corporal, standing close by, crouched down with a grimace of pain. Pannechon, laughing, pointed it out to the others, "Did you see the corporal? What a dive!"' Meanwhile

Paul Tuffrau remembered a comrade going into no mans' land to retrieve a wounded officer: 'Fromond has returned. He's brought back the aspirant. Poor boy, he's badly wounded. He wept when we lowered him [into the trench]. "Lieutenant," said Fromond, "if you carry on like that, I'm taking you back to the Boches."'

'Every soldier is afraid ...,' thought Jean Norton Cru, 'but the great majority demonstrate admirable courage by doing their duty despite their fears.' Guy Hallé (74th Infantry) was one such. Haunted by a vision of his own death, Hallé longed to escape: 'There'll be a huge flame, a cry, then my legs will be smashed, my chest all torn up and bloody, my eyes wide open, and my face completely white ... Oh, to get away from here ... to flee ... like a hunted animal, to escape to the rear somewhere, to the corridors of Fort Souville, to the Ravin de Bazile, anywhere but here.' Lieutenant Robert Desaubliaux (129th Infantry) was a cavalryman when war broke out. Having transferred to the infantry in search of action, he was wounded before Fleury in May: 'Ten months ago, I resolved to become an infantryman. What an absurd decision! I'm regretting it [now].'

'This terrible war,' wrote Charles Delvert, 'with its endless gun-fire, strains the nerves to such an extent that the veterans are becoming more afraid rather than less. And they're all the same. I'm sure they no longer pay much attention when a shell or a bullet whistles by. But every time we set off for the trenches again, I see a little more tension in their faces.'

'The sole purpose of the infantryman', concluded Sous-lieutenant Raymond Jubert (151st Infantry), 'is to be killed; he dies without honour, with no great outburst of feeling, at the bottom of a shell-hole, and far from any witness. If he goes on the attack, his only role is to mark the zone where the artillery reigns supreme ... to accept and celebrate the excellence of the gunners. War today is an exercise in time, not space. It's less about winning terrain than holding your place.'

'Courage consisted of holding on,' thought Jacques Meyer, 'and nearly everyone was brave ... Almost all had the courage of men with no alternative, and they showed it time and again ... They weren't heroes, they only left the trenches when they had to, but leave them they did, and for the rest of the time they held on.' Pierre Chaine went further: 'Having courage isn't [a matter] of holding on for eight days, but for twenty; not for twenty days, but for two or three months; and not simply for three months, but six months, no a year, and double that, and even more, as long as it takes.'

But a determination to 'hold on' hardly explains the acts of heroism produced by the war. What motivated men to risk their lives for others? For

Drs Huot and Voivenel, it ranged from 'fear of punishment to the purest of idealism, via esprit de corps, setting an example, and feelings of anger and rage'. Soldiers like André Maillet (23rd Infantry) were dubious of ideas of 'glory': 'Glory ... cannot be wooed by muddy creatures like us ... we know nothing of her; she knows nothing of us. We ask nothing of her; she promises us nothing.' Major Jean Henches (32nd Artillery) agreed: 'those most deserving of pity are those expecting personal renown. I don't think military glory will be the final outcome.'

Yet many soldiers still took pride in their achievements. On the left sleeve they wore a chevron for every six months served in a combat unit; on the right, a chevron for each wound. In April 1915 Deputy Bonnefous, seconded by Emile Driant, suggested that all those mentioned in despatches should also receive a medal. The award, the Croix de Guerre, was available to individuals and to units. Units wore distinctive lanyards indicating two, four or six citations; two regiments – the Régiment d'Infanterie Coloniale du Maroc and the Régiment de marche de la Légion Etrangère – received so many that they were presented with a special double lanyard.

But ordinary soldiers wanted awards to be distributed fairly: there was nothing to distinguish the stars or palms awarded for bravery from those conferred for some other service. 'Their Croix de Guerre,' thought Philippe Barrès (12th Cuirassiers, later 31st Chasseurs), 'there's no way I would wear it ... The way it gets handed out is a disgrace. It's dreadful to see it gleaming on some men ... while others get nothing.' Jacques Meyer was awarded the Croix de Guerre for his part in capturing a German battery during the battle of the Somme; artist Guirand de Scevola – who never went near the front – received his for 'perfecting the army's camouflage procedures'. Fifty years later Meyer could still recall his indignation on hearing the news.

Many soldiers thought the award of a medal too often depended on whim. 'One commanding officer showed himself generous, another ... haggled,' later claimed the Fédération Nationale André Maginot des Anciens Combattants. 'They imposed such a modest quota [for the Croix de Guerre] that platoon leaders despaired of making a choice. Meanwhile the wounded had been evacuated and tended to be forgotten about.' 'The men at the front fought in great confusion,' concluded Gabriel Chevallier, 'with no witnesses, no referee to keep the score. Only they were capable of deciding who was worthy.'

For *La Mitraille* (64th Division) the amount of publicity given to the soldier compared unfavourably with that received by the airman:

'Dressed in their Sunday best, beflowered, beribboned, beflagged, befuddled.' Conscripts take their leave to report to their regimental depots.

'Women tossed flowers; we stuck them in the muzzles of our rifles.' Somewhere near Tours, an infantry regiment marches off to war.

'The grape harvest didn't suffer. It went off as normal.' Pickers take a break as the infantry march past.

'Your huge horse and your shiny cuirass [are] a magnet for shells.' Cuirassiers on patrol.

'A pitiful exodus of country folk driven from their villages by the invasion.' Refugees struggle to make their way southwards.

'Women have gathered up their husbands' scythes . . . loaded the sheaves, spread the manure, guided the harrow.' Some even took over the ploughing.

'Have a shot of yourself taken in full dress and send it off to us as soon as you can.' Private A. Prades and chum, of 35th Infantry.

'Night after night they were riveted to the wheel.' Transport drivers pause for a photograph.

'Mud up to your knees – it's pitiful.' In the trenches of Artois.

'Comfortable rooms with all mod cons.' The Villa Monplaisir, built into a rocky hillside of the Woëvre.

'In the days preceding the attack they crowded into the small village church every evening to pray.' A padre conducts a field mass.

'Holes with groups huddled in the bottom . . . often closer to the holes occupied by enemy infantrymen than to those of their own section, formed the front line.' Manning the trenches at Fleury, 1916.

'That's the way to use your terrain! These are men who know how to fight.' Soldiers take shelter in the Tranchée des Calonnes sector of the Woëvre.

'If only our poor wives could see us now.' Territorials about to go up to the line.

'We already have a mask and goggles. I'm certainly not cut out for this kind of war.' Grenade in hand, waiting for an attack.

'We lit the fuse and then ran as far away as possible from this dreadful weapon.' A primitive trench mortar made from shell cases.

'The glorious 75! Bravo!' Gun-crews crouch over their weapons during the German 1918 offensive.

'The colonel stood motionless on the parapet, holding the colour . . . for five minutes, five long minutes.' Colonel Desgrées de Loü (65th Infantry), Champagne, 25 September 1915.

'We've become bandits!' Moppers-up in action at Verdun.

'A modern army smells of petrol, not horse droppings.' Some FT17s and their crews.

'There's a lot of chatting in the shelters, often even during bombardments. Talking makes the time pass more quickly and the waiting less trying.'

'Do I look better with the beard or without? Without!' A barber attracts an audience.

'We [ate] whenever we were able in case we couldn't eat when we wanted to.' A hurried meal and drink before moving up to the line.

'Water, the ordinary drink of the soldier; wine, the extraordinary drink of the soldier.' A delivery of wine.

'Women thought this type of work their patriotic duty. But it was very hard graft.' A woman munitions worker, wearing a very modern divided skirt.

'We really have been liberated!' French troops arrive in Roye (Somme), February 1917.

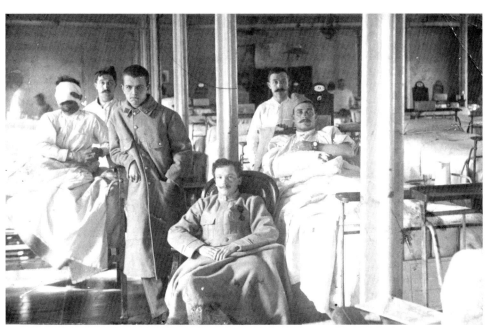

'What wouldn't we have given for a "lucky wound".' Casualties recuperate in Val-de-Grâce Hospital, Paris.

'The locals watched with interest as we passed by.' Captured Frenchmen are marched through the streets of Douai.

'They did not have Alsace and Lorraine.' French troops enter Mulhouse, November 1918.

'It is our duty to show our gratitude to our brave compatriots who died on the field of honour.' Young women dressed in the traditional costume of Alsace and Lorraine about to lay wreaths at a specially constructed cenotaph, Paris, July 1919.

There are many aces in the aviation service. The newspapers celebrate their victories every day. We really do pay tribute to the heroism of our brother soldiers. They have our greatest admiration. But have our so-called 'newspapers of record' not yet found aces within the infantry every bit the equal of our airman comrades? Many simple infantrymen hold five, six, seven or eight citations. Thirteen of them have been awarded the Légion d'Honneur. Why does the press never mention them at all? Could it be that, in some eyes, the infantry is the 'poor relation' of the French army?

And, for all their much-vaunted courage, Adjutant André Chainat (Spa3) knew that some pilots actively avoided combat:

I discovered two comrades wearing the group insignia. I signalled to them, 'Follow me.' They did so reluctantly. I put myself in among them, I pushed them, I found my Boches again, I worked out a plan, I signalled, 'I'm attacking'. I was lucky enough to be up against the last of the Boches and I sent him down in flames. I turned and looked for my comrades. They were no longer around ... There are some who are true and some who are false; some who go [into combat], some who don't [and] some who pretend ... some who disappear and can't be found until it's all over, when all danger is past; their engine began to sputter, their gun was jammed, they were attacked by an enemy superior in number, and they don't know how they managed to get out of it ... if they go out on their own they never meet [an enemy plane].

Paul Tézenas du Montcel (102nd Territorials) was another who believed that the infantry contained its share of 'aces':

The men I admire most are harder to find; they look at me calmly and seem effortlessly composed. That's the trick of it; they are the aces. They weighed up all the risks and sacrifices long ago: they were on the Somme, in Champagne or in the Argonne; they have achieved a degree of self-mastery which allows them always to be true to themselves, and trial after trial has not exhausted the deep well of devotion that lies within each of them.

Joseph Varenne (414th Infantry) was one of these men, mentioned in despatches as 'a really first-class NCO, brave and full of go'. Yet even Varenne had his limits. When ordered to lead his men into another attack, he was reluctant to do so: 'They called me over. It had been decided that I would by-pass the village to the left while one of them did the same thing on the right. I rebelled for a moment – it's not my turn, you know I've just led a fighting patrol ... I was surprised I'd expressed my indignation so openly. I didn't recognize myself any more ... What a dirty trick! I've got to go back. It's always the same mugs who cop for it!'

The broken nature of the ground and the isolation of the battlefield put a particular burden on regimental officers and NCOs leading their men in action. 'It is highly desirable for officers to know their men, and to know how to handle them at all levels of command. In fact, I would say it's an absolute necessity. But really, isn't it utterly stupid to make them take their first steps, to start their education, at the head of a unit? Is three months apprenticeship sufficient? To lead a unit in combat, bravery alone is not enough, you must know your trade.' When one hapless junior officer launched into a patriotic speech in an attempt to enthuse his men, the response from his veterans was immediate: 'That's fine, rookie. [Now] shut your trap and lead.'

Fresh out of St Cyr, Aspirant Bernard Croste (144th Infantry) was deeply affected by the burdens of command:

> I admit that I didn't always accept [orders] with good grace, and in some cases even amended them. I did it precisely because I was in command. Because I felt responsible for the lives of my men; because I judged an order impossible to carry out without incurring heavy losses; because I was better placed in the front line to spot a less costly solution than the CO in the rear. Nothing very military in all that! Perhaps. I always felt justified by the circumstances and the results. My men didn't blame me [and] neither did my friends.

Some officers were anxious to conceal any weakness from their men. Captain Henry Morel-Journel (74th Division staff) wept – but not openly: 'The news that we would be relieved had come through the previous day ... You know there are times when I cry like a child in this black hole where my men can't see me.' 'Will I get used to it?' wondered Aspirant Croste. 'I hear people talking, "he's no guts ... the aspi." I think that'll be my epitaph. I know sometimes I'm scared stiff and can't eat very much.'

Casualties among officers were often very high; for example, 115th Infantry lost twenty-four officers in a fourteen-day period in July. The toll on junior officers was particularly heavy. 'Since all the company's officers were dead,' recalled Quartermaster Sergeant Rendel (20th Infantry), 'Lieutenant V. arrived about six o'clock to take command. He was killed at ten.' In 101st Infantry Charles Delvert reported a similar experience: 'Lieutenant V., who arrived a few days ago as a reinforcement, has just been killed ... he shook my hand and two minutes later a piece of shrapnel hit his knapsack full of grenades and blew him to bits.' That same day Delvert lost three more young officers: 'Aspirant S. (aged nineteen) was killed. Aspirant M., the same age, and Adjutant C., ditto. My poor comrades, there they all are, lying stiffly side by side, in front of my dressing-station.'

Sergeant Gaston Gras (Régiment d'Infanterie Coloniale du Maroc) thought there were two kinds of leader, '[those] who galvanize their men and ... those who need watching carefully. The judgement of the men is the best guide ... the discipline [normally held to be] the principal strength of an army is really just an essential accessory: an army's real strength lies solely in the intelligence and mettle of its leaders.'

Sadly, the kind of bravado shown by Captain de Rohan at Douaumont was not an isolated instance. On 5 May 1916 Lieutenant Colonel Odent (68th Infantry) led two half-strength companies (from 77th and 290th Infantry) into the counter-attack: 'An outstanding officer, very bright. But how did he lead this counter-attack? He followed what he'd seen in pre-1914 manoeuvres, the companies all in dressed columns. The result – inevitable.'

The officers who needed watching also included the petty tyrants, considered careless of their men. 'No one likes Gaudry, the captain of 17[th Company],' confessed Sergeant Justin Giboulet (215th Infantry).

[He] told me off twice in one day about my beret and threatened to put me on a charge. He thinks the men are too noisy and unwilling to salute. He's the sort who's steeped in the military ethos, which according to him consists of following regulations to the letter and carrying out any damn-fool order. Very courageous in his dug-out and a deep strategic thinker in his room, very taken with his looks, thinks himself irresistible ... Everyone tries it on in the army [and] honesty is sometimes lacking. The result is the "report" in which everyone tries to cover their own back. People want to do sweet FA, and everyone grouses when a friend gets a promotion or an award. Many officers care too much about themselves and not enough about their men and their well-being.

Some officers could be a trial both in and out of the lines. In June 1916 a battalion of 67th Infantry halted for a time outside the village of Belrupt, en route to its rest area. A colonel passing by on lines of communications duties took offence at their scruffiness and warned he would take disciplinary action. Fortunately, their commanding officer had an ace up his sleeve:

'Colonel, instead of threatening my men, you should be down on your knees in front of them.'

Unimpressed, the colonel asked the name of the CO.

'Gouraud,' came the reply.

'Like the general? [General Gouraud was then GOC Fourth Army].'

'My brother.'

And that was the end of the conversation!

'Bloody bureaucracy!' fumed an officer in 95th Infantry. 'Bloody paperwork! Even in wartime, HQ never leaves us alone, and wherever we go we're hounded by the need to submit reports. Amidst all the turmoil of Verdun, who hasn't seen a captain, beset by all the difficulties and dangers of his post, receiving a request like this, "Submit without delay details of the number of boots in poor repair; urgently needed by Division."'

Le Filon (34th Division) later surveyed the amount of paperwork received in one month by the four companies of a single battalion: 'in addition to daily returns, each was sent fifty-seven notes from the staff, including battalion HQ. These companies were also asked for forty-nine returns, not counting those for the number of men on leave – these included four requests for the number of men with three or four children, three for the number of those who were tailors or cobblers in civilian life, and eleven for the state of ammunition stocks.' The same issue also asked 163 soldiers what swear-words they used in a variety of situations. What did they say, for example, when they arrived on relief to take over a trench, only to find the duckboards were broken and they were up to their knees in water? A handful muttered dark imprecations against the heavens, the staff and the pioneers; a quarter said '*zut*', plus several other words, 'more or less coherent'; but the vast majority opted for the '*mot de Cambronne* ['Shit!']'.

When front-line soldiers were dispersed among the shell-holes, treating and evacuating casualties presented particular problems. From a collecting point in the first line the wounded were carried in relays to a dressing-station in the second – using a stretcher, a tent section or, if the ground permitted, a wheeled hand-cart. Until 1916 casualties were carried lying flat on their backs; from then on they were carried half-sitting or lying on one side to prevent blood from pooling in the mouth and affecting the breathing, and/or to relieve pressure in the skull.

As in the British army, the regimental musicians normally played the role of stretcher-bearer. Laurent Pensa (31st Infantry) was called on to play both roles in one day during an attack in the Vauquois in February 1915:

About 12.30 pm, we advanced to the ridge and sheltered behind a shallow slope during a short bombardment. When the shelling stopped, we started to play the *Marseillaise*; the colonel, who was on the ridge, called us forward with the band of the 76th and we started to play again. We played the *Marseillaise* nine times; we watched 31st Infantry go into the attack, but they soon withdrew, sheltering behind ruined walls and folds in the ground. Finally we stopped playing, jumped into a communications trench and went back to where we started. We had the colonel and his ADC with us, both of them wounded. In the evening, we found ourselves in a bad spot; they woke us in the middle of night to retrieve the day's casualties.

Stretcher-bearers faced many of the same dangers as the rifle companies, but some fighting men still treated them as shirkers. Ernest Brec (77th Infantry) recalled 'being told off by Major Mariani, who described the stretcher-bearers as a "bunch of rotters", when we'd done everything that was asked of us'. Nevertheless, Brec and his chums 'became a team of twenty good pals, with two good MOs, one a doctor, the other a medical student'.

Some wounded soldiers were able to make their own way from the battlefield. Lucien Gissinger (174th Infantry) was hit in the left knee on 4 March 1916, shortly after a counter-attack at Douaumont: 'The pain was so intense I had to lie down. A moment later, it eased a little, so I stood up and managed to walk back to my comrades. At that moment a bullet hit me in my left buttock.' Diving into a shell-hole, Gissinger jettisoned his rifle and equipment. He thought he might be taken prisoner. If not, he planned to hold out until nightfall and try to regain the French lines.

Snow was falling, I was losing blood and starting to shiver. I had to escape from there at all costs, get to the rear and have my wound bandaged; but there was no trench or sap so I had to move in the open. Machine-guns constantly swept the ground. A wounded man crawled past in front of me, but a bullet took him out. That didn't give me much incentive to leave my hole. Entrusting myself to God, I finally took my chance. A comrade who'd been wounded in the arm shouted cheerfully across to us: 'That's it lads, let's go and see those little nurses!' The words had scarcely left his mouth when a bullet struck him in the head. I took advantage of a bit of a lull and moved forward slowly on my stomach as far as a little fold in the ground. No bullets whistled past. I carried on, stopping from time to time to rest my leg, which was causing me great pain.

Gissinger crawled for almost 500 metres through the mud and bodies, with the occasional bullet still flying overhead, eventually reaching a small wooded valley. Grabbing a stick to use as a crutch, he finally found a dressing-station. But his ordeal was not yet over: the station belonged to the neighbouring 153rd Infantry, who refused to treat a man who wasn't one of their own. The stretcher-bearers pointed him towards his own post, where he eventually arrived at midday, soaked to the skin by a nearby shell-burst. Here he was bandaged by two medical students, serving as assistant medical officers.

From the dressing-station, Gissinger went on to the regimental first-aid post, where the medical officer added new dressings or renewed the existing ones (badly wounded men were taken here direct). MOs could do little more with the means available to them but the treatment they offered at least reduced the risks of asphyxia or pneumonia. Serious cases were then taken, by motor vehicle whenever possible, to a field ambulance. Antiseptic measures were first applied here, and casualties were triaged and sent on to appropriate units. At this stage Gissinger would receive anti-tetanus shots and his wounds would be rebandaged.

Further specialist treatment meant re-evacuation to a forward hospital. Gissinger was taken by a motor ambulance driven by an English volunteer to a hospital in Chaumont-sur-Aire. Ambulance driver Pierre Muenier (SSA226) was also serving with an English volunteer unit:

> The medical service always suffered when things were frantic and, just as at the Marne, it was in complete disarray.
>
> 'You've got wounded?' the MO asked me. 'Stretcher-cases? What do you want me to do with them, my friend? All my huts all full. Keep those men in your ambulances.'
>
> 'But I've got to get back, sir. Really I must. I'm in a hurry. It's very urgent.'
>
> 'Well, you can't put them down in the snow. I'm telling you the huts are full to bursting.'

The drivers often came under fire. William Barber (SSU3), an American volunteer straight out of college in Toledo (Ohio), graphically described the dangers he faced:

> The road from Verdun to Bras is dangerous, filled as it is with deep shell-holes, and it leads along a very difficult way. There is a choice of two roads to Bras; but one was under constant fire, so we were forced to take the other, proceeding along this road up to the very top of a steep cliff, below which are the French guns and beyond which

are the trenches. It was at this point that we heard explosions the din of which more than doubly eclipsed anything we had previously heard. They were simply tremendous. We were at that point which is the very muzzle of some big French guns, and because the Germans are most anxious to get the 'battery', they direct their heaviest firing against it. We had to go as fast as we could in order to escape the shells, and yet we had to go cautiously enough to avoid the terrible holes in the road, some of which were five or six feet deep and as big as the machine itself. I was almost hurled from the back to the front seat of the machine when Mr. Hill, going twelve miles an hour, hit one of these holes. We got out of it soon, however, and approached a bridge, about the only bridge that the Germans have not taken in that locality, and they want that badly. It was under intermittent fire all the time, and we were supposed to stop if shelling were going on and wait for it to cease. All along the roadside was a deep trench into which we could go if the shelling became too severe. We soon approached Bras, where great rockets kept flashing out green, yellow, and red star-bombs, lighting up the sky and exposing the enemy's trenches.

Survivors were finally taken to a railhead for evacuation to a hospital far behind the front lines; Lucien Gissinger ended up in Grenoble. Corporal Blaise (216th Infantry) was another evacuee. After spending almost seven days fighting off German counter-attacks from a shell-hole in the Bois de Camard, he was 'evacuated to Château-Chinon, to the peace and clear air of the Morvan, eyes bloodshot, kidneys aching, face pale, and hair white. A month's convalescence put me back on my feet and I returned to the depot at Mâcon, but I still have bouts of irritability, and at forty years of age, I'm an old man.'

The pre-war network of military hospitals was plainly insufficient to cope with the number of casualties. Extra hospitals were added, either by co-opting civilian hospitals or by creating new 'auxiliary' hospitals, run by the French Red Cross or one of its subsidiaries (the Société Française de Secours aux Blessés Militaires, the Association des Dames Françaises and the Union des Femmes de France), in large public buildings such as schools, dance-halls or casinos.

Julien D. found himself in one of three hospitals set up in the small town of Yzeure (Allier): 'The hospital is dirty [and] some of the chaps in my room are in a real mess; there are no orderlies in our ward and, as I'm one of the less seriously wounded, I have to do a lot of the fetching and carrying. Although I'm always happy to help out, I reckon I'm in hospital to be cared for, not for me to care for others.' Abel B., meanwhile, was in the spa town of Aix-les-Bains, where he was missing the food of his native south-west: 'The food's no good; the soup's rubbish – nothing but warm water, no potatoes, no cabbage, a little scrap of meat which half the time is inedible. The rice, macaroni and vegetables are better – and we nearly always have rice or noodles or macaroni – so I'm getting used to them.'

Hospital No.44 (Second Military Region) was created in January 1915 in the seaside resort of Le Crotoy, on the Somme estuary, making use of a hotel, a private house and the presbytery. In April the Aviation Service moved into the two houses, and the hospital also took over the local casino, doubling the number of beds available. Angéline Baillon was anxious to do her bit: 'The priest spoke to the chief medical officer, offering to take up a collection to raise money for material to make shirts, and made 200 francs ... The army asked for charitable ladies to make them up ... cutting them out and sewing them ... good God, I had to do something for the war.' Angeline also volunteered at the hospital itself. With no medical training, all she could do was wash and sew, cook treats for the patients, and try to bolster their morale. 'He was delirious,' she wrote of one man, 'but I did my best to console him; he spoke of his mother and said that he loved her. I gave him a kiss in [her] place ... he was happy, my kiss settled him down [and] my words comforted him.'

Volunteering was the only way for women of a certain social class to make a contribution to the war effort. One young woman in Mende expressed her frustrations at the situation. 'I hate being a girl,' she wrote to a friend:

> ... I think I'd be strong enough to carry a rifle ... and I wish I was like the Serbian women, brave enough to follow our soldiers, rifle in hand, and later claim a small part in saving my country. When we're asked, 'What did you do while the whole of France confronted the enemy, while the blood of our men flowed on the frontiers, while women cared for the wounded, sometimes at risk of their lives?', I shall reply, 'I embroidered, I sewed, I taught my little brothers, and to relax (just imagine) I played the piano for a while and then went for a walk with my friends.'

Combatants suffered from mental as well as physical wounds. Georges Gaudy and his chums were shocked by one encounter: 'Helmetless and without a weapon, a soldier from 119th Infantry watched as we approached. "Have you seen my wife and children?"' he asked in a voice which chilled us to the bone.' They directed the man back down the line, but he stopped every soldier he met to ask the same question. The condition known as *obusite* ('shell-shock' to the British) was recognized by the French as early as March 1915, and psychiatric centres were set up as part of the military hospital network. But diagnosis and effective treatment remained haphazard – some military officers continued to regard shell-shock as shirking. For most of the war no single treatment was generally accepted: some doctors used electric shocks, while others preferred a system of isolation and one-to-one therapy.

Some men hoped for a 'lucky wound' – serious enough to merit a hospital stay and a long convalescence, but not so grave as to lead to permanent disability. Among them was Pierre Pasquier (67th Infantry): 'As we went up to the line the Germans were shelling us the whole time. What wouldn't we have given for a "lucky wound" before we got there.' Others resorted to self-harm in an attempt to escape the trenches. Men shot themselves 'accidentally' in the hand or foot when cleaning their rifle, injected petrol under the skin to produce an abscess, or gargled with a mixture of hot wine and pepper to mimic the symptoms of angina. Those who did so faced draconian punishment. Since September 1914 the crime had been judged the equivalent of abandoning one's post, and those found guilty faced the death penalty.

So, in April, when Victorin Bès (161st Infantry) deliberately stood in an icy puddle, he ran the risk of being arrested and shot:

> It's cold and snowing [and] a few men have been taken to the rear with frostbite in their feet. It really browned me off seeing them leave a couple of days ago, all smiles despite the severity of their complaint, hearing people say ... "You lucky blighter, you're doing all right!". Round about midnight, I made up my mind: by tomorrow I'd have frostbite too.

Bès put his right foot into the icy water:

> The pain was excruciating, my determination began to waver, it was hurting too much ... I got out and put my boot back on. Shit, shit, and a thousand times shit. Too bad, a shell or a bullet might kill me, but I'm not brave enough to give myself frostbite. From the point of view of the patriot, self-mutilation is considered cowardice; but I, an unwilling soldier, can hereby confirm that you have to be extremely brave and incredibly determined to take this desperate action.

Assessing a soldier's guilt often depended on the testimony of the regimental MO. Some were very strict. Others, like Dr François Perrin (36th Division Field Ambulance), were not:

I had other more difficult [cases]. Soldiers court-martialled for self-inflicted wounds. I made them all admit [what they had done], but I always left room for doubt in my forensic report. The disabled soldier was acquitted; once he'd recovered, he was returned to the trenches – even minus three fingers – but with another unit. I believed in all conscience that I was doing the right thing. Nobody can say what they would have done in the sometimes atrocious conditions our soldiers lived in. And most of the time these poor souls, driven mad by depression, risked a firing squad to go home to a woman they knew to be unfaithful. Shoot a deserter who goes over to the enemy, yes. But don't put in front of a firing squad a young lad who's already seen action and is temporarily demoralized by despair because life seems impossible. A man suffering from depression is ill. And if you compare his life with that of countless shirkers in Paris, then you can understand his illness and excuse him.

Others sought to escape the conflict by disobeying orders, or simply by deserting. An attack on the Bois de Malancourt in March 1916 inflicted heavy losses on 57 Brigade, which subsequently faced allegations of cowardice. Claims were made that an unusually high proportion of men had allowed themselves to be captured without putting up much of a struggle – 2,800 men and 59 officers were taken prisoner. Action was taken against the regiments in the brigade: 258th Infantry was disbanded immediately, while 111th Infantry was taken out of the line and brought back up to strength with drafts from other regiments. But censorship controls revealed that morale remained low, and the 111th was disbanded in July, the only regular regiment to suffer this fate during wartime.

That same month 140th Infantry was finally relieved after four weeks in the front line. Shelled throughout the twelve-kilometre march to its rest area, the regiment was immediately sent back to the line, and shelled again throughout the return journey. After another forty-eight hours in the front line, it was then relieved again. Three days later twenty-one men were arrested for abandoning their post; one of them was shot.

Conditions in the front line were equally bad for Germans and French alike, and on some occasions opponents made a tacit agreement not to fight. A patrol from 205th Infantry had a chance meeting in no man's land:

This happened in a quiet sector. A thick fog blurred everything that morning. Impossible to see two paces in front of your face. We had set up an outpost in front of our lines. It was cold and mizzling; suddenly a Boche patrol loomed out of the fog. They were walking unhurriedly, hands in pockets, rifle over the shoulder, pipe in mouth. Dumbfounded, our soldiers hesitated for a moment. 'Sad war, gentlemen! Sad war!' said the Boche NCO mournfully. Then the fog swallowed him up.

'All we know for a fact is that the Boche are sick of the war,' wrote Louis Bénard on 15 April. They're using bottles or placards raised above their trenches to let us know: "No more victims. No more bloodshed" ... I'm telling you this in confidence but it seems things like this are happening all over.' Some German soldiers surrendered rather than carry on fighting, and any who seemed reluctant to do so were not necessarily motivated by patriotism. 'Our prisoner made us understand that he was happy to be captured,' wrote Private Suteau (91st Infantry), 'that his war was over, and that, if he'd seemed so unsure about giving himself up, it was because on the other side they were told that the French bayoneted their prisoners to death.'

Men trying to surrender were undoubtedly killed in the heat of battle, but when cooler heads prevailed an underlying humanity usually won through. Dr Léon Barros, medical officer of 217th Infantry, watched a number of German prisoners file past:

Some were wounded [and] were bandaged by our men en route. They were hungry [and] thirsty, their faces drawn, and their clothing muddy and tattered. They asked for something to eat and drink. Our soldiers, who had just suffered so much at their hands, forgot all their bitterness and, in a great outburst of generosity, gave them bread, chocolate and water. The Boches ... wept and offered us everything they had: pocket-knives, cigars, boxes of matches.

The French had succeeded in blunting the German offensive, but at a terrible cost. They had also begun to realize that courage alone was not enough to secure victory. The number of casualties sustained at Verdun, plus the requirements of the Somme offensive, created an insatiable demand for manpower. Young and old alike were called to the colours: the class of 1917 had already been called up a year early in January 1916, and the 48-year-olds of the class of 1888 followed in March and September. Joffre also resorted to other expedients, removing an infantry regiment from each division to create new formations. But still he was unable to satisfy Pétain's insistent requests for more men and hold back sufficient troops for the Somme.

However, Pétain never simply threw men into the attack. 'Victories ... will come only when [people in] the rear resolve to work harder,' he commented in the aftermath of the failed Artois offensives. 'We don't need 20,000 shells a day, we need 200,000 ... the same goes for equipment.' His thinking was incorporated into a new official manual for small-unit combat published in January 1916. 'You don't pit men against matériel,' it stated – a dictum soon proved correct by the experience of Verdun. The new manual was the death-knell of pre-war tactics. 'Tradition evaporated in an instant,' wrote Jacques Duhelly. 'Desire, heroism [and] resolve have been eclipsed by the cold-blooded machine-gun. We're going to have to accept that you don't pit men against matériel. It's the triumph of matter [over mind].'

By May Joffre was envisaging any future offensive as a series of 'powerful, slow, methodical, repeated' blows, designed to use up German reserves before eventually breaking the enemy line. Although Pétain was not renowned as an attack-minded general, he was recognized as an excellent trainer of men, and in his new role as army group commander he took on the task of training formations, three corps at a time, in the 'methods of combat appropriate for modern offensive warfare'.

These new methods were supported by new weapons. During the summer of 1916 infantrymen began to receive new rifles, the superior 1907 Berthier replacing the awkward, obsolete Lebel. The Berthier was loaded with three-round clips rather than single rounds and could be fitted with a grenade cup-discharger. Each infantry platoon received the brand-new CSRG (or Chauchat) machine-gun. Inexpensive to make, the Chauchat was produced in great numbers: when it worked, it worked well, but it was always liable to jam. The heavy Hotchkiss machine-gun was also supplied in greater numbers, each infantry battalion receiving sufficient to equip a machine-gun company.

The artillery too continued to expand, if only slowly. Heavy weapons remained in short supply, and the French continued to rely on the 75mm field-gun. The infantry received a small 37mm cannon as a close-support weapon, but trench mortars only became available in any number at the end of 1916. Georges Demonchy first encountered the 37mm on the Somme in 1916:

> Like grenades, no-one knew how to use them, though with these you also had to know how they worked. But how could you learn in the front line, up close to the enemy ... Our platoon commander Lieutenant Salles was killed as a result; so too was Sergeant Salles (a sad coincidence – [they were] unrelated but shared the same name and died together). And several men were wounded, principally by the 37 itself, which injured its crew if badly placed within the battery

... I was one of the new sergeants ... Without instructors [and] knowing nothing about artillery, we taught ourselves. Instructions in hand, the lieutenant, sergeants, corporals and men combed through the details of this gun ... This 'little 75' was an extraordinary weapon if served properly. But it was too heavy for the poor soldiers who had to carry it for kilometre after kilometre. The sergeant gun commander carried the shield (28kg); the two gun numbers, the tripod (38kg); and the firer and loader, the barrel (48kg). These five men were armed with a pistol and didn't carry a pack. Other men carried the ammunition.

The primitive trench-mortars operated by Aspirant Vaillant-Couturier in 1915 were replaced by more reliable models. The infantry were not always great fans of the crews of these '*crapouillots*' (derived from the word for toad), who would set up their mortars in the front line, fire off a few rounds, and then disappear before the Germans could retaliate. When the inevitable retribution arrived, 'it was always the infantrymen who paid for the breakages'.

However, soldiers in need of rest did not always appreciate the need for training in new weapons and tactics. This was certainly true of Sous-lieutenant Roger Campana (151st Infantry):

Our rest ends tomorrow, but how can we call this 'rest' when we go off on exercises every day? When men come out of the trenches they need to forget they're at war for a while ... to banish the obsessive vision of death which so haunts them. So why are we on manoeuvres morning and evening? Arms drill, platoon exercises, bayonet fencing – are any of these still of use in the war we're waging now? In my view, the exercises serve only to annoy the men; but orders are orders and we have to follow them.

The new combat instructions replaced the single wave of attack with a succession of waves: the first now consisted of riflemen and rifle-grenadiers, with some supporting engineers, whose task was to cut any unbroken wire; a second wave of bombers and rifle-grenadiers followed them, and finally came a third wave of riflemen and bombers. Behind these three assault waves came the 'moppers-up'. 'The assault waves will cross the captured trenches without stopping,' explained Lieutenant Emile Morin.

The 'moppers-up', as their name suggests, will 'tidy up', that is to say neutralize the occupants with gun-shots, grenades and even knives! Hence this distribution of new weapons. Some men do a kind of scalp-dance, brandishing their knives; but, despite this exuberance, many are reluctant to use them and almost everyone intends to throw theirs away when they leave their own trench. 'We're not murderers!' they say.

Armed with grenade and knife, Anatole Castex (288th Infantry) was repelled by this new style of warfare: 'It breaks your heart to see it. We watch each other as if we're lying in wait for rabbits. We throw bombs and torpedoes at each other. We're only forty metres apart and we can't see each other. We've become bandits.' Antoine Redier was also dismayed: 'A barbaric operation, this so-called "mopping up" of the trenches. It's not pretty! Everyone's a soldier, but not everyone's been a butcher.'

'No truce nor any rest' – the Somme

Britain and France had originally planned their joint offensive on the river Somme for August 1916, with Joffre contributing as many as forty divisions, but the German attack at Verdun forced a rethink. To relieve the pressure in the Verdun sector, Joffre asked General Haig, commander-in-chief of the BEF, to bring the date forward. Haig agreed to do so and the offensive began on 1 July. But the French could now offer no more than sixteen divisions, five of which, all from Sixth Army, were scheduled to take part in the opening attack.

For many French soldiers the British offensive couldn't come soon enough; their immense effort at Verdun had left them feeling that they were fighting the war on their own. 'The British boast they have 5,000,000 men,' wrote one member of Third Army, 'but what have they done, apart from their lamentable Dardanelles expedition and their surrender at Kut-el-Amara. They've certainly taken firm control of one portion of our territory; they hardly ever leave the boulevards of the capital.' Another soldier from Fourth Army agreed: 'What gets our goat is that the British don't give a damn, they claim to have a wonderful army, very large and very strong, [but] instead of giving us a hand, they stand by with their arms folded.'

Aspirant Louis Mairet (127th Infantry) was on the Somme in mid-June, trying to stop the Germans reinforcing the area in front of the British zone of attack: 'It's time for Verdun to get some help. It's time for the Russians to launch their offensive and for the British to declare themselves ready to go.' Even the Germans thought so. Towards the end of June a rocket landed in the trenches held by the 127th: 'What's happened to the British offensive?' read the attached note. 'Are they still your allies?'

General Foch (Northern Army Group) and General Fayolle (Sixth

Army) – both artillerymen – were the French commanders in the sector. Fayolle was the closer in temperament to the cautious Pétain and had a clear idea of the kind of battle he wished to fight: 'We're not talking about a dash through the enemy lines, a general assault conducted at headlong pace, but an organized battle, which leads from one objective to another, always with an accurate artillery preparation, an accurate and thereby effective preparation.' But Fayolle's views did not necessarily accord with those of his commander. 'Foch! He'll be the death of me,' he complained to his chief of staff.

Positioned at the southern end of the allied line, the French achieved greater success than the British on 1 July – the terrible first day of the offensive. The advantage of the ground, weaker German defences, a more intensive barrage and more flexible infantry tactics allowed the French to capture the German first line with some ease. By 3 July the breach in the front south of the Somme was almost eight kilometres wide and the French held the high ground overlooking Peronne. But to the north the British advance had stalled and Foch declined to press his advantage for fear of exposing his flanks. His hesitation allowed the Germans to reinforce their defences, and any further French gains were marginal.

Major Aubert Frère (1st Infantry) was at Maurepas. After calmly removing his helmet and replacing it with a red side-cap (a souvenir from ten years' service in Algeria), he gave a cry of 'Now, my friends, forward, for France', and led his men into the attack. Despite his flamboyant gesture, Frère survived, only to perish in a Nazi concentration camp during the Second World War.

Joseph Foy (265th Infantry) took part in the follow-up wave in front of the village of Fay:

Our artillery preparation was wonderful. It completely destroyed the German defences and our assault waves managed to cross the lines without much resistance. Only an enemy counter-barrage claimed a few victims. As soon as the first wave had set off, we advanced over the heavily cratered ground, ready to help out those in front. The enemy continued to send over a heavy barrage so we dug in when we reached the outskirts of Fay to avoid taking too many casualties. The shells fell very close by, but we were right at the bottom of our trench and they didn't touch us. The next day we moved further forward until it was time for our turn to lead the advance. That moment arrived about 3.00 pm on July 3. We accomplished our mission without any trouble, and it was a real miracle because we had to cross 1500 metres of open ground to reach the point assigned to us. Our shells had cut a way through the enemy wire ... A barrage of shrapnel greeted our arrival at our objective; we dug in for a few minutes and quickly secured our position. Our company suffered no losses during the advance. We set up our machine-gun straight away. In the ground we covered, several artillery batteries had been flattened. Some pieces were still in good condition and we've even turned one against the Boches. We were lucky we didn't meet any resistance. Fortune was smiling on us all. We stayed there under artillery fire for thirty-six hours. Even the bravest don't have much to say in moments like these.

On 4 July the men of the Foreign Legion had to cross nearly 200 metres of open ground to reach their objective, the village of Belloy-en-Santerre. Rif Baer spotted the American poet Alan Seeger, 'his head erect, and pride in his eye, I saw him running forward, with bayonet fixed. Soon he disappeared and that was the last time I saw my friend.' Machine-guns cut down the first wave, including Seeger, but the second wave crawled through a wheat-field, bombed their way into the village, and captured it after two hours of house-to-house fighting. Seeger died of his wounds. 'I have a rendezvous with Death / At some disputed barricade,' began the celebrated poem he wrote shortly before the battle.

The French tried to launch a gas attack the following day, with disastrous results, as Léopold Noé (281st Infantry) recorded:

We're alongside 256th Infantry, which released the gas at 10.00 pm, with the wind in our favour, but [it] veered and blew the gas back on our side. Eight men from the 256th suffocated and one hundred and twelve had to be evacuated. The ration party, which hadn't been warned, was coming up at that very moment and they all died in the communications trenches.

Jacques Meyer (329th Infantry) was among the troops facing a German counter-attack:

This was one of those rare moments when we were gripped by an intoxicating desire to kill. Our men – even the mildest of individuals – wanted to take part in the slaughter ... [They were] on edge [and] drunk with killing. [They] no longer paid any attention to shouts of 'Kamerad', still less to the compassionate words that Father Sainte-Marie [the padre] was trying to get through to them. It's not my wish to seem to be excusing these soldiers; they are far above any excuses. They were simply obeying human nature, maddened by fatigue and the death of so many friends, including the admirable Father Sainte-Marie.

The Somme offensive certainly buoyed the spirits of the troops behind the line. Lucien Cocordan (22nd Dragoons) had been in pessimistic mood in late May. He was coming to the end of a leave period, due originally in February but postponed on account of the Verdun offensive: 'I'm really down in the dumps ... Please let the war end quickly. I've had enough.' But by the end of June his mood had changed: 'The Russian offensive is now into its eighth day and making excellent progress. Offensives on all fronts: the British in the north, the French at Verdun, the Italians and Russians on their respective fronts; they're all attacking with good effect. We firmly believe that by winter the war will be over. Some predict August or September. That'd be great!' An army morale report in mid-July noted that news of the action had been greeted with enthusiasm: 'The rapid advance of the Russians has raised hopes to giddy heights. Franco-British co-operation was going to achieve devastating results. People have been talking about a breakthrough, and a push that would boot the Germans back home.'

Bandsman Victor Christophe (150th Infantry) was a native of Lille, in enemy hands since 1914. He too was hoping that the Somme would prove more than just a tactical victory: 'A brilliant Anglo-French offensive has made a good start in the north. Will it be the first step in the liberation of our country? Let's hope so!' And there was another benefit to his transfer from Verdun: 'It's good to hear Picards talking. It reminds me of home. In the morning I'm going to have a drink in a cafe called *"Al Ch'koukou Ki Kante"* ['The Singing Cuckoo'].'

In early September the French resumed the offensive, capturing five kilometres of ground before their attack came to a halt for lack of reserves. On 15 September they tried again, this time in co-ordination with the British. But two weeks of heavy fighting produced few gains, and bad weather brought the action to a halt. Pierre Paraf (92nd Infantry) was among those who went over the top:

Waiting for zero hour. The platoon commanders pass by looking preoccupied and seem to be overcome with emotion. We wish each other luck, putting on smiles we've borrowed like white gloves for a celebration ... My heart thumps harder and harder. We try to distract ourselves with a bit of intellectual conversation, arguing without conviction. Just think how many people have never experienced these glorious moments ... poor souls! ... My men are quiet ...

wearing their tent sections bandolier-style ... they've been waiting for nearly three hours. Come and take a look at them, you newspaper warriors and armchair strategists, you academics baying for blood, you well-meaning readers attributing to them all the venom of your little minds ... they're too big to hate [the enemy] but they're big enough to despise [you]. They're not drunken brutes who go into the charge singing 'There's still a drop to drink' [words fitted to the regulation bugle call 'Charge'].

The 92nd attacked a trench known as the Demi-Lune, near Chaulnes. When it was all over, Paraf looked out over no man's land: 'As night fell on [the] Demi-Lune, I clambered out of the communications trench to contemplate the field of honour for a while ... Then I thought I heard the voice of my brothers-in-arms: "Well, old boy, you've seen the battlefield. Grand, isn't it, what they call glory? Will you dare tell the truth one day ... [or] will you forget us when you leave the trenches, wounded, ill or shirking?"'

The Somme offensive began to change soldiers' views of their British allies. 'The British are doing good work', reported one man. 'Our near neighbours, the British, are also doing well,' wrote another. Yet approval was sometimes grudging: 'I was expecting more from them, I admit ... it seems quite clear that our advance was superior to theirs. But they are only beginners.' '[They're] astonishingly brave and calm,' wrote Major Jules Henches (46th Artillery). 'They're very nice, take no precautions at all, and seem to think well of us. They'd apparently rather be killed than get themselves dirty. They remain standing rather than throw themselves to the ground like us; it's all very grand but not very intelligent. Lying flat on the ground no doubt seems cowardly to them.' Meanwhile, former cavalryman Major Pierre Bréant (90th Infantry) thought the British much smarter than the French, but not necessarily better soldiers: '[The British] look superb. ... And yet our soldiers are the best in the world. How can I reconcile this? Clothing doesn't make the man. Despite their untidiness, I know only too well what my soldiers will be capable of in a few days' time, and I'm very fond of them, even if their unmilitary bearing often annoys me.'

In early November Joffre finally called a halt to any further attacks; his armies needed time to recuperate from a long and harrowing year. For some, it was not a moment too soon. Guy Hallé (74th Infantry) described the men who survived the battle of the Somme: '[they] arrived robust and full of life, [but] the hunger, the thirst, the fear, the horrendous exhaustion of these hours in hell turned them into strange ghostly figures, with dark bags under their eyes, wracked with fever, gaunt-cheeked, walking slowly and wearily, like old men.'

If the experience of Lucien Cocordan was typical, few infantrymen would have turned down an opportunity to join the cavalry. On his move to Lorraine in August, Cocordan found himself in 'a really quiet sector. Not a shot from rifle or cannon. We sleep in the open, no shelters. We're bedding down in what remains of a tile factory. We're spending five days here and five in reserve.' But on his return to the barracks at Lunéville he was soon champing at the bit: 'What a bore to be back here again after two years of war. Our old barracks life begins again, fatigues, roll-call etc. Everyone is fed up.'

As the rains set in during October, soldiers could even summon up some sympathy for the enemy. 'The Boche trenches were completely flattened and our men occupied the shell-holes,' wrote Victor Christophe.

> What could be more terrible than the position these poor souls [found themselves in], out in the rain and machine-gun fire without any cover. And, with everything we were sending over, the Germans were at least as badly off as us. Comrades from 73rd Infantry told us, 'These poor souls look so scared when they shout "Kameraden" that not even the hardest among us ... can fire on them.' We're all men, after all, with minds and consciences always disposed towards pity.

'One soldier remains' – the rise of Nivelle

By the end of 1916 Joffre had made his plans for the coming year: another Franco-British offensive on the Somme in February would be followed by a further French offensive in Champagne. But the high reputation enjoyed by Joffre as victor of the Marne had slowly evaporated as casualties mounted with little to show for the sacrifice. As criticism in the press and in parliament began to gather pace, Joffre tried to save himself by scapegoating Foch – but his attempts were in vain. Joffre and Foch were both sidelined into advisory posts, Joffre becoming a Marshal of France (the first since 1870). Castelnau was sacked and Franchet d'Esperey replaced Foch as commander of the Northern Army Group. On 12 December Robert Nivelle was appointed commander-in-chief.

Nivelle, another artilleryman, first came to notice during the battle of the Marne. In December 1915 he was promoted to the command of III Corps and further enhanced his reputation in some of the French counter-attacks on the right bank of the Meuse. Replacing Pétain in command of Second Army in April 1916, the energetic Nivelle differed markedly in temperament from his cautious predecessor. On a visit to GQG a group of deputies asked whether the Germans would break through. 'I hope not,' replied Pétain. 'Never!' responded Nivelle.

Nivelle was half-English, auguring well for future joint projects, and a Protestant, pleasing the strong anti-clerical element in the French parliament. Nivelle also claimed he held the key to breaking the stalemate on the western front, and the politicians were convinced they had found the right man. Corporal Charles Nordmann (5th Artillery) thought highly of Nivelle as a regimental officer: 'This colonel is the most accomplished "leader" I've come across in this war ... his military and manly qualities go hand in hand with his humanity ... he is worshipped by the entire regiment, and he takes pains to conduct his own reconnaissance, to go and observe the fall of the shells in the front-line trenches. He proves that he "knows his artillery".'

But Nivelle's sudden rise had made little impact on other front-line soldiers. Dr Louis Maufrais (94th Infantry) had certainly never heard of him: 'Our new commander is General Nivelle. Well known apparently among the staff, but not among the soldiers; I've never heard them mention his name.' Amand Saint-Pierre was equally bemused: 'This evening we learned of the appointment of General Nivelle. I'm still very surprised and I'm wondering what sort of pull he has because it seems extraordinary to me.'

The newspapers continued to report nothing but good news. *Le Canard poilu* (XV Corps) had access to British newspapers, among them the *Daily Telegraph*, whose correspondent had commented favourably on the morale of the French army, without setting foot beyond GQG. 'The morale of the French soldiers is magnificent,' he reported. 'I was able to talk to four of their generals, whose composure amazed me.' *Le Canard* drew its own sly conclusion: 'We do indeed have every reason to believe that the morale of French generals is magnificent.'

Looking back at 1916, Paul Tézenas du Montcel (102nd Territorials) had no time for the men in charge of his war:

> We never see the divisional staff in the trenches; we never get any compliments or praise. But when we think we've earned a bit of a rest, they swamp us with notes, circulars and reprimands. They're always fussing. All this produces a kind of loathing we find increasingly hard to fight. The senior commanders aren't really up to the job, particularly when it comes to keeping up morale. They do nothing to make themselves liked; they're never around when danger looms, and we've got nothing good to say about them. Our opinions

about them are far from the respect and affection they should deserve.

The president and the commander-in-chief certainly met with a mixed reception when they visited the front on 5 November. 'We were billeted in Belleray [(Meuse)],' wrote Abbé Joseph Magnien (66th Chasseurs). We were coming and going in the main street of the village, when suddenly we had to move aside to allow some staff cars to pass by. In one of them, we recognized President Poincaré and General Nivelle. Some men cheered, but you could also hear cries of "Shirkers!". There were even some stones thrown at the cars. I can still see Monsieur Poincaré, in his sailor's cap, leaning out of the car door to watch.'

Soldiers also continued to be wary of those in the rear – suspecting that they were not doing their bit, in some cases even profiting from the war. Georges Caubet (214th Infantry) remembered a village which 'although only a few kilometres from the German lines had never been shelled. This reassured the locals who had no qualms about indulging in the odious practice of profiteering, robbing the soldiers while pretending to provide for their material needs.' April saw Charles Delvert in Paris, enjoying a short period of leave: 'Sailed on the lake in the Bois de Boulogne in the afternoon. A wonderful time. Plenty of people around. You'd think it was a public holiday or race day at Longchamp. They tell us that that the nation is suffering; that all its energies are directed towards eventual victory. The strain hasn't reduced the number of strollers [though].'

But in many places everything was geared to war work. Juliette Eychenne was in Carcassonne (Aude):

> The schools were turned into military hospitals – Saint-Stanislas, André Chénier, l'Ecole Normale des Garçons and other places ... Saint-Stanislas was always full of the seriously wounded; no-one knew what to do with them, the schools and even the big shops were all full. The men were away ... so women were brought into the factories to make shells ... [They] thought this type of work their patriotic duty. But it was very hard graft.

Juliette's mother worked in the garment industry: 'There was also a big laundry in the Rue Pasteur which did the washing for the barracks: the machines were basic and many things were done by hand; the worst job ... was hanging out the washing in all weathers, even if it was freezing cold. There were also lots of women making up uniforms at home. None of this paid well; my mother worked every day but, despite all her efforts, we were still poor.'

As another winter of war approached, soldiers were becoming ever more disheartened. Although he had been promoted to the rank of captain and awarded the Croix de Guerre, Charles Delvert was thoroughly weary of the fighting: 'I make no secret of it, all I want now is to be a shirker. I've had enough of this war. It's gone on too long.' In Bressuire (Deux-Sèvres) the sub-prefect wanted to ban all home leave because he felt that soldiers were poisoning civilian morale. Conversations overheard on trains indicated that 'our soldiers have been driven to an incredible level of war-weariness'. They had also been heard advising people not to subscribe to war loans 'so as not to prolong the fighting'. This kind of attitude did not appear to be general, the official added, but it certainly did exist.

Quartermaster Corporal Henri Fauconnier (273rd Infantry) wrote regularly to his fiancée: 'What enthusiasm I must have had to begin with to put up for so long with the things I find the hardest – the cold, the dirt, the need to obey, and the idiots everywhere ... If the war lasts another year, I'll start to seem very downcast and pessimistic to you.' He later continued in a similar vein:

> We should expect no mercy here. Our suffering matters little, provided we can still march. Cannon fodder [like us] have no right to complain. In fact some find it annoying that they can't prevent us thinking ... Once I would have given my life quite gladly, now I prefer to hang on to it. Why? I think it's the newspapers which killed my idealism. All they contain are lies, hypocritical praise [and] articles appalling in their stupidity and bad taste. And they speak on behalf of France ... (they'd end up by making you hate the place!) And if they do contain the occasional glimmer of truth or common sense, the censors are quick to black it out.

On 28 October Edouard Coeurdevey (167th Infantry) was resting behind the lines when the unit postman arrived: '[He] delivered some postage-paid cards with the Abel Faivre drawing of a recruit shouting "*On les aura!*". These once magical words now do nothing but demoralize us ... We can't take any more.'

Chapter 4

'Hold'

1917

Chronology

21–26 Feb	Battle of Verdun
12 Dec 1916	General Nivelle succeeds Joffre as the French commander-in-chief
16 March	German troops begin their withdrawal to the Hindenburg Line
6 Apr	United States declares war on Germany
9–16 Apr	Canadians capture Vimy Ridge
9–15 Apr	Third Army attacks towards Saint-Quentin
16 Apr–15 May	Second Battle of the Aisne: Nivelle's offensive is halted within four days
29 Apr	First outbreak of mutinies in the French Army
15 May	Pétain succeeds Nivelle as commander of the Armies of the North and North-East
31 July–10 Nov	Third Battle of Ypres: First Army attacks in the north of the Ypres Salient
23–26 Oct	Battle of La Malmaison: the Germans are driven off their positions on the Chemin des Dames

'We are all condemned' – Nivelle's offensive

In early February 1917 the Germans decided to make a strategic withdrawal to straighten their line and remove any vulnerable salients projecting into allied positions. This planned retreat took the Germans back to the heavily fortified positions of the Hindenburg Line, constructed over the winter, and liberated a number of towns. Among them was Noyon (Oise), where the occupying force had spent the best part of two months preparing for its departure; priests and doctors were taken hostage, and young men and women sent to Germany as forced labour. 'We wept, we were afraid,' wrote one anonymous citizen. 'But the soldiers were telling us, "You're going to see your fellow countrymen again" ... The [Germans] left during the evening of Saturday 17 March ... The fact that they left in a hurry and in the dark seemed to bode well.' Before long French cavalry had moved into town: 'We cheered them as soon as we dared. And we knew where we'd hidden our French flags and dug them out to hang them at the windows.'

But to the surprise of Edouard Déverin (48th Chasseurs), some civilians appeared unmoved by their new-found freedom: 'At Guiscard [and] Guivry, the remaining inhabitants – women and old men – showed no enthusiasm as they watched us march past. They still seemed to be sunk in a kind of apathy. There was one emotional moment though: as we entered one village, some pale, gaunt-faced children ran up to grab hold of our hands.'

'Events hurry on apace,' wrote one fervent optimist. 'The front has been pierced. It feels like the end. This retreat is very bad for the Boches. It's proof of their weakness. We'll be in Berlin in a week.' But this was far from the case. As the Germans pulled back to their prepared positions, they adopted a scorched earth policy, poisoning the wells, demolishing buildings and cutting down crops and trees. French soldiers – particularly those from a farming background – were appalled at the devastation wrought in the former occupied zone. 'Have you seen in the papers that those bastards cut down all the trees as they cleared off,' wrote one man. 'We've got to get our own back.' A member of 355th Infantry also witnessed the destruction: 'What really makes us mad is seeing all these trees – fruit trees and others – hacked down to the base. Only cold fury and a desire to destroy for its own sake can have inspired this decision by the German high command, and the troops carried out their orders to perfection.' Artilleryman Firmin Bouille summed up the general mood: 'It's just barbarous, I don't know what more you'd need to demonstrate the crimes the [Germans] committed during their retreat.'

The withdrawal had little effect on the new commander-in-chief, for Nivelle had already decided to scrap Joffre's plans for 1917 and begin again. The supporting British would go on the attack around Arras on 9 April, followed a week later by the main French offensive on the river Aisne. Nivelle created a new Army Group under General Micheler expressly for this purpose; named the Reserve Army Group, it would be made up of Fifth Army (Mazel), Sixth Army (Mangin) and Tenth Army (Duchêne). Meanwhile Third Army (Humbert) would attack around Saint-Quentin in an effort to fix the German forces in that sector and prevent them from reinforcing their comrades further south.

Nivelle described his strategy in a briefing to his subordinates on 30 December 1916:

> Our goal is nothing less than the destruction of the major part of the enemy's forces on the western front. We will achieve this only as the result of a decisive battle which engages all his available forces, followed up by an intensive exploitation. In the first and second phases, this means that we will have to break through his front, then beyond that breach engage any of his forces we have not yet fixed in other regions, and finally turn the bulk of our attacking force against his main lines of communication, forcing him into speedily abandoning his current front lines or accepting further combat under the most adverse of conditions. We will achieve these results by ... using a portion of our forces to fix the enemy and breach his front, then by committing our reserves beyond the point selected by me for the breakthrough.

Nivelle also claimed that he 'now had the formula' to put his strategy into effect. These were the assault tactics he had copied from the Germans at Verdun and used there successfully in a series of limited attacks. Following the preliminary bombardment, the artillery would open the attack, concentrating its fire in narrow zones to clear a number of corridors for the infantry advance. Shortage of long-range artillery had doomed previous attempts to use these tactics on a larger scale, but Nivelle was convinced he now had the guns he needed for his forces to penetrate as far as the enemy's heavy artillery in a single twenty-four to forty-eight hour thrust. Keeping the heavy artillery moving forward – almost as if it were field artillery – was vital to maintaining momentum and achieving the breakthrough.

The infantry also had its part to play in maintaining the impetus of the attack. Lieutenant Colonel Theron (132nd Infantry) explained to his company commanders that their men must resist any temptation to go to ground:

> It's important that everyone realizes that the only way to overcome any pockets of resistance not destroyed by our artillery is to stay on their feet. A machine-gun with three or four men in a shell-hole shouldn't be able to hold up an entire company. The attacking wave floods forward; it moves through the breaches and closes up again behind the islands obstructing its passage and soon to be submerged in their turn ... Sections in reserve close to roads have an over-riding duty to keep them open by filling in the shell-holes: it's the only way

of ensuring that the mobile cookers and the wine ration get to [the troops].

In a time of uncertainty – France had a new government in March 1917 – Nivelle's air of self-confidence quickly won over allied political leaders. President Poincaré supported the plan, as did the new British prime minister, David Lloyd George, and his French counterpart, Alexandre Ribot. However, the professional soldiers were harder to convince. Generals Pétain, Franchet d'Espérey and Micheler repeatedly expressed their doubts. So too did General Lyautey, the French minister of war: 'It's a plan worthy of the Duchess of Gerolstein!' he exclaimed, in a reference to Offenbach's light opera, a current Paris hit, its plot a satire on unthinking militarism. Lyautey's successor, Paul Painlevé, also tried to argue for a more limited series of attacks, but Nivelle remained unmoved. By a combination of the carrot and the stick – he promised a breakthrough within three days and threatened to resign (and bring down the new government) if support was not forthcoming – Nivelle brought the doubters into line.

Surprise would be essential to any successful attack. 'The only way to achieve significant results in the forthcoming offensive is surprise. Nothing must therefore alert the enemy to the preparations we are making' read the attack orders for 2nd Division. General Mazel agreed wholeheartedly. 'Beyond the drive and discipline of the troops, the key to success is surprise, born of secrecy and speed,' he told his men. And in the same spirit GQG issued a warning to every soldier: 'Stay quiet! Stay alert! Stay hidden!' But, having first ignored the opinion of his fellow generals, Nivelle now disdained basic rules of security. His plans were widely discussed in Paris and so reported in the newspapers, and a copy of part of his attack orders fell into enemy hands. The Germans made good use of aerial reconnaissance to plug any gaps in their knowledge, then made their plans accordingly. '[They] seemed to know everything we were doing,' wrote one front-line soldier. 'They sent over a note saying that all the work we were putting in on a big offensive would be in vain; the peace agreement would be signed before it started.'

Worse still, the sector chosen by Nivelle could scarcely have been less suitable for a full-scale offensive. The French would be attacking uphill, in difficult terrain, against enemy forces who were extremely well dug-in. High chalk ridges dominated both sides of the marshy Aisne valley, rising on the largely German-held north bank to a height of some 180 metres. The Chemin des Dames, the road which later gave the battle its name, ran along the top of this northern ridge. The countryside beyond was studded with farms and villages, and included two forts, once part of the outer defences of the city of Reims. It was also dotted with thickets and small woods, with numerous re-entrants and areas of dead ground, which the French (short of howitzers) would be unable to dominate.

The French had already experienced the difficulties involved in attacking in this sector in September 1914, and subsequently in several smaller-scale encounters. The intervening months had provided the Germans with further opportunities to strengthen their defences, and the intelligence leaks gave them ample time to make their final preparations. In March, a full month before the attack, they virtually abandoned their first line of trenches, setting booby-traps and poisoning the water sources. Behind this came a series of concealed machine-gun nests and concrete machine-gun posts, all with overlapping fields of fire. Further back still were strong reserves of infantry and artillery.

Perhaps because of the experience of 1914, the Aisne had been a relatively calm area of the front: 'The Boche were quiet enough. They sang or whistled songs from Montmartre; they told us they liked the French a lot and that they were only getting meat once a week now.' When the men of 67th Infantry arrived in their trenches, the Germans tossed them a note: 'We're in a rest sector not an attack sector. If the 67th wants to fight it can go back to the Somme.'

The preliminary bombardment on the Aisne opened on schedule on 8 April. On the following day so too did the British attack around Arras, supported by Humbert's Third Army. However, apart from the spectacular success achieved by the Canadians at Vimy Ridge, it produced few gains. While Haig continued on in support of Nivelle, the French broke off their supporting attacks on 15 April, on the eve of the main offensive.

Nivelle had adapted Pétain's phrase from the previous year – '*On les aura!*' (We'll get them!) becoming '*On les a!*' (We've got them!) – and his confidence permeated the army at all levels. Georges Bonnamy (131st Infantry) shared the general mood of optimism: 'This offensive? It's got to be our final effort, the end to all our suffering; it's got to bring a quick victory and put the enemy to rout. Everyone's talking about it and we're all confident ... Everything's been carefully planned and any problems anticipated. High command has even had the forethought to tell us where, when and for how long we must pause while moving forward! That might perhaps be taking it a bit too far.'

On the eve of the attack Georges Gaudy (57th Infantry) was just outside the little town of Fismes: 'Big groups of zouaves and Colonial troops were strolling around. The whole French army appeared to have gathered there for the victory push ... We were in the grip of a tremendous fever. Officers and men refused to go on leave to make sure they didn't miss the great offensive.' Louis Désalbres (128th Infantry) also thought morale was high: 'You might even say the men are enthusiastic. They're joking and shouting across to each other in every platoon. This'll be the breakthrough. The Boche are going to be hit by an avalanche. It'll be the end of the fighting for this year.'

Jules Ninet (89th Infantry) was behind the lines with his regiment: 'For several days now the amount of noise from the front has been steadily increasing. The roads are full of soldiers in blue and yellow [i.e. the yellowish khaki of the Colonial troops], all marching off in the same direction, along with whole columns of artillery, and lorries filled with ammunition and stores. We watch these huge convoys pass by, shake our heads and think, "Those Boches are going to cop it!"' But ominously the weather was beginning to turn. 'Since yesterday,' wrote Ninet, 'a whole section of the Craonne plateau has been swimming in a fog which is only getting thicker.'

On the night of 15/16 April Maurice Pascal (67th Infantry) and his men made their way forward to the start line:

> Left for the assembly area at Ribaudon at 6.00 pm on 15 April. An extremely difficult march down rutted lanes in the pitch-black night. The men were in single file and each had to hang on to the skirt of the greatcoat [of the man in front]. It was raining [and] the wind was blowing furiously. Soaked to the skin, laden down like mules with grenades, pyrotechnics and sandbags, the men did very well. I didn't lose [anyone] on the road and I was happy with 3rd Company. At the halfway point, an incendiary grenade exploded in the knapsack of a man in 2nd Company. Two soldiers were fatally wounded. A moment later, while we were taking a break, the same thing happened in my company. A soldier was thrown three metres, blown to smithereens; four others, including a sergeant, burned like torches, screaming in agony from the effects of the phosphorus. "Nothing to be done," said the doctor. "It just has to burn itself out." It's gloomy and horrible on this dark night. I ordered the phosphorus grenades to be thrown away. Arrived Ribaudon. We settled into our trenches and I received the order "Zero Day = 16 April, Zero Hour = 0600".

Although the guns opened fire on schedule, the bad weather forced Nivelle to postpone the start of the main offensive. Planned for 14 April, it finally began at 6.00 am on 16 April, the attacking waves setting off in the face of driving rain and sleet. On the left eight divisions from Sixth Army formed the first wave; on the right, sixteen divisions from the Fifth. Meanwhile, Tenth Army was held in reserve to exploit the breakthrough.

The 2nd Chasseurs were expecting an easy passage through to Laon: 'A bombardment of several hours will begin at Zero minus X; at Zero Hour, Bengal lights will show the reserves which route to follow. The first wave will reach Braye-en-Laonnais at Zero+30. The reserves will pass through it at Zero+40 to dig in along the [river] Ailette, which they will reach at Zero+2 hours; and at Zero+6 hours we will take possession of our billets in Laon, for which the sergent-majors have already received their instructions.'

One soldier described his experience for *L'Argonnaute* (25th Infantry):

And then I thought of nothing. I went over the top. I ran, I shouted, I hit, I can't remember where or who. I crossed the wire, jumped over holes, crawled through shell craters still stinking of explosives, men were falling, cut in half as they ran; shouts and gasps were half muffled by the sweeping surge of gunfire. But it was like a nightmare mist all around me. ... Now my part in it is over for a few minutes. ... There's something red over there, something burning. There's something's red at my feet: blood.

Corporal Jean Portes (1st Infantry) recalled:

Our morale was excellent as we crossed the parapet. Nothing could stop us: [in our minds] we'd already reached Craonne, California Plateau, the Ailette, which we would cross with thick ropes to make sure no one drowned. What disappointment! What slaughter! From the start of the first phase – the plan had six of them – the machine-guns stopped us dead. Within ten or fifteen minutes the company had been cut to pieces; among the dead, many veterans of Verdun and the Somme.

Pinned down all day under withering fire, the survivors waited in no man's land until nightfall and then scraped holes for cover. Portes's company gained a toe-hold in the village of Craonne but was later driven out; the regimental war diary recorded that 396 men were lost that day.

The objective of 5th Colonial Infantry was the village of Martigny. Maréchal de logis Bastien (5th Hussars) was attached to the regiment:

Colonel Marroix had ordered the musicians to bring their instruments: they were to play the *Marseillaise* when we entered

Martigny ... We were all confident, indeed eager: the war was coming to an end ... We arrived at a plateau which was in chaos. I couldn't run with the load I was carrying; I dumped the knapsack with my rations in it. Bullets whistled past. We were walking on a carpet of packs and equipment; here and there puddles of blood ... "Forward! Dump your packs and double forward!" The sprint lasted several seconds. After about fifteen metres I found myself in the first line of German trenches ... On every side the wounded were trying to crawl away amid the mortar fire. We couldn't advance or pull back. We hugged the ground ... We knew what kind of trouble we were in: we waved our arms or legs so we wouldn't be mixed up with the rows of corpses. The major looked at his watch: it was midday; we should have been in Martigny, marching behind the band.

The opening day of the offensive also saw the French deploy tanks for the first time, at the eastern end of the line, around Berry-au-Bac. The very sight of them contributed to the air of optimism which surrounded the forthcoming attack. 'What a machine!' commented Jules Ninet (89th Infantry).

Tanks: steel monsters, pierced with loop-holes, with machine-guns and even field-guns poking through! Gruesome inscriptions are written on their black bodies – "The Grasping Hand", "Death Cheater" etc., accompanied by strange drawings, the skull and crossbones, the ace of spades ... The aces are the men who climb aboard these tanks. ... We stare goggle-eyed with admiration. It doesn't make the men in leather jackets [i.e. the crews] at all cocky. They speak simply, without boasting, and their confidence wins us over. Can anyone stand up to these machines? No, it's absolutely impossible. So victory is certain! ... The end of the war! ... With tanks, why not? Can you stop a tank or kill it?

But in action the tanks proved largely ineffective. The local tank commander, Major Louis Bossut, thought they should be used as a breakthrough weapon, striking deep into the enemy lines. However, General Mazel (Fifth Army) disagreed. Mazel wanted them to play a much more limited role, providing close fire support to the infantry, and his view prevailed. One infantry battalion – 17th Chasseurs – had been trained specifically to work with tanks in this close support role, but in the event it was deployed elsewhere and replaced by two inexperienced detachments drawn from two different regiments. Bossut expressed his reservations in a letter to General Estienne, the overall commander of tank forces:

You are aware that the plan for the first French tank attack is far from the one I advocated. Nevertheless, it still has a chance of success, thanks to the magnificent spirit of our crews. If the opposite comes to pass, I don't want the survivors blaming me because their comrades have died to no purpose. Leading the way myself will allay my fears. I will therefore give the order to attack only on condition that I am the first into action.

Corporal Jean-François Perette and his tank were also part of that first attack:

A deafening din fills the tank, the 75 thunders, the two machine-guns spit fire continuously. What [are they firing] at? Truth to tell, I don't really know because I can't see anything much … Then the inevitable happens, something I've been expecting at any moment since this morning. A flash of lightning and a roar of thunder! I'm thrown to the base of the central pit, knocked out, dead! Yet, after a few moments of unconsciousness, I realize I'm still alive … I'm broken, bleeding and my left arm is trapped; I'm bleeding all over without really knowing where the blood is coming from under my torn clothes. Miraculously, the cupola and my body have provided a protective shield for the rest of the crew.

Tank officer Charles Chenu was another in the midst of the action:

Oh, there are some things you'll never forget. Sights which will be forever engraved on your mind, despite all the horror already burned there. The tank on the left suddenly becomes an inferno. In front of it is the shell which set it alight. Two torches get out, two torches making a mad, frantic dash towards the rear, two torches which twist, which roll on the ground … A tank burns on the right; another one, behind. And on our left, it looks as if someone is setting our line of steel alight like a row of floodlights. Fires, explosions. All at once flames envelop the tanks, and immediately after, with a dreadful crackling sound, everything is blown apart, is thrown up into the sky: sixty exploding shells on board, and thousands of bullets!

The French deployed a total of 132 Schneider tanks at Berry-au-Bac, in two groups commanded by Majors Bossut and Chaubès. Fifty-seven of them were destroyed by enemy artillery, and a further nineteen either broke down or got bogged down in the marshy ground. Only Bossut's group succeeded in crossing the German trenches but, in the face of the enemy counter-bombardment, the accompanying infantry unit was unable to follow them up. With nothing to show for their advance, and so many tanks out of action, the survivors could only fall back to the start line. Bossut himself was killed.

Meanwhile Georges Bonnamy (131st Infantry) was waiting in the reserve trenches for the order to advance: 'A very young officer came past us, holding himself very stiffly. He had a terrible wound to his jaw with no dressing on it; we asked him if things were going well; he made a sign to say yes. But within a few moments we'd picked up so much contradictory information we didn't know what to think.' The order to advance never came: 'We spent the whole day like this watching the wounded passing by, and convoys of all kinds, tanks, cavalry, streaming back in disarray.'

As Xavier Chaïla (8th Cuirassiers) discovered, evacuating the wounded had not formed part of the pre-offensive planning:

> We picked up a number of wounded men to carry them to the rear. It was no small matter trying to get down blocked communication trenches ... We arrived at an aid post manned by divisional stretcher-bearers who refused to take our wounded because we weren't from their division ... We had to go as far as the canal ... There were at least 400 seriously wounded men on the banks. The chief MO was fuming. Although this attack had been planned for a long time, no provision had been made for the evacuation of the wounded ... It was the Boche prisoners who had to carry the stretchers over a considerable distance. Some of our wounded had to spend forty-eight hours on the canal bank, in the rain, the cold and the shell-fire. Many of them died there because they couldn't be treated in time.

In the rear Dr Benoit (155th Infantry) was hard at work: 'There was a dreadful procession of wounded men. We bandaged them one after the other, at top speed. Our young padre took confession and gave absolution to the dying. We were well protected in our huge concrete aid post; but it wasn't the same for the wounded out in the shell-holes ... The[ir] wounds continued to bleed in the cold. I can still hear those who had the strength and breath to shout, crying "Stretcher-bearers! Stretcher-bearers!"'

The field hospitals for the more seriously injured were further to the rear. René Naegelen described the scene at Prouilly:

> Stretchers cover the courtyard and the surrounding area. Greatcoats are thrown over immobile bodies, and the stretcher-bearers look for the gleam of rank braid under the dried mud. We'll bandage those, we'll do the others later. But the medical officers are overworked; there are too many wounded and not enough doctors. The walking

wounded crowd round, demanding attention, pushing in front of their comrades moaning on their stretchers. Blood-soaked linen is deftly removed, despite the cries of pain, [and] bottles of ether empty quickly, spreading their atrocious odour of suffering; soiled dressings pile up ... And still the ambulances keep arriving. Drivers search for empty stretchers. We've run out. You see them in the courtyard, lifting up greatcoats, checking faces, and sometimes turning over a stretcher. A man lies on the ground. He doesn't need a surgeon any more.

'Why [did it happen]?' asked Jean Ybarnégaray, a parliamentary deputy fighting with 249th Infantry. 'Like everything else, it was because in this offensive we'd planned for everything but defeat. We began from the idea that the offensive would be a success ... That's why nothing had been organized: no evacuation routes, too few aid posts, impossible to get the field ambulances to the wounded.'

By midday the French attack had come to a full stop right along the line. On the French left Sixth Army found that the extensive preliminary bombardment had inflicted little damage on the enemy defences; in the chalky ground the deep German dug-outs and strongpoints remained largely intact. The men of I Colonial Corps captured the mill at Laffaux, but were too exhausted to carry on. On the right, before the village of Craonne, Fifth Army gained no more than a toe-hold in the German first line, a particularly savage battle for the Cerny sugarworks producing nothing but heavy casualties. The only French success came further right still, towards Juvincourt, where some units managed to reach the German second lines. Jean Ybarnégaray later summed up the fighting before a parliamentary committee of enquiry: 'The battle began at 6.00 am; by 7.00 am it was lost. Fifteen minutes after the assault waves set out across the huge Aisne plateau, nothing could be heard but the stuttering of machine-guns and a single cry escaping thousands of anguished breasts, "the machine-guns haven't been destroyed". The victory we thought was in the bag was going to be a bloody reverse.'

Georges Gaudy (57th Infantry) and his comrades were at the front near Vassogne on 17 April when they began to realize that things were going wrong:

We were shaken awake. Every man stood up and rubbed his eyes. It was raining now and the snow had melted. We heard whispers that the regiment was returning to the rear ... The battalion marched in silence down unfamiliar tracks ... passed by troops going up to the line. Why were they going up when we were coming down? ... That's when our misery overwhelmed us. We didn't speak for fear of bursting into tears. We no longer thought for fear of understanding what was going on. Somewhere within our ranks a voice groaned, "It's never going to end, never!"'

After two days of waiting without orders, 131st Infantry marched off to another part of the line. 'The morale of the troops is growing steadily weaker,' reported Georges Bonnamy. 'Yet three days ago it was solid; I'd never seen it so good. These men and their officers went into the attack full of enthusiasm, confident of their own strength and of defeating the enemy ... after three days of marching, orderless in every sense, difficult and deadly, we haven't seen the enemy. We don't even know where he is and we've taken heavy losses!'

Nivelle did what he could to retrieve the situation. General Anthoine's Fourth Army was ordered to attack around Moronvillers in Champagne, and Fifth Army moved its axis of advance north-eastwards in an attempt to join up with them. Camille Vilain (1st Artillery) took part in the advance as part of VIII Corps (Fourth Army):

A whispered command, 'Forward!' Shapes leap up! The first wave dashes forward. It's still dark, and against a background of dull rumbling, there's something close to silence, deep [and] disconcerting. How long can it last? Then there's the pitiless thunder of shells, the roar of a barrage growing louder and louder, masking the bark of the machine-guns. Suddenly, everything's trembling, everything's on fire. Rockets shoot up from all sides, in groups, in lines, in bunches: green and red on the enemy side, white on our own. Their bright trails light up an apocalyptic landscape, with great black clouds rolling around in the pale dawn light. Dense flakes of snow begin to fall. Shells crash down constantly around us, shell-holes appear, men fall down. On all sides the whistle and crack of bullets, so many that they seem to be coming from everywhere at once. The wounded, covered in mud and blood, are screaming in pain and looking for the dressing stations. Prisoners go by, flinging themselves down in the mud at each shell-burst.

The attacks met with some early success, with the Moroccan Division capturing a hill given the name Mont-Sansnom ('Nameless Hill'). Among them was Sergeant Louis Bac (8th Zouaves), serving with the machine-guns:

At the appointed time, and under cover of the last shadows of a dark and rainy night, 6th Company ... leaped out of the departure trenches. Their progress was slow and difficult on this churned-up ground, bristling with barbed wire, pitted with trenches almost impossible to pick out in the darkness. The Germans, taken by surprise but tough as usual, welcomed us with grenades and machine-gun fire. We got past the first redoubt and descended into a valley the Germans called the Hexenweg, where the first light of day helped us on our way. It was the sight familiar from every battlefield: bodies, saps collapsed, trenches destroyed, weapons and equipment scattered over the ground. At 7.00 am we reached our objectives after capturing the Bethmann-Hollweg Trench, plus several 77mm and 105mm cannons, and entering the wood in the direction of Moronvillers. Our losses seemed relatively light, and to the rear, a jumble of wounded and prisoners took the route of the old front lines.

But ultimately this advance too came to nothing: vigorous German counter-attacks checked the progress of Fourth Army, and the Fifth stalled when it failed to capture Fort Brimont. On the left of the main offensive Sixth Army made only minimal gains, and on 17 April the whole offensive ground to a halt. Many troops were now struggling to cling on to the scraps of ground they had gained. On 18 April Captain Felix Boillot (43rd Infantry) reported to his commanding officer from a position in front of Craonnelle:

Towards 1830 hrs, the Germans launched a counter-attack against my company. Lieutenant L., commanding the centre platoon, was wounded, and his men fell back. I headed immediately to my first line; a French machine-gun was falling back and I tried to get it to turn round, but in vain. I ordered an immediate counter-attack with grenades to retake the section of the communications trench we had lost. The two parts of the company managed to get back together: I had the position in Section L recaptured. I ordered a heavy rifle-grenade bombardment on Ranstadt Trench which allowed me to push the enemy back and, I believe, destroy a machine-gun they had brought up. My men are crippled with fatigue. With the best will in the world they can't attack tomorrow. They're completely exhausted through lack of sleep [and] the frenzy of work I've forced upon them every night to get them organized, along with the cold and rain. I urge that this be reported to the colonel and I ask, most insistently, that my company be relieved and spared an effort which will inevitably end in failure.

Painlevé did his best to persuade Nivelle to call off the offensive, but the commander-in-chief refused, throwing Tenth Army into the battle in support of the Fifth. This too produced no noticeable gains and on 20 April Nivelle finally had to give way. Running out of ammunition, his exhausted troops could do no more.

Between 16 and 25 April Sixth and Tenth Armies lost around 134,000 men: 30,000 killed, 100,000 wounded, and a further 4,000 missing. Nivelle's gamble had failed. At Verdun he had used the same tactics in pursuit of limited objectives and also had the advantages of surprise and adequate artillery support. On the Aisne, however, all these elements were missing. The Germans were expecting the attack, and the preliminary bombardment, despite its length, inflicted little damage on their network of machine-gun posts. When the French infantry advance slowed down, the creeping barrage simply rolled on ahead and left them unsupported. And the French were still short of guns and shells, lacking the long-range artillery they needed to counter the German reserves once they were committed to the battle, as well as the ammunition required to sustain a prolonged bombardment.

Among the dead were many Senegalese tirailleurs: twenty battalions (or around 15,000 men) formed part of General Mangin's Sixth Army, and 1,400 of them were killed on 16 April alone. Small numbers of Senegalese had fought in the front line since the conflict began, but the Chemin des Dames saw their first deployment en masse. Facing an ever-worsening manpower crisis, France had turned not only to its veterans and youngsters but also to its colonies. Over 50,000 troops had been raised among the indigenous inhabitants of France's west African colonies in 1915 and 1916. Mangin, a veteran of colonial warfare, had long argued for the greater use of a '*Force noire*' (Black Force) and this was his chance to put his ideas into practice.

However, the Senegalese battalions failed to live up to his expectations. Deployed on either wing of Sixth Army, some battalions lost up to three-quarters of their officers and men in the attacks on 16 and 17 April. After the war it was alleged that Mangin had 'cold-bloodedly allowed all his black regiments to be slaughtered'. Known to his men as 'The Butcher', Mangin certainly had a well-established reputation as a fire-eater: 'Those in Paris – civilian or military – who say I get too many men killed are misinformed,' he wrote to his wife in 1916. 'They wouldn't say that here. The fact is that bombardments are appalling and there are hardly any shelters. Whatever you do, you lose a lot of men. If the combat takes place between the infantries you lose fewer to the artillery and more to the rifle and grenade. But the number of casualties stays about the same.'

But in fact there were deeper, structural, reasons for the failure of the *Force noire*. Major Trouilh, who commanded 5th Senegalese Battalion, blamed the officers and NCOs: 'The European cadres they've been given have little or no knowledge of their men. They seem convinced that black soldiers can only be taught how to march by beating them; they see only their faults and not their good points. In other words, they've no confidence in the tools they've been given.' Meanwhile Captain Gosset, commanding 48th Senegalese Battalion, highlighted their inadequate weapons: 'The battalion only has 1907-pattern rifles, with 120 rounds per man, and six light machine-guns ... It's been impossible to maintain the [latter] to a high enough standard to permit rapid or sustained fire. No grenades, no signal flares ... In sum, the tirailleur only has a few bullets, a bayonet and a machete. The rifles are in too poor a state of repair to be used [even] in good conditions.'

In close-quarter fighting the Senegalese could still wield their machetes to lethal effect. 'Along with a few Senegalese we surprised several Boches from the Imperial Guard at the bottom of their dug-out,' wrote one anonymous soldier. 'They were heating up their coffee. The Senegalese used their machetes on them and we drank the coffee.' And the very sight of black men certainly made an impression on some Germans, as Sergeant Costes (144th Infantry) discovered. Costes was among a party which had moved forward to take over some captured trenches:

> We were surprised to see a German emerge from another shelter, with his hands in the air, then two, then three, eventually twenty-two in all. They belonged to the Queen Augusta Regiment [4th Guards Infantry Regiment] [and] were eager to get out of there. On the way back to HQ, I asked them why they'd waited several hours before surrendering; using sign language they made me understand that they were waiting until white men had replaced the blacks.

Like their French counterparts, most of the Africans just wanted the war to end. 'They want to go home to their villages,' commented one anonymous observer. 'They're quite happy to express their feelings in front of those who are strangers to the army, but they're careful to hide them from their commanding officers.' Serving with a Colonial regiment, Lieutenant Tézenas du Montcel thought the Senegalese in a neighbouring battalion, 'cold and unhappy ... disoriented and sad'.

Despite spending the winters in the south of France or north Africa, the Senegalese and other soldiers from warmer climes suffered badly on the western front. At least 1,100 Senegalese were evacuated before the attack on the Chemin des Dames suffering from pneumonia and frostbite, while almost half of the Guianese who served on the western front died of illness, half of them from chest complaints. 'All the creoles had frostbite,' wrote Philistall Médus (4th Zouaves). 'The cold ate them up. And I was evacuated with frostbite in both my legs. I was sent to the hospital at Bar-le-Duc for three or four months because I couldn't walk.'

After its success at Verdun, the performance of the French Air Service also proved a disappointment. Instead of fighting the Germans in the air, the three new groupements de chasse now sought them out on the ground. But while they met with great success in hunting German aircraft over their own airfields, they also left the French army co-operation squadrons seriously exposed. In snow and rain the German planes which escaped the attentions of the French fighters played havoc with those aircraft trying to spot for the artillery. In the view of some corps commanders, their squadrons had simply been abandoned by 'glory-hunting aces'.

Victor Christophe (150th Infantry) watched as German aircraft shot down a French observation balloon: 'A few more thousand-franc notes go up in smoke. It's a good job we have mastery of the air. Heaven knows what would happen if we didn't! Meanwhile our "aces" are no doubt taking their ease!'

The name on everyone's lips, however, was no longer a French ace but a German who daily strafed the French lines. The soldiers christened him *Fantôme-As* (the 'Phantom Ace'), after Fantômas, the criminal anti-hero of pre-war novels and films, although his real identity (if he was indeed a single pilot and not a succession of enemy aviators) was never established. As they headed into the line near La Malmaison, Jacques Arnoux and his comrades were certain that they had spotted him: 'Fantôme-As! Fantôme-As! It's him. I've seen him. He glides down, opens fire, spins round and launches his rockets. Except for the incline of his wings as he banks, you'd think he was running along the ground. We open fire on him as he turns to attack ... At the first bullets he shies away and in a flurry of wings speeds off northwards ... It's a trap.'

Over the next month Nivelle launched a number of small-scale attacks, with mixed results. The French made no gains around Soissons, but they did manage to clear part of the Chemin des Dames and reopen the important Reims–Soissons railway line. At Laffaux mill, at the western end of the ridge, tanks – Saint-Chamonds this time – went into action again.

Among them was Lieutenant Marcel Fourier (AS31): 'My tank pushed forward slowly but surely, crushing the wire and the stakes; on either side it caught up whole lines [of wire] and dragged them out. The heavy mass of my vehicle crushed, flattened and destroyed everything in its path.' After the battle he took stock of his machine: 'the Japanese scenery which camouflaged its huge sides has almost completely disappeared; with the explosions [and] the bullets, the painting which must have so delighted the "camouflager" is burned and peeling, nothing more now than a memory. Boche shells flattened themselves against the armour or ricocheted from it; the steel, stripped bare, is speckled and scored with bright scars.'

The Laffaux attack achieved its objective, but this was largely through the efforts of the infantry, and heavy tanks were henceforth deemed a failure. The Schneiders and Saint-Chamonds had proved too difficult to manoeuvre over broken ground, and even in the flatter terrain around Berry-au-Bac their achievements were dwarfed by the number of casualties incurred.

In the aftermath of the battle the scene around the Chemin des Dames was one of total destruction. Moving up to the line on 29 April Aspirant Lucien Laby (249th Infantry) reached the village of Chavonne: 'One of our men – who comes from this area – looked in vain for his house: he couldn't even find where it used to be.' The failure of his offensive marked the end for Nivelle. Rumour only exaggerated the level of casualties – already high enough – sending civilian morale plummeting in Paris and forcing President Poincaré to take action. Fearing another bloodbath, the politicians were reluctant to permit Nivelle to resume the offensive in the Chemin des Dames sector, or against Fort Brimont. Nivelle at first protested, then decided to scapegoat General Mangin, who was sacked on 29 April. Henry Morel-Journel had no sympathy: 'Like the great player he is, [Mangin] had chanced his arm and lost.' On the same day the government appointed Pétain as chief of staff of the army, to rein in Nivelle and perhaps force his resignation. But Nivelle remained obstinate to the last, hanging on until 15 May when he was finally sacked. Pétain became the new commander-in-chief, with Foch replacing him as chief of staff of the army. Four days later Nivelle handed in his resignation.

'No-one wants to march any more' – the mutinies
The generals and politicians were not the only ones dismayed by the failure of the much-trumpeted offensive on the Aisne; so too were ordinary soldiers. Maurice Faget (129th Territorials) was part of a detachment charged with identifying the dead. 'When will this slaughter come to an

end?' he wondered. 'They haven't reinstated leave,' grumbled Joseph Varenne (414th Infantry), 'and those who were counting on getting away from the war for a time to reimmerse themselves in the peace of family life find themselves angrily contemplating a possibly fatal return to the lines. Despondency is taking hold in the ranks. The failure of the recent offensive has dealt a rude blow to morale.'

Captain Paul Tézenas du Montcel (102nd Territorials) talked over the situation with the regimental padre: '[We discussed] what the colonel had said about the letters sent by our men and the regrettable frame of mind they sometimes revealed. [Father Plus] wasn't at all surprised and even defended them. He had this reply for the generals who were complaining, "What have you done to bolster morale among the men ... they'd have to be angels not to moan."' Even Tézenas du Montcel was feeling down: 'The most determined and optimistic among us are saddened and depressed. All we can see is chaos, confusion, a lack of agreed strategy, no firm leadership, quite the opposite to the other side!'

Lucien Cocordan (22nd Dragoons) had so far experienced a relatively easy war, but he too was profoundly affected by the catastrophe:

16 April ... Such carnage in an age when progress and civilization reign over us. It's incredible to think that this slaughter has now lasted two and a half years. 19 April. We'll never break through their lines in conditions like these. Why then sacrifice so many precious human lives? How careless! 20 April. What a change in my political ideas [in June Cocordan claimed he had for some time been a complete anarchist] and in my state of mind! It's certainly taken me by surprise, but I'm not feeling down any more.

On 29 April unrest broke out amongst 20th Infantry, a regiment which had spent four days in the front-line trenches from 17 to 20 April. The 20th was eventually relieved and sent to the rear on 25 April, two days late, and then passed four days resting at the Camp de Châlons. When the regiment paraded prior to returning to the trenches, 2nd Battalion did not fall in with their comrades, and 208 men once more failed to answer at roll-call that evening, although all were present again the following morning. Charged with mutiny, six men were sentenced to death, and another eight to ten years' hard labour. The CO, Major Lavall, was reduced in rank to captain, and other officers were replaced.

From these small beginnings a wave of disobedience spread through other regiments, all in the same 'difficult' sectors of Craonne and Cerny. Shattered by the first few days of combat, the regiments involved began to waver when asked to go on the attack once more. All the incidents took place close to the front lines, and in every case the regimental officers managed to get their men moving again. GQG was aware of what was happening but concluded that the officers had simply lost control.

Over the next month things seemed to settle down, but on 1 June more disturbances broke out among the infantry of 41st Division. After losing over a quarter of their effectives in the recent battle, the four regiments which made up this division had been promised a long rest. When this failed to materialize the trouble began. Two of the regiments – 229th Infantry and 363rd Infantry – remained unaffected throughout, but men from the 23rd and the 133rd formed a mob, carrying a red flag at its head and singing the *Internationale*. The brigadier, General Bulot – tagged a 'murderer' and a 'blood-drinker' by the soldiers – simply fanned the flames of discontent. It took the divisional commander, General Mignot – and a promise that the division would not return to the front line — to restore order. The following day a second demonstration took place within the same two regiments, and the whole of the division was moved to the rear. Nine men were condemned to death and five capital sentences were carried out.

From here the disturbances spread yet again. In all, 250 incidents of disobedience took place, differing in type between regiments and involving perhaps as many as 30,000–40,000 men in sixty-eight divisions. Nine of these divisions were classed as 'very seriously' affected, and a further five 'profoundly' affected. The immediate trigger was provided by military grievances – returning to the line, fear of an unknown sector, the possibility of heavy casualties, the incompetence of officers, or lack of leave – often compounded by copious quantities of alcohol.

The 162nd Infantry had also suffered badly on the Chemin des Dames, losing almost half of its 65 officers and 2,510 men between 16 and 22 April. Back in camp at Coulonges, rumours of an imminent return to the front were enough to prompt some men to start stoning regimental headquarters:

> Officers positioned in the front row tried to intervene. No good came of it since all they did was start a fight. Some of the hotheads pounced on them. Suddenly there was a bright light: it was a Ruggieri smoke pot, intended to set fire to the floorboards. That produced a stampede for the exit. Outside a crowd had grown, shouting and gesturing. There were cries of 'Down with war!' 'Rest and leave!' 'Death to shirkers!' 'Death to officers and NCOs!' 'To Paris! To Paris!' ... A good thousand soldiers had gathered. A few

metres from the entrance to the camp stood a sentry, bayonet fixed. As everyone moved off, one of the ringleaders snatched [the man's] bayonet, returned it to its scabbard, grabbed hold of the poor devil, who was quite dumbfounded, and forced him to follow the column of men, which left amid shouting and angry cries.

Tempers also ran high in 63rd Division. One soldier grabbed hold of an officer, bawling: 'You're no man. I'll smash your face in, I'll break your jaw, I'll knock your head off. You're a kid, a little shit. If you're a man, come outside with me.'

A socialist from 36th Infantry wrote home to his wife:

We refused to go up to the line on Tuesday night, we didn't want to march. You might almost say we went on strike, and many other regiments have done the same thing. It'll be easier to explain when I come home on leave. They drive us like animals; they don't give us much to eat, and they want us to get ourselves killed again for nothing. If we'd gone into the attack, only half of us would have come out alive, and we refused to go forward. Perhaps you won't receive my letter. Perhaps they'll open them and keep back the ones which say what happened, or burn them. I don't care, I'm fed up of their war.

'Great guilt and heavy responsibility is borne by a commander who suddenly and belatedly realizes that the morale of his men has been affected,' Nivelle had observed in 1916. And Henry Morel-Journel, on the staff of 74th Division, knew exactly where to place the blame: 'It was the generals, like Nivelle, Mangin and their kind, who were responsible for this state of mind; they were never sufficiently concerned about what a man was thinking or feeling; he was just a rifle to them, nothing more. The strongest morale cannot withstand such treatment for too long, and the jug can only be taken to the well so often before it breaks.'

Charles Delvert thought the problem lay not with the commanders themselves but with their staff:

The four sections of the general staff included among its members some of the most highly qualified officers, but many of them had little experience of fighting, and some none at all ... The poor infantryman coming out of the trenches heard them coming up with some very disconcerting military theories ... One of the section heads, a man with brilliant qualifications, grabbed hold of a bayonet one day and said 'This is the only thing I believe in!' We couldn't bite back our reply, 'Major, how can you say something like that after thirty months of war!'

Although leave had been extended in September 1916, it continued to provoke discontent among ordinary soldiers. Each man was now entitled to three seven-day leave periods each year and the limits set on the proportion of each unit which could be absent at any one time increased to 9 per cent (with some sub-units allowing a slightly higher level for short periods). But as usual in the run-up to a major attack, leave had been cut dramatically immediately prior to the Chemin des Dames offensive. The permitted level of absentees was reduced to 5 per cent on 21 March and to just 2 per cent eight days later. This was only a temporary expedient: in late April the rate was restored to the pre-offensive norm, and during May some units raised it as high as 25 per cent. But this was still not enough to clear the backlog. In June one woman wrote to her husband, serving with Second Army: 'Five months without leave, it's scandalous ... If you're not home soon, I'm going to write to the minister of war, and I'll have something to say to that scoundrel. He ought to be sent to the front.'

Leave trains were 'filthy, squalid [and] unimaginably slow', and a journey to and from the front could be a dispiriting experience. 'With my leave period over, the evening of 13 June saw me on the platform at Bayonne station,' wrote one artilleryman. 'On the outward journey, and on my return, I was struck by the indiscipline which held sway both on the leave trains and at the mainline stations.' The trains were covered in graffiti: 'Our leaders are the pigs. Not us or the Germans', or 'Long live the Boche, they're not as dozy as we make out.'

In some cases the inhibitions imposed by army discipline were also loosened by drink. 'The 18th Company marched about with a red flag to cries of "Down with war!"' reported one soldier. 'Most of them were drunk.' The same was true of 131st Territorials, remembered NCO Georges Murat:

> One evening, when we'd drunk more than usual, [trying] to get ourselves blotto, we were ordered for a relief. 'We won't go,' said the hotheads; the others followed and then the whole battalion was up in arms. Here and there, former trade unionists and former pacifists [might have chosen] that moment to remember their old dogmas, shouting 'Down with war!' and waving the red flag. However, in the majority of units, [the mutinies] happened [just] as I described them, and always when the [soldiers] were ordered back to the trenches yet again.

The drinking habits of soldiers had been causing concern in certain quarters since the start of the conflict. In August 1914 six Breton territorials reportedly drank themselves to death in a single incident, and in the Côtes-du-Nord the prefect decided to close the cafés at 8.00 pm to curb drinking. The local newspaper supported the move but pointed out that it would still do nothing to tackle the problem of home brew: 'Apart from absinthe our Bretons face another terrible enemy, apple jack – all the more dangerous because ... they produce [it] at home in large quantities.' By 1915 some observers were suggesting that alcohol was behind half the crimes committed by soldiers.

However, alcohol was readily available at the front. Since November 1916 every man had been entitled to three-quarters of a litre of wine a day, but not every soldier would drink his full ration, so there was plenty to spare for those who wanted it. 'The soldier talks much more about *pinard* than he actually drinks,' commented Abbé Marcellin Lissorgues (287th Infantry). 'He thinks there's nothing better than a glass of wine, especially a glass of white wine. To tell the truth, he doesn't knock it back ... one litre is enough for half a dozen men. I'm convinced that the joy of eating means more to him than the pleasure of drinking.'

Soldiers could also buy wine behind the lines. There were still several shopkeepers around behind the Aisne front and they were willing to sell to the army – at a price. 'In Dommiers, they were selling wine for 42 sous a litre at 8.00 am,' reported Jean Marot (334th Infantry).

> At midday [it was] 45 sous. In the evening 52 sous. The only wholesaler is the mayor [and] he lets every retailer have a barrel each. He himself sells us wine for the colonel's mess at 22 sous ... At Glennes there's a profiteer selling wine in the bottle at 6 francs [a time]; it's an Aramon worth no more than 12 sous a litre. But the profiteer is risking both his neck and his bottles; there are big shells bursting over his huge cellar every minute and they break something every time.

Soldiers were also concerned about the progress of the war and the welfare of their families at home. Some soldiers were desperate for peace at any price – 'I'd have surrendered Alsace and Lorraine and even the Lozère to bring peace,' confessed one southerner. Georges Murat agreed:

> We attacked with enthusiasm on 16 April and it ended in defeat. If we failed then, we were never going to succeed. The Boche wouldn't get through, but [then] neither would we. ... We needed to make peace at once because our leaders were incapable of leading us to

victory. But that was never going to happen when those in the rear had no interest in peace because they weren't the ones doing the fighting. Well, we soldiers had had enough; we were going to say what we thought.

'I don't know what kind of soldiers you've seen, perhaps those weak with loss of blood,' wrote the philosopher Alain (3rd Heavy Artillery) to his friend Elie Halévy, a medical orderly. 'I've only seen rebels; they're always looking for ways to end the slaughter and when they can't find any their minds turn to thoughts of revenge.' Army Intelligence believed a number of different strands of thinking had come together: victory was now impossible; the high command had run out of ideas; it was vital to come to terms before Russia sued for a separate peace; the war would lead to famine; the foreigners flooding into the country would take the jobs of the combatants; [and] the women and children at home would run short of food and coal.

War-weary civilians were also hit hard by the catastrophe on the Aisne. '[It] has greatly demoralized the soldiers at the front and [civilians] in the rear areas,' wrote postal censorship officials in Bordeaux. 'The morale of the troops is the lowest we have seen for some time ... [and] civilian morale is no higher. Everyone has had enough.' In Le Creusot it was becoming harder and harder to persuade people to subscribe to war loans. 'The collectors, the fund-raisers, all those who in any way request [something] for others face an ever more thankless task,' wrote the chief secretary to the mayor. 'War has almost become the norm, blunting [people's] feelings.'

The prefect of the Isère thought 'country people remained the most steadfast and the most patient', and accused soldiers of undermining civilian morale: 'Comments made on trains, in stations, in cafés, then in the village, give a terrible impression of the state of mind of far too many front-line soldiers ... They get hawked around from one person to the next and exaggerated on the way, increasing anxiety and discontent ... What we need to revive flagging spirits [and] renew people's confidence in the future is a military victory, a major Russian offensive, or simply for the Germans to pull back.'

But soldiers were also affected by civilian disquiet, picked up while they were on leave, or from comrades, letters or the press. Their training complete, members of the class of 1917 (called up in January 1916) were beginning to arrive at the front in some numbers, and exaggerated rumours from the rear further fed the soldiers' fears. A minor disturbance triggered when a Paris shopkeeper tried to short-change some Vietnamese tirailleurs had become a full-blown riot by the time the news reached the trenches.

Various sources claimed wives protesting against the war had been fired on – by the Vietnamese, the Senegalese or the gendarmes – and many killed. Other rumours claimed women had been demonstrating in Paris, with cries of 'Give us back our husbands and children!' and 'Down with war!'

In the rear, opposition to the war was becoming increasingly overt and strikes more common. The *Union sacrée*, the temporary truce called between the political parties in 1914, had soon begun to founder. In the Limousin anti-war sentiments were apparent as early as 1915, with calls for 'an end to the war in the interests of socialism, of the working class and of our country'. By 1917 industrial unrest was widespread in many of France's cities and major industrial areas, partly the result of wage demands prompted by rising prices. In the Dordogne the sub-prefect dismissed such concerns: 'Since [the peasants] have been told there's no longer a chance of peace, all they ask is to sell their produce at the highest possible price and collect their allowances ... The countryside overflows with savings. Wives ... who are willing to work lack for nothing, disposing of sums of money unknown to them before the war. In these circumstances, any criticisms and complaints are merely superficial.'

However, the introduction of meat and sugar rationing had failed to stem the rise in the cost of living. In Paris the purchasing power of the franc had fallen by about 10 per cent since the beginning of the war. Elsewhere in the country the rising cost of food was far outstripping any wage increases; for example, in the Loire-Inférieure, around Nantes and Saint-Nazaire, the cost of food had risen by 169 per cent since the start of the war, wages by only 119 per cent.

In January 1917 some 400 women staged an anti-war protest in Limoges, while in May strikes in Paris reportedly involved about 100,000 workers. The following month trouble broke out in the mining and metalwork industries in the Gard. At a mass meeting a speaker denounced the *Union sacrée* as 'an expression as magnificent as it is fraudulent ... its sole aim is to safeguard the coffers of capitalists'. In June one soldier's wife wrote with news to cheer her socialist husband: 'We must wish with all our hearts for an immediate peace. There are 15,000 women on strike. So much the better ... it's sure to bring peace.'

Paris, Limoges and the Gard were all strongholds of the left, but the war was also losing its ability to anaesthetize normal political impulses in other parts of France. In the heart of the Dordogne female workers at the explosives works in Bergerac came out on strike. 'For the most part they're women of loose morals, with Kabyle [Algerian] lovers,' reported the local *commissaire de police*. 'The managing director was afraid that the women and Kabyles would terrorize the rest of the workforce and wanted me to do everything I could to protect the freedom to work.'

Socialists – soldiers and civilians – also took inspiration from the February Revolution in Russia and the planned Stockholm Peace Conference. Among them was a member of 36th Infantry: 'We have to put an end to this war, which is destroying the working class and consolidating capitalist interests. We must have peace or revolution.' A comrade in 3rd Infantry agreed: 'It's been like this throughout the war. It's the capitalists, who aren't at the front and whose money brings in three times the interest it did before the war, who keep it going to annihilate the workers.' Louis Barthas reported that some men wanted to create a soviet within his regiment. But for all his trenchant criticism of the war, Barthas refused to join, although he did write a petition protesting about the lack of leave. A detachment of cavalry soon arrived, and the regiment was forced to march off 'like convicts being led into forced labour.'

Against this background, many generals were convinced that the mutinies were the product of a conspiracy involving socialists and internationalists, financed by Germans or Bolsheviks, and much was made at the time of the presence on the Chemin des Dames of a turbulent brigade of the Imperial Russian Army. Their revolutionary views may have influenced some French soldiers in the immediate vicinity, but overall they played a minor role in the whole affair. For Georges Murat (131st Territorials) there was no left-wing plot: 'We thought it quite wrong that our general staff ... should blame discontent in the army on the evil influence of the rear areas [or] of revolutionary tracts and pamphlets. ... Many of us thought that, in the present circumstances, the actions of the stateless and the revolutionaries counted for little.'

Why did French soldiers feel they could ignore military discipline and take direct action in this way? Part of the answer lay in the particular relationship which existed between the soldier and the republic. Soldiers were citizens under arms, retaining all their political rights, and had already shown their readiness to protest against injustice when the occasion arose. In December 1915 GQG published a communiqué announcing that men in the trenches would receive warm clothing and better food over the winter. In reply they received no fewer than 200,000 letters from all areas of the front, from soldiers knee-deep in water and mud, eating cold food, without access to fresh water and sleeping on verminous straw.

Soldiers were willing to submit to the loss of personal liberty required in serving their country, providing their commanders did not squander this sacrifice by throwing their lives away in pointless attacks. The level of casualties sustained at Verdun was admissible to them only if it resulted in victory, and a speedy victory at that. The Aisne offensive was the tipping point, its results contrasting so starkly with the promises made beforehand.

As citizens in uniform, soldiers turned to conventional civilian remedies for their grievances – demonstrations and strikes. Protesting soldiers not only displayed the symbols of industrial conflict (the red flag, the *Internationale*), they treated their demonstrations like a labour dispute. 'The soldiers are thinking like employees,' wrote the postal censors. 'They concern themselves with laws governing recruitment, pay, command structure, the guarantees afforded to them by the state ... Moreover the soldiers are convinced that by acting collectively they can determine their own fate, if need be by imposing their will at the front as do workers in the rear, by striking.'

Major Vuillemin (152nd Infantry) argued that this social contract applied in particular to officers: 'Everybody – soldiers and officers alike – should obey the law (which represents the will of the people) and the ... commander-in-chief (who represents the country as a whole). This is particularly true of officers who should set an example to their subordinates.' But senior officers had broken their side of the bargain. Men saw no sign of the promised rest periods after they were relieved from front-line duties, still less of leave. 'They're giving the soldiers a load of old eyewash ... After Verdun, after Mort-Homme, after Maison-de-Champagne, after Four-de-Paris, we didn't get any rest periods at all, or else they were a sham.'

Many of the ringleaders among the mutineers were arrested and tried. Those found guilty were sentenced to death. The youngest was 17 years old; the oldest, 48. Four out of five were veterans who had been fighting since the war began. In terms of their peacetime employment, they were roughly typical of the army as a whole: around a quarter came from an agricultural background, while another two-thirds were factory hands, artisans, clerks and shopkeepers. They came from radical and conservative areas of the country, but most were northerners. There seems to have been no link between the mutineers and socialist anti-war movements, since few of them hailed from the major industrial centres. In the event most of the executions were stayed by presidential decree (almost certainly under pressure from Pétain). Of the 452 who were convicted, 22 men were eventually shot.

The majority of incidents were settled by negotiation, suggesting that the mutinies were not indicative of a deeper malaise within the army. At

Blanc-Sablon camp Joseph Varenne (414th Infantry) thought his officers coped well with the situation: '[They] did their best to calm everything down. They went from one group to another; they didn't talk about patriotism, but spoke to the man rather than the soldier; they quickly sketched a picture of of the despair and dishonour their families would feel if the worst were to happen [i.e. the soldiers were charged with mutiny].' Indeed, it seems likely that some senior officers over-dramatized incidents thought trivial by their regimental counterparts, who had a better knowledge of their men and their foibles. 'Fortunately', concluded Philippe Barrès (12th Cuirassiers), 'the French high command worked out that it was faced not simply by a subversive rabble in a movement it needed to break, but by an irresistible cry of anguish from the French people.'

What would have happened if the Germans had attacked? War-weary or not, the overwhelming majority of soldiers were quite prepared to carry on fighting. '[We have to make sure] that all these brave soldiers didn't die in vain,' wrote one southerner in June 1917. Even a dyed-in-the-wool socialist thought the French had to 'bar the way to the Boches, hard though it is'. Many mutineers maintained that they too would have taken up arms to defend their positions. Fortunately, their claims were never put to the test. Given the notoriously leaky signals discipline of the French front line, it is hard to believe that the Germans had no idea what was happening. Yet they chose not to take advantage of French disarray. Why? Perhaps the German troops in the immediate area were in no fit state to mount a major operation so quickly. Or perhaps they hoped that the French, like the Russians, would simply collapse from within.

'And yet we still have hope' – Pétain takes command

Pétain was now faced with the enormous task of rejuvenating both the army and the war effort. Rejecting any idea of achieving a breakthrough in 1917, he announced that further offensives would take place only in pursuit of limited objectives proportionate to the likely number of casualties. Drives deep into enemy territory – which often produced dangerous salients, death traps for those within – were also abandoned. Instead Pétain proposed a series of attacks, each restricted in scope, with the aim of wearing down the Germans and limiting their freedom of action. Careful, intensive artillery preparation would precede each attack; supported by tanks, the infantry – preferably outnumbering the enemy by three to one – would then occupy the ground. 'The artillery kills, the infantry occupies,' was the general's dictum.

Changes in infantry organization aimed to provide greater flexibility and substitute firepower for men. From September 1917 each infantry platoon was divided into two 'combat groups', each further subdivided into two fire teams: 'Automatic weapons capable of entering quickly into action and laying down a large quantity of fire will form the core [of each team] ... Around them, bombers armed with hand- or rifle-grenades will keep the opponent at a distance. And finally, skirmishing around the whole, beating the cover, ready at any moment with rifle, bayonet or grenade, will be riflemen, agile and alert.' The new system seemed to promise more responsibility for NCOs. But Louis Bobier (11th Chasseurs Alpins) was disappointed. He felt the NCO counted for nothing at the front: 'Only officer's braid commands respect and obedience.'

Units withdrawn from the front would in future pass through battle schools, where they would receive further training, taking part in all-arms exercises which concentrated on close co-operation with artillery and aviation, and movement in and around enemy positions. The artillery received extra guns, plus dedicated observation balloons and reconnaissance aircraft, and tank units were inserted into each army group. Despite the tanks' poor showing on the Chemin des Dames, Pétain remained an enthusiastic proponent, and threw his support behind the introduction of the new FT17 type, lighter and more manoeuvrable than the Schneider and Saint-Chamond, and equally important, easier to manufacture in large numbers.

In June Pétain spoke to the officers of 215th Infantry. 'As if in obedience to the word of command, every newspaper is talking in favourable terms about the soldiers and the need to improve their living conditions,' wrote Sergeant Justin Giboulet.

> Several rumours are circulating: whole divisions have mutinied [or] refused to go into the trenches. Trainloads of men going on leave have demonstrated ... At an officers' meeting at the town hall in Granges, Pétain acknowledged that the situation wasn't wonderful; we had to try not to aggravate the men, especially when they were at rest, an hour or two of exercises at most, watch the food, mingle with them a bit more and avoid any trouble. The colonel himself, a vile bully with a Boche view of discipline, advised us to be very restrained: he said the mutinies had decimated some army corps, that a regiment had been disarmed and was being held at Mailly, and that even the Colonial troops had refused to fall in. Some regiments had mutinied because of the general staff. Believing the promises made to them, these regiments had been expecting to attack just

once; then they were asked to do so a second time, and a third. On the fourth occasion they refused to march. You couldn't expect anything else.

Pétain further advised his officers to combat defeatism among their men by emphasizing the advantages now held by the allies – the naval blockade of Germany, and the entry of the United States into the war in April, with its potential to field a large army to reinforce the allied cause.

He also set about improving the living conditions of the ordinary soldier. One of his first moves had been to reintroduce leave, and he then took steps to make sure it was actually granted. 'Pétain really reined in those commanders who were reluctant to allow leave,' wrote one anonymous commentator. 'His orders were that far from postponing leave, they had to do their best to grant it more often, taking advantage of every opportunity to up the percentage.' In Louis Barthas's regiment, this alone had been sufficient to get the mutinous troops moving, although Barthas was sure that they had forced the concession: 'In the afternoon, we received the order to depart immediately [for the front]. We were given official word that leave would resume at a guaranteed rate of 16 per cent from the following day. The military authorities, so arrogant and authoritarian, had been forced to capitulate. Nothing more was needed to restore order.'

Each leave period would now last between seven and ten days. Shuttle buses would take the soldiers from the camps to a local railhead, served by better, faster, leave trains. The sheer number of trains heading to and from Paris – then as now the hub of the French rail network – often led to unexpected jams and delays, so canteens and dormitories at all major stations would provide facilities for soldiers delayed en route. Advance notice of leave would give the soldier and his family time to prepare. And, from October 1917, leave would be paid, each soldier receiving an allowance of two francs a day.

Some peasant soldiers found a spell at home a mixed blessing. It served only to depress the men of 117th Infantry: 'The sight of poorly cultivated land and the hardships endured by their loved ones in keeping the family property going leave a most painful and lasting impression on this type of soldier and severely test their morale.' But soldiers from 48th Infantry came back to the front in much better spirits: 'After ten days our Bretons came back happy because they've been able to work, to plough [and] to sow. None of them are down in the dumps. The harvest was better than last year's. With wheat to sell, there'll be no need to buy bread. There are apples and they're selling well. Those at home will lack for nothing.'

Providing better rest for soldiers coming out of the line was another aspect of Pétain's reforms. Lieutenant Goutard (30th Infantry) remarked on the improved conditions of a rest camp near Soissons: 'We appreciated the peaceful nights, the relative comfort of the billets, and above all the noticeable improvement in our daily food produced by a settled position and the resources of the rear areas.' Putting Pétain's instructions into effect, he and his fellow officers tried to get to know their men somewhat better, especially the new recruits: 'Dealing with their little troubles, taking an interest in their families ... During the dark hours of battle and despair, this sort of intimacy will strengthen the bonds between soldier and officer.'

However, promised improvements were sometimes slow to materialize, as soldiers from 1st Zouaves discovered in October 1917. '[Our camp] is a perfectly organized and self-sufficient unit,' claimed an article in the regimental newspaper, *La Chéchia*.

> The zouaves are cleverly lodged in berths which can also serve as company shop, saddlery, stores depot or the office of the sergent-major ... It's easy to fetch drinking water which is usually 500 metres from the camp – but ... [only] between 5.15 am and 6.22 am, and 8.30 pm and midnight ... very practical. The showers are in the next village. On the ground, however, there's water everywhere ... the only water supply whose use isn't strictly regulated ... No profiteers visit the camp. It isn't worth their while [because] a canteen lorry comes on the 12th and 25th of each month, just before pay-day. That apart the regimental co-op is normally only one or two kilometres away ... the camps in the woods are generally known as rest camps.

The 321st Infantry found something similar when it rested up in a village behind the lines: 'To their anger and surprise, after forty-one months of war the set-up in the villages was no less primitive than in October 1914 ... the organization was poor and the billets were still appalling, with all the good places snapped up by the staff and the Automobile Service.' Nevertheless, one soldier (68th Infantry) thought that several days' rest in a village, mixing with the locals, 'does more to raise the morale of the men than a longer stay in a camp'. A chasseur (21st Battalion) suggested that it was personal contact – particularly with the opposite sex – which made all the difference: 'What draws men into the bistrots isn't so much the wine they drink in the only bar in the village: it's the feeling that they're in a family home, where the lady of the house, helped by her daughter, her niece or a servant like "Madelon", is happy to let them tell the tale, or catch her by the waist or the chin.'

Meanwhile, in village or camp, drilling continued unabated – much to the disgust of the ordinary soldier. 'Knowing how to parade isn't going to help us chuck the Boche out of France,' grumbled one member of 133rd Division. *On progresse* (9th Dragoons) observed: 'The only two things which can really give you an idea of infinity are the stupidity of the army and the vastness of the sea.' However, additional courses in combat drill or weapons handling were better appreciated. 'We needed some kind of healthy activity to ward off the dangers of idleness,' commented Lieutenant Goutard. 'Well-planned exercises, performed with all the officers present, some specialist instruction which the men themselves felt need of, and games under the benevolent eye of a sports-loving officer ... chased away boredom and allowed us to bring the regiment back under control.'

In the north Anthoine's First Army had remained unaffected by the mutinies and made the first attacks under Pétain's new regime. On 31 July units crossed the river Yser in support of Haig's Passchendaele campaign. The French quickly captured their objectives in a two-kilometre advance, and the allies continued the offensive in a series of set-piece attacks preceded by long bombardments. By the middle of October Anthoine wanted to put a stop to French involvement, but Pétain insisted it continue for the sake of allied co-operation.

Pétain also had in mind another offensive on the Chemin des Dames, but the Germans beat him to it. Raoul Brunon (6th Chasseurs Alpins) was among those in the line of fire:

11 August. A very hard day's fighting. The Germans attacked us violently, Verdun-style. Naturally we stood firm as a rock. Three formidable bombardments followed by three attacks. During the preceding six days, I had quickly organized our defences, digging everything out and placing barbed wire a few metres from the Germans, along with one or two other good men (I lost one of them during the course of the operation). It all bore fruit since the Boche weren't able to get near me.

The officers and men of 359th Infantry were among those badly hit by the German counter-attacks. Captain Henri Desagneaux soberly recorded their losses: 'a memorable day for the regiment. In Champagne, in 1915, we lost twenty-two officers. At Verdun, twenty-three. By tonight or rather tomorrow we can reckon on at least thirty-two, plus two battalions, the 5th and 10th ... completely wiped out.' The regiment had to be relieved immediately.

Pétain's second offensive began on 20 August. General Guillaumat's Second Army mounted an assault on the Verdun front, retaking Mort Homme and Cote 304. Louis Désalbres (128th Infantry) was among those waiting for the attack: 'the wood is crammed with artillery. If there are this many guns all the way up to the front line, then the Boches will be hit by a real hurricane. Up above, there's the continual drone of dozens of aircraft criss-crossing the sky. They pass back and forth like flies on the ceiling of a room.'

Désalbres and his comrades made their way to the jumping-off point laden with gear:

'[We're in] assault order – no greatcoat, no pack, but a tent section rolled across the chest. Two days' rations and two days' reserve, a waterbottle of coffee and one of wine, and they've finally given us some spirits, which give off a slight smell of ether. As a rifle-grenadier, I'm carrying four grenades, proper little shells that can travel up to eighty metres. These grenades do good work. I've also got some rifle-grenade flares; flares to request a barrage, flares to lift the range, as well as my issue cartridges. When I get back to my tent, I feel more weighed down than if I was wearing my pack. That's what they call light assault order. Indian file, the platoons enter the woods. It's 11.00 pm.

One soldier described the aftermath of the attack on Mort Homme and Cote 304 in a letter to his local newspaper, the *Messager de Millau:*

This afternoon I visited Mort-Homme. There's nothing left of the Boche lines. The first line has been 'mortared'. Shells of all calibres have wrought even greater destruction on the others; craters, big and small, appear one on top of another. It's unbelievable ... an incredible chaos [where] seem to float pickets, barbed wire entanglements, the logs from shattered shelters, German grenades, fragments of planks, unexploded shells, and a thousand of those pitiful wrecks you find on every battlefield, as if on a raging sea ... The Boche second line in particular has been pulverized. I say 'second line', but it should be 'where the second line used to be' because you'd search in vain to find the slightest trace of it ... You wonder how any man could still be found [alive] in this precarious landscape. Not a single square metre of earth remains untouched. Everywhere the guns have excavated craters, some of them six metres deep by eight metres across and more. Everywhere avalanches of stones and lumps of earth, brought up from deep within the ground, have crushed anything beneath them. All this land, these fields of wheat, whose soil is still visible within our own lines, has been completely destroyed.

'Bravo the gunners,' enthused *Poil ... et plume* (81st Infantry) in a rare example of fellow-feeling, 'you are our brothers!'

Pétain's offensive on the Chemin des Dames finally got under way in October, Maistre's Sixth Army achieving a notable success at La Malmaison. As part of the assault wave, the men of the Régiment d'Infanterie Coloniale du Maroc found themselves facing a lunar landscape:

> The lie of the land became more distinct as dawn approached – a huge crater field, barren, laid waste, the look typical of our battlefields. A paler line, scarcely visible, unrolled beneath our feet, doubled along its entire length by a line of shelters and trenches, from which our fighting patrols were now driving the first prisoners we spotted. There we were, masters of the notorious, the formidable Chemin des Dames. We suddenly felt a great urge to stand upon it at last; our pace quickened. Captain Dardenne was killed at the head of one company; so too Lieutenant Chatel, who had taken his place, and his successor Lieutenant Dumonteil. Lieutenant Casse then rounded up the remains of this fine company. In hand-to-hand fighting, using their grenades, they took the Préfet quarry, whose western and southern flanks ... formed a considerable strongpoint. Goaded by the deaths of their comrades and commanding officers, Dardenne's Colonials showed no mercy in cleaning the place out with grenades and bayonets; only thirty prisoners were spared.

Like many of his brother officers, Lieutenant Goutard (30th Infantry) had wondered how his men would react. How would they perform in another attack, despite its limited objectives? 'Our brave Savoyard soldiers ... certainly stayed true [i.e. during the mutinies in June]. However, the very recent memory of their prolonged suffering on the Chemin des Dames, the bloody losses they sustained at the Cerny sugarworks, long-postponed reliefs, suspension of leave and privations of all kinds have diminished their enthusiasm and shaken their faith in a new offensive.'

In the event he need not have worried: 'We entered the line that night. Everything was ready. I saw my men again, good lads ... plus the other young men of the class of '17. Heading for their first battle, they'd no appreciation of danger and needed to be prepared; they were all good soldiers, rough navvies, a bit too fond of the bottle when at rest, but they marched well and stood shoulder to shoulder in combat.' Scrambling through the bombardment, under enemy rifle and machine-gun fire, Goutard's men pressed home their attack:

> Then, from right beneath our feet, the Germans emerged from the Guerbette valley, with their hands in the air. ... In the middle of the track a burnt-out shelter, a furnace, a fiery hole in the slope – the work of our flame-throwers. You had to run past it ... The only ones still flooding towards us were prisoners ... Panic-stricken, running through the fire of their own side, they jumped down into the sunken lane. Wounded Germans dragged themselves towards us, poor blighters we helped down [too]. Our men called out to them while they worked – 'Hello there, you Germans!' [or] 'We've got 'em!' – laughing in a sort of nervous release ... One by one the enemy machine-guns stopped ... This time around you could stand up and look out over the battleground, at the big bowl of Allemant, which we now dominated, at the entire Chemin des Dames front and, over there, La Malmaison.

Tanks again went into action and once more they failed to live up to expectations. Supported by two wireless tanks, and accompanied by infantry, one group of Schneiders managed a three-kilometre advance, while a second group of Saint-Chamonds advanced a kilometre before halting and taking up defensive positions. A total of sixty-three machines were engaged in all; of these, only twenty completed their mission and nine were lost to enemy action.

Marching over the battlefield the following year, Marcel Prévost (XXI Corps staff) could scarcely believe what had happened there, nor indeed that he had been part of it: 'Suddenly one of my comrades stopped and said, "The Chemin des Dames?" It's true ... we'd just crossed it without even noticing. Let's go back ... Let's have a look ... which of these craters swallowed him up? Impossible to decide. Let's check the map ... "Ah! There ... look!" [He] showed the others a narrow triangle of broken stones. ... That's it ... Thousands of human beings were wiped out to control this.' A contributor to the first issue of *L'Horizon* (Fourth Army) was equally bemused: 'I cannot believe, I shall always refuse to believe, that so much youth, so much ardour, so much vigour could be mown down, obliterated, lost in time and space for ever more.'

In addition to his limited offensives, Pétain also sought other ways of damaging the enemy. Among them was the trench raid – launched to destroy a machine-gun post, gather information or prisoners, or cut the enemy wire. Previously a British speciality, trench raids became increasingly common in the French lines from the summer of 1917. Nevertheless, some French soldiers continued to view them with suspicion, regarding them more as an unwelcome interruption to trench life than a means of carrying the war to the enemy. 'Periodic raids disturb the peace and quiet,' complained Sous-lieutenant Torquat (41st Infantry), holding the trenches around Calonne near Les Eparges; while in Alsace Jean Daguillon (3rd Artillery) found that 'the only disturbance in the sector is caused by raids which take place every ten days or so'.

The failure of Nivelle's offensive also produced repercussions in Paris. Following stormy debates in the legislature, Painlevé replaced Ribot as prime minister in September, retaining his portfolio as minister of war. But only two months later he too was forced to resign amid political scandals and calls by some politicians for a negotiated peace. In desperation, President Poincaré turned to Georges Clemenceau. Clemenceau immediately took control, implementing a number of reforms designed to reassert political supremacy over the army, so effectively undermined by Joffre. Among these were mandatory retirement ages for senior officers – 60 for divisional commanders, 58 for brigadiers and 56 for colonels. Pétain retained his post as commander-in-chief, but his relations with the belligerent Clemenceau remained uneasy. The new prime minister thought Pétain over-cautious and increasingly turned to Foch as a more congenial spirit.

By the autumn of 1917 the men of 222nd Infantry fell into three distinct groups, typical of the army as a whole: veterans, youngsters from the class of 1917, and a small number of *récupérés*, casualties who had recovered from their wounds and returned to the lines. The veterans were judged to be men who, 'given leave and good care, [would] hold on to the bitter end', the youngsters most likely to rebel if the war continued for very much longer. Meanwhile, the *récupérés* 'need[ed] to be watched' – perhaps because they were up to all the old soldier's tricks, or perhaps because their injuries had affected their morale. If all else failed, the most incorrigible could be posted to north Africa, where they could do no further harm.

An officer from 115th Infantry thought good regiments were built around their veterans: 'You find among them the coolness, the measured courage, the esprit de corps that form the heart of any unit.' He also felt they had an important role to play in toughening up young soldiers: 'Contact with their elders is good for them ... it gives them the staying power they need.' An officer from 49th Chasseurs held similar opinions: 'the young are happy to listen to the [veterans] and believe what they have to say.' The youngsters themselves were often given short shrift. 'You've no right to speak until you've served three years in the trenches' was the terse advice received by one new recruit to 108th Infantry. Nevertheless, an officer in 229th Infantry found them much harder to handle than the veterans: '[They're] much more demanding, more argumentative, less disciplined. They don't understand this war of attrition [and] are more prone to depression.'

By now the mutual support found in units from the same locality had also been lost. Disbanded and reformed as the situation demanded, regiments had long taken drafts from any available source. For example, a section of 128th Infantry, ostensibly from Picardy (its pre-war depot was in Amiens), was by 1917 made up of men from the Charente, Normandy, Picardy, Brittany and the Ardennes. For Colonel Bertrand (162nd Infantry) the rapid turnover in men and mixing of soldiers from different regions made the job of the officer even more difficult: 'Commanding officers can only influence their men when they know them; for some time now, [the extent of our] losses means that ordinary soldiers, and even NCOs, are replaced too frequently [for this to happen].'

Pétain's attempts to restore morale already demanded much of the officer. 'It's become trickier dealing with the troops, their morale is more brittle than before,' reported an officer in 18th Infantry. 'The commanding officer must never let his guard drop [or] neglect the slightest detail. He must be loved by his men; he will get much more from them [that way] than ruling by fear.' Good officers were thought by their men to be familiar but not condescending, offering a cheerful 'Morning, lads!' in greeting. 'The officers treated us very kindly,' wrote one gunner (8th Artillery), 'as if we were somebody, not like the officers ... in the training schools.' Others were variously described as 'a decent and honourable man', 'the best of men', or someone 'who spoke to his men like he spoke to his officers'. 'We have a good, fearless officer,' commented another artilleryman (225th Artillery). 'You'd happily go to your death with him.'

But other soldiers remained disdainful of their superiors. One man (45th Territorials) had little time for his CO: '[He]'s a bit of a fire-eater, but actually he's not much good. He's an autocrat who plays the hard man; but he's a dead loss as far as the ordinary soldier is concerned.' One republican soldier dismissed officers who remained aloof from their men as 'a new aristocracy'. NCOs were thought to have been promoted only through length of service and the lack of any alternative. Regimental medical officers were 'nothing more than machines ruled by circulars'.

Soldiers continued to reserve particular scorn for generals and their staff officers: generals 'look[ed] to the honour of their division without taking into account the exhaustion of their men'; staff officers were 'incapable of leading a company under fire but la[id] claim to the command of regiments and divisions'. However, Pétain himself was a notable exception to the rule. '[He] seems to be a very decent sort of chap,' thought one infantryman (19th Infantry). '[He's] a tall, good-looking man, sturdily built, a direct look, he made the best of impressions.' Even a committed communist like André Morizet admired the general. A Flanders veteran and no lover of the military, Morizet published a book in 1919 designed to expose 'the incompetence of the general staff before and during the war'. But he made a notable exception for Pétain: 'It took one man to reach the head of the army for methods to change ... I'm not here to praise [him] – I've no intention of praising any general – but ... [he] alone among the great leaders understood something of the character of modern warfare. That man was General Pétain.' By late 1917 many Frenchman had begun to view the simple victor of Verdun as something of a miracle worker, a man who could transform base metal into gold. It was a role he would be called upon to play again in 1940.

What motivated men to carry on fighting after three long years of war? In a conscript army like that of the French, opinions were as varied as the soldiers themselves. 'If the troops fall in, it's because they're forced to do so, not out of patriotism as claimed by the bollocks-for-brains in the rear,' thought one gunner (22nd Artillery). Sergeant Jean Bec (96th and 107th Infantry), a peasant farmer from the Hérault, was Catholic by confession and conservative by nature. On his call-up in July 1915, Bec had declared himself 'happy to fulfil my duty towards my country, which requires so many hands to defend it against an invader who now occupies part of its territory'. But by February 1917 he had been radicalized by war: 'Here yet again some of our comrades in misfortune will surely pay with their lives at the bidding of some brass-hat at the other end of a telephone some twenty or thirty kilometres away ... That's how you do away with a few more of the working class.'

For some the war had become simply a matter of routine: 'It's been our everyday life for nearly three years now and it becomes a habit.' Others emphasized their sense of duty, although this was sometimes a duty reluctantly borne: 'when all was said and done, you had to do your duty'; 'we poor buggers spit in disgust and set off obediently to do our duty'. But others considered it a patriotic obligation proudly undertaken in their country's hour of need. 'I was wounded in both feet today and my boots are full of blood,' wrote one infantryman (149th Infantry). 'But I'm still not downhearted. I'm standing firm to the end, I'm doing it for France.' An anonymous voice agreed: 'Despite all the nonsense, all the mistakes, all the blunders, are there any other soldiers as good as the French?'

Certain individuals continued to feel the weight of history and the defeat of 1870: 'We're fighting to avenge our grandfathers who fought in this very place. They're sleeping here beneath our feet and following everything we do. They stopped [the Germans] here and we won't let them get any further!' Some fought on to avenge friends, family and countrymen. 'All minds have but a single thought – avenge those who are no longer here,' wrote a member of 408th Infantry. 'You can be sure I've avenged my two poor brothers who've been dead since 1915,' promised a comrade in the 73rd. And one member of 116th Infantry was already thinking about exacting a further toll when the war was over: 'Gazing sadly upon all these ruins and thinking about the despair of those who'd lost everything, I understood better why peace without reparations was a crazy idea which had to be vigorously opposed.'

'It's our national duty to hate the Boche' read the strapline of *Le Voltigeur* (12th Division), and a soldier from 344th Infantry was in no mood for compromise: 'Their soldiers live by plunder and trickery, they're a treacherous race which deserves to be wiped out.' Philippe-Jean Grange (30th Infantry) would have agreed wholeheartedly. October found him back on the Chemin des Dames, at Laffaux:

> Many bodies still lie unburied after previous attacks. Bones litter the ground. I find the grave of the son of our corps commander, a sous-lieutenant killed at the age of twenty-one. A bit further away a cross rather bigger than the rest is set upon a collapsed dug-out. A colonel and all his regimental staff are buried under this mass of earth and stones. I swear I'm going to kill the first able-bodied German I meet on the day we attack. That's how I plan to avenge all the dead. I truly hate the Germans.

Yet when Grange came face to face with his victim two days later, he was persuaded to back down: '[The Boche] must be able to read in my eyes that I really do intend to kill him. What do I care about his wife and children? How many family men on our own side will be dead by this evening? Let's get it over with! But Dusdat lowered my arm: "Leave him, come on, you'll have plenty of chance to kill others!" The whole episode lasted no more than thirty seconds. Why did I give way?'

Others needed no reminder to treat their enemy with compassion or respect. 'Why do people think we should be better than them?' wondered Georges Murat (131st Territorials). 'They're tough fighters, the Boches.

All you hear about the enemy being demoralized, it's a joke.' One member of 1st Division was happy to give a prisoner something to eat and drink. 'They're still somebody's children even if they are our enemies,' he reasoned, 'and it breaks my heart to see such awful things.' A gunner from 276th Artillery put it even more succinctly, 'after all, they too are just men'.

Meanwhile instances of fraternization were still taking place in quiet sectors of the front: 'The Boches gave us some cigarettes today and we got some bread over to them,' reported Charles Ballet (75th Infantry). 'They [also] offered to swap six packets of cigarettes for a canteen of wine, but it was warm today and we didn't take them up on it. Not that this stops us when we take it into our heads to chuck over a few grenades. Yesterday morning [the Boches] came within six metres of me. They'd have been easy meat if we'd wanted to nab them. But they didn't want to surrender; they told us the war would be over by August.'

To the soldiers of 222nd Infantry peace still seemed a distant prospect: 'The men don't think we'll be defeated but overall victory still seems a long way off, which frightens them a little. Only the elite are bothered about Alsace-Lorraine. The [men] think it will be [a] long [war] and are resigned to it.' Their comrades in 346th Infantry had also grown used to the idea of a war of attrition: 'The men no longer expect to crush the Germans, but to wear them out and force them to agree to peace terms dictated by the allies.' Everyone wanted peace, commented one gunner (8th Artillery), but it had to be 'a good French peace, and for this ... the soldiers will stand firm'. Meanwhile some members of 131st Territorials had a novel idea for bringing the conflict to an end: 'They're tired of the war,' reported one of their NCOs. 'The[y] all tell me they're farmers and that if their wives do a good job the war will [only] last longer. Don't grow anything and the war will have to end sooner. That's their theory.'

Men returning to the trenches remained as apprehensive as ever:

How quickly the rest period has gone. The war that seemed so distant is gradually sinking its claws back into us ... As we left the peaceful village more than one man was thinking, 'Will I be back here again next time?' No one pursued the idea any further, but in the back of each mind lay a hazy image of crosses leaning to one side and bodies lying out in the open. The lottery was starting up again. Lucky those who drew the winning numbers.

To the despair of the ordinary soldier, newspapers – and now the cinema – continued to peddle a hopelessly inaccurate view of the fighting. *Le*

Crapouillot provided a pithy summary of the plot of the 'innumerable patriotic films': 'with amazing panache, squads of discharged actors storm the bastions of Vincennes. Leaping boldly over harmless fire-crackers ... raising their arms to the heavens, [they] die happily with a smile on their lips, while the orchestra plays a catchy little number.'

But, as they marched off to the front, even the hardened cynics of *Le Crapouillot* were charmed by the attentions of the Paris public:

> They welcomed us from the windows of houses, from cafe doorways, from pavements, from trams going down the avenues; they clapped and they cheered. Overcome with emotion ... we puffed out our chests with pride to think that it's thanks to our efforts ... that these women, children [and] old people can take a peaceful Sunday stroll through the sunlit streets. We were thrilled by the admiration, by having an 'audience'. ... In the mud and mortar fire yesterday, the soldiers scorned the facile optimism of those in the rear who would never understand the hardships of the front. Today these same men, disarmed by the applause ... were keen to parade before the spectators ... as light-hearted, cheerful, heroic poilus! Suddenly, as a train glided slowly into the crowded station, and without a word of command, the column burst into song from one end to the other ... 'The Republic calls us! We must conquer or we must die!' With tears in our eyes, we ... sang at the top of our voices, drunk with the applause, proud of our muddy greatcoats, insanely proud of a renown so painfully acquired, and genuinely prepared for any sacrifice ... We felt we were setting off to defend Paris out there under the grey skies of Artois.

Chapter 5

'Victory!'
1918

Chronology

21 Mar–5 Apr	German offensive on the Somme (Operation *Michael*)
26 Mar	Foch appointed Allied Co-ordinator
3 Apr	Foch appointed as Supreme Allied commander-in-chief
9–30 Apr	German offensive on the Lys (Operation *Georgette*)
27 May–6 Jun	German offensive on the Aisne (Operation *Blücher*)
9–13 Jun	German Noyon-Montdidier offensive (Operation *Gneisenau*); battle of Matz, and the French counter-attack (11 June)
15 Jul–2 Aug	German *Friedensturm* offensive in Champagne
8–10 Aug	Allied offensives in Picardy and around Matz
20 Aug–3 Sep	Tenth Army attacks north of the Aisne
12–16 Sep	Reduction of the Saint-Mihiel salient
26–30 Sep	Allied offensive against the Hindenburg Line
4–12 Oct	Germans pushed back to the Hunding Line
8 Oct	Germans pushed back to the Hermann Line
14–26 Oct	Attack on the Hermann-Hunding Lines
11 Nov	Armistice signed

'Four years of hope' – the end approaches

Pétain's perceived leniency in response to the mutinies of 1917 had not met with universal approval. Among the critics was Major Gémeau, a French liaison officer serving at BEF Headquarters: 'Gémeau ... declared that the general should have shot two thousand men and not just thirty during last year's mutinies. The French army was in a very serious situation at that time and required drastic measures to excise the ulcer. Instead of driving the men, he gave them leave and rest.' However, time had proved Pétain right. During the autumn and winter of 1917 internal government bulletins noted considerable improvement in morale: 'Uniforms more correct, discipline better observed, fewer cases of drunkenness. Incidents on trains and in stations now very rare ... Morale among the troops seems to have firmed up recently, however great their desire for peace.'

Determined that France should play the decisive role in Germany's defeat to justify her enormous sacrifices thus far, Pétain framed his plans for 1918 accordingly. He proposed that the British extend their front to include the Aisne, while the newly arrived Americans entered the line in Lorraine – keeping the two apart to prevent the two English-speaking nations from dominating the campaign. The main French offensive would take place further east again, in Alsace. If possible it would also include a thrust down the Rhine valley to attack the Saarland, a key German industrial area. Success here would give France a much-needed victory, help regain the lost provinces of Alsace and Lorraine, and provide a useful bargaining chip in any future peace negotiations.

But the collapse of the Russians and the defeat of the Italians at Caporetto in late October threw Pétain's plans into disarray. He saw no alternative but to go on the defensive until the Italian front was stabilized. The Bolsheviks' seizure of power and the subsequent armistice also released large numbers of German troops for service on the western front, just as France was facing an acute shortage of manpower. Each infantry company, 250 men strong in 1914, now had a theoretical strength of 194, but many could in fact muster only half that number. The class of 1918 had been already been called up in April 1917, and France's last reserve of manpower, the class of 1919, was called up in April 1918. The Americans now arriving on French soil in some numbers required further training and would not be ready to enter the line in force before May. Until sufficient reserves of manpower and equipment were built up on the western front, Pétain would continue to wait for 'tanks and the Americans'.

Feelings about the Russians ran high. 'We should never forgive their cowardice,' grumbled one factory worker. 'They dragged us into the war in 1914 and now they're betraying us.' In December one Russian officer was jeered at in the streets of Paris: 'Hey, look at him. That lily-livered Russian. He'd be better taking off his uniform than appearing dressed like that.' The Russian brigade which had mutinied the previous summer had since been disbanded and those not directly implicated were incorporated into the Foreign Legion. However, Lieutenant Colonel Rollet (CO of the Legion's

Régiment de marche) felt th Russians' conduct under fire left something to be desired: 'As soon as they came under a violent artillery barrage, they found a shell-hole and stayed there all day, letting their neighbours attack on their own. This has made their existing legionnaire comrades very angry with them.'

France's new allies received a very different welcome. The first American units had disembarked in June 1917, but the build-up over the autumn and winter was slow, and by January only 161,750 men had crossed the Atlantic. By September, however, there would be over 1.5 million American troops in France. Jean de Pierrefeu (GQG) compared the newcomers with their French counterparts:

> Around Coulommiers and Meaux, they passed by in column after column, crammed onto lorries ... almost all bare-headed and bare-chested ... singing songs from home at the top of their voices, amid enthusiastic crowds. The sight of all these magnificent young men from overseas, these kids of twenty, clean shaven, bursting with energy and health, all kitted out in their new equipment, produced an extraordinary effect. They made a striking contrast with our regiments, with their faded uniforms worn out by so many years of war, and their gaunt soldiers, hollow eyes shining in dark sockets. ... Everyone felt they were about to witness the magic of a blood transfusion.

Private Legentil (74th Infantry), a machine-gunner, was also eagerly anticipating American support: 'Let's hope they hurry up and join us in the line. We won't be offended, it'll lighten our load!' So too was a member of 220th Artillery: '[The Americans have] plenty of fire in their bellies, [and are] longing only to measure themselves against the Boche. In short [they're] the French in 1914.' But another infantryman (103rd Infantry) recognized the size of the task faced by the newcomers: 'Those with no experience of war who start out now can't help but find it astounding, or else they need to be pretty astounding themselves.'

As part of his reform of army structure and doctrine in 1917, Pétain had also prescribed changes to French defensive organization. The second line of trenches, situated at least two kilometres from the Germans and thus out of range of their artillery, was now to be the principal defensive position. The role of the front line would simply be to slow down the enemy, not to stop him, and troops would no longer be concentrated here. Meanwhile reserves were to be located close to transport links to make them easily available for counter-attacks.

Prescribing schemes of defence at GQG was relatively simple; constructing them in the winter mud was another matter entirely. *Le Bulletin désarmé* (44th Chasseurs) described one muddy sector:

> An oily pond, disconcertingly deep, awaits you, draws you towards it; duty pushes you onwards. In one of those foolish decisions [like those] which throw you over the parapet on the morning of a big offensive, you venture into this foul bath. The water gets into your boots with the glugging sound made by an emptying bottle, while behind you the skirts of your greatcoat balloon gracefully like the veil of a water-nymph. Sometimes the two lips of the trench ... come together in a ghastly embrace, the wattle sides crushing the life out of each other ... And for the reserve company there are the detested digging fatigues, a real labour of Sisyphus to get a clear broth to stick to the parapet when it's determined to run off ... The mud hides a man from head to foot, snuffing out ... all distinguishing signs of age and appearance, the smile of the rookie and the gravity of the reservist – the rosy cheeks of the 20-year-old and the wrinkles of the 30-year-old.

As the fifth year of fighting began, *Le Canard du boyau* (74th Infantry) struck a wry note: '[The war will end] when every man has the Croix de Guerre ... When we get a litre of wine a day ... When every regiment knows every sector ... When all the shirkers are at the front and all the soldiers at the front are shirkers ... [and] when all the daddy's boys on the staff are serving in a front-line company.' Other trench newspapers took a more stoical line, typified by the first issue of *La Musette* (409th Infantry): 'Take heart. Let's put an end to the ridicule. Silence the criticism. We'll apportion blame later. Now's not the time to do it. First we must win. The hour is grave but not without hope. Have faith, we will win to avenge our dead and [to ensure] we don't betray [their memory].' But no-one was willing to expose themselves to needless danger. In the words of the New Year edition of the *Gazette du créneau* (134th Territorials), 'The unlucky soldier who is last to be killed will regret it all his life.' The holder of that sad distinction would be Private Augustin Trebuchon (41st Infantry), a battalion runner killed near Vrigne-sur-Meuse (Ardennes) at 10.50 am on 11 November 1918.

'Soldiers of France' – the German offensives
Pétain and Haig were well aware that Germany would use the divisions newly released from the eastern front to launch a spring offensive, but

effective German security measures prevented them from identifying exactly where the attack would take place. The British focused on the Albert–Arras area, while the French were more concerned about the Champagne front, around Reims. As a result, neither army had its reserves in the right place when the Germans eventually launched Operation *Michael* on 21 March in the Saint-Quentin–Barisis area, close to the junction of the British and French sectors. Mounting evidence of a German attack in Champagne, as well as Pétain's suspicions of British motives (he feared they might simply use French troops to hold off the enemy while they retreated to Dieppe), meant that Haig's urgent plea for twenty divisions fell initially on deaf ears. But later that day Pétain changed his mind, sending thirteen divisions and a number of other reserve formations to assist.

What the French most needed in the hour of crisis were mobile units to plug the gap between the two armies. But, just when its time had come, the cavalry was elsewhere, drawn away 'in aid of the civil power' to tackle industrial unrest in a number of French cities. Many soldiers were apprehensive, fearful of a 'new Verdun'. But one member of 166th Division welcomed the attack: 'We can't carry on like this for long, so it's [got to be] the last of the killing.'

It fell to Third Army to plug the breach. Units were fed desperately into the gap as they arrived on the scene, sometimes without supporting artillery, the men carrying only the ammunition already in their pouches. Georges Gaudy (57th Infantry) and his comrades were near Babouef when 'an endless convoy of motor ambulances with English wounded passed us and headed down to Ribécourt ... groups of men were perched on the roofs of the vehicles, infantrymen, their heads and arms swathed in white bandages, their faces drained of blood'.

Despite the experience of the Somme and Passchendaele, Pétain was not the only Frenchman suspicious of his British allies. 'As far as the Tommies are concerned,' commented one infantryman (74th Infantry) in October 1917, 'I don't know what they're capable of ... They're with us, but we'd like it better if they went back where they came from.' After the disaster at Caporetto, a comrade in 5th Infantry wrote: 'That just leaves us and the English to go after the Boches, and we can only rely on ourselves.' And now, while exceptions were generally made for the Scots or for British colonial troops, many felt their ally had abandoned them. 'The British are hopeless and it's costing us dear,' commented one soldier (70th Division). Another thought the British commanders were not up to the job: Foch would have to 'shake them up and get them to manoeuvre properly.' 'Where is their fabled cleanliness, their English hygiene?' queried a member of 37th Division. 'And their decency? And their phlegm? And their guts?'

In Paris panic reigned, and stations with lines leading west and south were crowded. 'You'd have to go back to August 1914 to find an example of a similar exodus,' remarked a member of staff at the Gare d'Orsay. Shelling from the 'Paris Gun' made it seem as if the Germans were almost at the city gates. This huge rail-mounted weapon fired its first round on 21 March. Only when all the fragments were reassembled were they found to have been from a shell and not a bomb. The gun was located some 120km away, and in all fired around 350 94kg rounds, killing 250 civilians and wounding a further 670. The very fact that the city was being shelled wrought even more damage to civilian morale than the shells themselves. Writing for the magazine *Everyweek*, Marie Harrison referred to the bombardment, with considerable understatement, as a period of 'acute unpleasantness', because the shells arrived unpredictably – unlike an air-raid, which at least had a definite beginning and end. 'Yet,' she continued, 'I found Paris brighter than London, I found it more alive, more interested and so more interesting.'

Paris was certainly accustomed to air-raids. The Germans had been launching intermittent attacks, by aircraft or zeppelin, since 1914. In March 1917 Benjamin Poupin (XIII Corps staff), stationed near Compiègne, watched as one of these raiders (Zeppelin L39) met its end:

What a handsome sight! Just as day dawned, scarcely three kilometres away, over Compiègne, we could clearly make out a huge airship at an altitude of about 3,000 metres, which looked almost stationary. It seemed to be moving, but very slowly. It was surrounded by shells, exploding one after another ... 'We'll get it!' we all said. Ten minutes passed, a quarter of an hour, with the shelling increasing, when suddenly an incendiary hit the monster. A long flame rose up, other flames seemed to break off and fall slowly to the ground ... the evil beast collapsed in flames ... three of the airmen threw themselves out from a height of 500 to 800 metres. One of them ... wasn't quite dead. A bold Compiègne mother wanted to finish him off with a big kitchen knife: 'Child killer, I'll rip you apart!' she shrieked. We stopped her in time. Besides, the Boche was so badly injured he soon turned up his toes. I picked up a small piece of the monster's framework. According to reports ... there were twenty-three crewmen, including officers, in the nacelle of the zeppelin, but the latter were hardly recognizable in the debris.

From 30/31 January 1918 it was Gotha bombers which raided the capital more frequently: in all, there were thirty-three raids, causing 787 casualties. Both air-raids and shelling ceased later in the year as the allies threatened German positions, but only in early August, with victory in the Second Battle of the Marne, did Parisians begin to return to the city in any great numbers.

Le Bulletin désarmé (44th Chasseurs) 'sympathized' with the plight of Parisians in their hour of need:

> Constantly exposed to the bombs of the sinister Gothas, forced to spend hours in a cellar when you could pass them more agreeably elsewhere, your life becomes unbearable. Long accustomed to life underground, soldiers would soon have turned your cellar into comfortable living quarters. But from here I can see that it's cluttered with barrels and bottles of wine. They've got to be kept safe. Since that's hard to do, the soldiers would polish them off as if they were gnôle. Sometimes you've just got to resign yourself to making great sacrifices. I [still] don't think these are shared out fairly though.

Further north, civilians fled southwards away from the fighting, just as they did in 1914. 'We caught up with a crowd of refugees which soon overwhelmed us,' wrote Georges Gaudy. 'Men, women, children, on foot, in carts, an enormous army of exiles ... I could sense all these unhappy faces staring at our men. For these people fleeing far from home we were the only ones who counted right then. They were even more upset to see that we were retreating too, before we'd even got to the front.' Gaudy had earlier entered one village to find a fierce argument under way between a local and a gendarme: 'The civilian wanted to put everything on his cart; you could tell he was heartbroken to leave his household effects behind; he'd have taken his whole house if he could.'

When Gaudy reached Noyon, liberated only twelve months earlier, he found the town empty: 'Several Englishmen suddenly appeared out of a shop of some kind and called out to us in French, "Come in! This is our canteen! Take anything you want!"' Sadly for Gaudy and his chums, their NCOs quickly appeared to restore order and prevent a free-for-all. Instead, the captain ordered a two-minute halt; three or four men per section were allowed to go inside, grab whatever they could and share it out afterwards. They all emerged 'laden with hams, bottles of beer and ... boxes of cigarettes'. But this left the lucky recipients with a dilemma – where could they put it all? Quickly they drank the beer, crammed as much as they could in their pockets, and then made more space by jettisoning their underclothes: 'We could always find more underclothes. What we needed [now] were things to eat.'

Even the city of Amiens was threatened. The mobility normally provided by the cavalry now came from the aviation service. By 25 March seventy-seven squadrons were mustered over Picardy, trying to slow the advance of the leading German troops: 'Although there were no ground troops capable of opposing the invasion, someone suddenly remembered the aviation service,' wrote René Fonck (Spa103).

> I don't know who came up with this brilliant idea ... or how the High Command was persuaded to accept ... [it]. But from the most distant points of the front, one squadron after another rushed to the danger zone. The roar of aircraft engines there was louder than had ever been heard before. We flew so low that we were almost on the tips of their bayonets, and our machine-guns rattled at point-blank range onto the dense mass of troops below. The bombers were more heavily laden [and] dropped their missiles on the columns and convoys of marching troops. Our attack spooked the horses; they threw their harness into the ditches, creating [a scene] of unutterable confusion.

But the French failed to make the most of their opportunity. 'Such a total and unexpected success took our battalions completely by surprise. Nervous at finding nothing but empty space in front of them, they hesitated to press home their advantage and lost vital hours.'

Elsewhere the Germans continued to press forward, taking Montdidier on 27 March. Georges Tardy (226th Infantry) and his comrades were on the far side of the town:

> We debussed near a little hamlet a few kilometres from Montdidier and slept there for two or three hours. We'd nothing to eat, so at daybreak we went round the area evacuated by the locals and pounced on the chickens, rabbits [and] potatoes etc. We set off again around noon, thinking that there were troops ahead of us, but we were on our own and found ourselves face to face with the Boche in front of a small village. We attacked three times during the day to [try and] take it from them, but in vain. We had some armoured cars to support us, and it was great watching them drive around untroubled by the bullets. In the afternoon my section was sent to seize a small wooden hut and capture a road junction. We succeeded, but the Boche gave us a rough time and [only] four out of the seven

of us came back. It was like that for two days, a war of movement with attacks and counter-attacks. Then another battalion arrived to relieve us and we fetched up at a little place three kilometres in the rear.

Convinced that the German attack had knocked out the British, leaving the French to fend for themselves, Pétain made his plans. He took what he felt was a realistic view, preparing to cover Paris rather than maintain contact with his allies. But such a pessimistic outlook was not to the taste of Clemenceau, who suggested Foch be appointed to co-ordinate British and French responses to the German assault. From there, it was a small step to promote him to the position of allied commander-in-chief. Foch would oversee overall strategy, with the three national commanders – Pétain, Haig and Pershing – responsible to him for the tactical handling of their respective armies. Foch saw the western front as a single theatre of war, where operations should be jointly planned and executed by all the forces available, not by each country going it alone. He was also instinctively opposed to Pétain's defence-in-depth arrangements. He had always found it difficult to countenance yielding any ground to the enemy. Even during the crisis of the First Battle of the Marne in 1914, Foch's response had been to counter-attack. 'The best means of halting a vigorous and sustained offensive ... is to launch a powerful [counter-]offensive,' he told allied chiefs of staff in January 1918. While costly in terms of French lives, his aggression did equal damage to the enemy, and prevented them from exploiting gaps in the French positions.

Although the Germans succeeded in driving back the allies, they were unable to achieve a decisive breakthrough. Their offensive ground to a halt on 5 April, and they switched the point of attack further north, to the area around the river Lys. The assault fell mostly on British formations, but the French were driven off the key position of Mont Kemmel with its exceptional views over southern Flanders. Arriving from Alsace on 15 May, the men of 28th Division came almost immediately under German bombardment. On the night of 24/25 May Captain Pinçon (99th Infantry) and his regiment were in support of the main position on the hill. The barrage began at 1.30 am:

> For more than four hours it was impossible to take off our gas-masks. The men remained as if petrified in their holes, under a deluge of iron, fire and poison, half-smothered, suffocating, overwhelmed by the noise and the concussions in ground and air, their vision blurred behind the misted lenses of their masks. The wounded were running like madmen, braving the barrage to reach the aid posts, flinging

themselves to the ground to try and catch their breath, seeking safety in flight; dark shadows you spotted among the flames of the explosions, like demons in a furnace.

By 7.30 am the Germans, supported by ground–attack aircraft, had managed to penetrate the front line of 30th Infantry. By 9.30 am the hill was in German hands: the 30th, along with a battalion of 99th Infantry, had simply ceased to exist. The regiment lost 48 officers and 1,688 men killed, wounded or missing.

On 24 April German forces crossed the Somme and retook Bapaume and Noyon. The French managed to halt the German advance just beyond Noyon, but only by committing all of Reserve Army Group, as well as elements of First and Third Armies, plus a new Tenth Army, created from divisions brought back from the Italian front. Among those newly returned from Italy was Louis Bobier (11th Chasseurs Alpins), a veteran of the class of 1914. Bobier found life under the barrage particularly difficult. He came out of one spell in the trenches 'so exhausted all I wanted was to die, not to keep on suffering any more'.

The arrival of French reinforcements halted the offensive. But, while Foch was anticipating a further attack on the Somme, the Germans switched focus again, this time to the Aisne and the Chemin des Dames. The attack, planned to draw French reserves away from the Somme and allow Operation *Michael* to continue, fell on General Duchêne's understrength Sixth Army. Contrary to Pétain's directives, Duchêne had placed the bulk of his force in the first line of trenches, unwilling to abandon ground so dearly won in 1917, and anxious to hold the heights rather than the river line. 'Save for a direct and exceptional order from a commander (général de division or higher),' he told his men, 'each element, regardless of its position, will remain in place until it is overrun.' Pétain was aware of Duchêne's insubordination, but he was always inclined to view the commander on the spot as the best judge of the immediate situation. And, in view of the impending attack, he decided to leave the general in place.

The blow fell on 135th Infantry. Four thousand guns began their preparation at 1.00 am on 27 May, shelling the French lines to a depth of twelve kilometres in a bombardment which lasted only two hours and forty minutes. 'I've never seen anything like it,' one survivor wrote to his parents:

What a dreadful – in the true sense of the word – bombardment. The poor division. You should see what it's like now, there's nothing left. As for the regiment, while we've been in the line 2,000 men have been reduced to just over 200. So you can see what kind of a storm these swine unleashed upon us. There are just ten men left from our poor machine-gun company, and it's still not over. We haven't been relieved as yet, we have to wait until the reinforcements arrive.

The 22nd Division was almost annihilated, and heavy losses were also inflicted on British troops who had been sent to the area for a rest after their experiences during Operation *Michael*. The gap in the French lines quickly widened to twelve kilometres and by 27 May the leading German units had advanced fifty-five kilometres.

Four days later the men of 57th Infantry were retreating through fields of standing crops, among them Georges Gaudy:

We each fall back in turn, pausing to fire when the black helmets appear from the pale fields. When a section gets up and moves off, the enemy mows it down from left, right and front. We can clearly see that Sirey is surrounded, struggling in the storm of grenades. If we can get two or three platoons to regroup, we can go forward to disengage a neighbouring company in trouble. Near the Saconin road, Lieutenant Chauveau defended himself for more than an hour. When the Germans got to him, he was lying wounded among his dead [comrades]; he refused to surrender [and] went to his death firing on his attackers with his revolver.

The remains of twenty-three companies from four different regiments fell back among the quarries to the west of Saconin (Aisne), where they managed to hold off the Germans over a long moonlit night, before falling back again out of harm's way.

By this point of the war nearly all the cuirassier regiments were serving as dismounted infantry. At 9.00 am on 12 June Yves Tourmen (12th Cuirassiers) and his comrades were in the quarries around Dommiers (Aisne). Caught between a French barrage firing too short and well-targeted German shells, the 12th were hugging the ground and hoping for the best: 'We needed new orders. Without saying anything to us, the major took the MO, the captain etc. and left with the staff to tell someone [about our situation]. Some of the walking wounded followed them – scared stiff. About fifty of us remained but then they too departed one by one, even those who couldn't walk properly. That just left me [wounded in the leg] and my chums Rabourdin, Bazin and Monnereau.' Falling back, the four friends found their way blocked by the French barrage: in one direction lay death; in the other, the likelihood that they would be 'caught like rabbits'. All they could do was stay put and allow themselves to be taken prisoner.

French morale plummeted in the wake of the German success. After surviving a further enemy attack, another member of 57th Infantry wrote to his wife:

Today I'm fine but the situation is serious, I wouldn't be surprised if I was taken prisoner tomorrow. ... I don't know how events will turn out in France. If things go too badly, try to get to Switzerland and I'll do my best to meet up with you there ... In any case remember this. If we emerge victorious it would be unfair. We don't deserve to win; we're too idle and too stupid. Damn Clemenceau and the bitter-enders whose blindness and obstinacy will lead France to ruin.

One member of 289th Infantry wrote home in such pessimistic tones that the censors confiscated his letter:

At the front, all that's left are poor little workers taking a beating for the big bosses ... and they're the ones demanding victory, saying in their newspapers that the Boches won't last much longer because they're running out of food. But I think it's the Boches who'll be victorious and us who'll soon have nothing left to eat. It's over now. It's the Boches who are going to win, we've no chance of kicking them out of France; we'd have been better to accept peace terms when they were offered. Now it's too late. To see so many men killed for nothing, especially when we don't know why we're fighting, that's still the saddest thing of all.

Desperate defence by the French, as well as the timely intervention of two American divisions, saved the day. By 6 June heavy casualties and logistical problems had brought the German attack to a halt only sixty kilometres from Paris. But a large salient now projected into the French lines. Duchêne was sacked and would not receive another command until 1920. 'Here, as elsewhere, the origins of the disaster were the same,' observed Jean de Pierrefeu at GQG. 'A new procedure which didn't receive the attention it deserved. Absolute proof of how hard the French – intellectuals in love with theories and ideas in general – have found it to adapt to this technical war, which also explains why our staff, so thoroughly educated in the art of war, have been so slow in developing new equipment.'

Resuming their offensive on the Somme on 9 June, the Germans quickly advanced east of Montdidier. Here Third Army, which had only arrived in the area during the emergency in March, had been unable to construct a position in depth and incurred heavy casualties in trying to hold a single line of trenches. Fortunately, the French were aware of the imminent attack, and had their reserves to hand, slowing the German advance. A counter-attack around Matz, led by General Mangin, restored to favour by Clemenceau, also shook the Germans, and they called off their offensive five days later.

The counter-attack at Matz marked the last independent appearance of French Schneiders and Saint-Chamonds. Once again losses were high: seventy-three machines (almost half the total number of tanks engaged). Clearly too slow and too vulnerable, they would in future go into action only when accompanied by the lighter Renault FT17. The FT17 had actually been in development since the end of 1916, but progress had been slow, and it only went into mass production, at Pétain's insistence, after the disaster on the Chemin des Dames. Light enough to move on the back of a lorry, the new tank had a turret which revolved through 360 degrees, providing far greater operational flexibility than its cumbersome predecessors. The infantry finally had the right kind of mobile support, although not everyone was convinced of the FT17's reliability. 'The Renault tank', commented one cynic, 'is by definition a machine which has broken down, but which nevertheless deigns to work occasionally!'

The final German thrust came in Champagne. By now the French had broken the enemy codes, and both signals and human intelligence alerted them to the forthcoming attack. On 28 June General Mangin's Tenth Army launched a pre-emptive strike towards Soissons, advancing several kilometres and capturing several thousand prisoners. Undaunted, the German attack went ahead on 15 July. Elements from four French armies tried to hold their ground, but they were slowly pushed back until the Germans achieved a foothold on the south bank of the Marne, near Dormans. However, the German advance had created a large salient, especially vulnerable on its western side. Led by Tenth Army, the counter-attack came on 18 July and, by omitting any preparatory barrage, managed to achieve complete surprise. Preceded by tanks and a rolling barrage, the US 2nd Division advanced eight kilometres, and by the end of the first day 12,000 prisoners had been captured.

The rapid advance of the specially trained German stormtroops during the spring had shocked many allied commanders. Characterizing them as 'an indication of the flagging confidence of the German high command in its infantry', Pétain had rejected the idea of creating similar units in the French army:

The[y] provide immediate and limited success, but it is to be feared that these results will be obtained at the expense of the cohesion and offensive capability of the army as a whole. Such systematic groupings in effect 'skim off' the best soldiers from each unit and end up by rapidly wearing them out. Ultimately, they risk undermining the collective spirit. Besides, the assault should not be the privilege of an elite, it is the supreme act in which each soldier is required to participate.

Nevertheless several armies had by 1917 created 'détachements d'élite', whose main role was to act as trench raiders. Through their pre-war traditions, a number of other units had also developed an esprit de corps which set them apart (particularly in their own minds) from their fellow soldiers. Among these elite units were the chasseurs, with their light infantry traditions of rapid movement and independent thought. 'It's always the chasseurs who grab all the glory,' grumbled one soldier. So too were the units of XX Corps (11th and 39th Divisions), which in peacetime garrisoned the German frontier. They were always kept at wartime strength and consequently were never diluted by a large influx of reservists returning to the colours.

Other regiments thought by contemporaries to stand out from the rest were those of I Corps (1st and 2nd Divisions), raised in the Nord and the Pas-de-Calais, whose home towns were now under German occupation, and the Bretons of X and XI Corps (19th–22nd Divisions). All these units managed to maintain their reputation despite the casualties of war. But the formations most frequently considered as corps d'assaut, despite Pétain's strictures, were those made up of regiments raised in north Africa: the Moroccan Division and 37th, 38th and 45th Divisions. Their regiments had created a formidable fighting reputation for themselves since their creation in the mid-nineteenth century and were now some of the most decorated in the army.

One of these north African regiments, 1st Zouaves, took part in the counter-offensive. Their objective was Villers-Hélon, to the west of Villers-Cotterêts. René Clozier (also the editor of the regimental newspaper *La Chéchia*) took part in this attack and saw how it differed from those earlier in the war – no fixed bayonets, but plenty of grenades:

> We're approaching the crest which our 75s are pounding. We're holding our rifles with both hands, clutched to our chests. We haven't even taken the precaution of fixing bayonets; but under the right elbow, we're carrying our haversacks of grenades. I signal to my men to make one ready, and transferring my rifle to my left hand I take one in my right. This is the real weapon of attack.

Captain Bally (125th Infantry) went into action at Pierrepont on 10 August:

> For the first time since the start of the campaign we were planning to attack without artillery support, not a single artillery round; progress would be made solely by our infantry who so manoeuvred, infiltrated and overran the Boches that the [enemy] abandoned the struggle in the face of flanking fire from our rifles and machine-guns ... The attack began at 3.30 am and only finished in front of Marquivillers (Somme) at four in the afternoon, after a twelve-kilometre pursuit ... On again! Marquivillers fell into our hands.

There Bally and his men met with some unexpected good luck, capturing a depot with plentiful supplies of mineral water. But the next day they made only two kilometres.

Marcel Fourier was part of a section of FT17s supposedly supporting a battalion of 233rd Infantry in an attack on the village of Le Plessier-Huleu (Aisne). Fourier was expecting a supporting barrage which failed to materialize; nevertheless, he attacked anyway: 'My men were worn out and sleeping soundly on the steel benches ... They were too tired to do any more and we didn't have so much as a crust of bread to eat before setting off.' At 3.55 am he started up his engine and moved out, the three tanks crossing a wheat-field, line abreast. Anti-tank fire had earlier been reported coming from a house flying a Red Cross flag. 'I stopped the tank [and] tapped my gun-layer on the shoulder ... "The house on the left with the red cross." "Spotted!" Bang! My gun-layer had well and truly spotted it. The shell went right through the front wall.'

The other two tanks fired as well, surprising the Germans, who sent up their red and green flares. 'Where had the infantry got to?' Unable to see anything through his vision slits, Fourier got out and returned to the start line, now deserted. One tank had been destroyed, while the other was working its way through the village, destroying the houses one by one. By 10.00 am the infantry had reappeared and reported the village empty. The counter-attack forced the Germans to withdraw. But the absence of a matching attack to the east, combined with heavy French casualties, allowed the enemy to fall back in good order. By 22 July the Germans were offering stiff resistance to French advances, but they continued to withdraw and by 3 August had completely evacuated the salient.

Behind the German lines Alfred Hue was mayor of Beuvardes (Aisne), a village north of Chateau-Thierry. Several Germans had been billeted on him; they had left him the use of one bedroom, but he thought it safer to sleep in the cellar. Apparently indifferent towards the invaders in public, in private he delighted in their misfortune. 'They tell me they're preparing to attack Châlons. In the west they can't get past Essômes. It's clear things aren't going well and no-one mentions Paris any more; we no longer hear them say "Paris in a week", or "Peace with France in a fortnight".'

At a meeting at the local Kommandatur on 9 July, Hue learned that the neutral Spanish–Dutch Committee was taking over the supply of food to civilians in the area. A committee of three local men, himself included, would hand out rations consisting of 2kg of bread, 350g lard or fat, 100g coffee, 100g sugar and 250g dried vegetables per person per week. The Germans were also evacuating 'useless mouths' – i.e. those considered incapable of work – away from the forward areas, to be repatriated via Switzerland to Annemasse or Evian. Altogether some 500,000 French people were displaced in this way during the war. Among them was Julienne Lor, pregnant and taking care of the family bistrot in the village of Chaillon (Meuse). In February 1915 she managed to send a letter to her soldier husband:

> I'm glad I can write to you because you must be wondering what's become of us. We've been with the Germans ... since August. A fortnight ago they took us as prisoners to Landau in Bavaria. We were there for ten days, then they sent us back via Switzerland. We arrived in Schaffhausen ... then on to Geneva and from there to Laroche-sur-Foron in Haute-Savoie. ... We've been prisoners, lying on a straw mattress with a blanket, like the soldiers. Everyone had a mess-tin. We had to go and fetch our own soup and coffee, like the soldiers. They took the whole village. Everyone. There are just Germans at home ... our poor village has been wrecked. Every day we had to hide in the cellars. Every day the French bombarded [us]. When we left, lots of houses had already been destroyed by the shelling. We've had a dreadful war, you know. Without knowing it, you were better off than us because we've been right in the firing line. Our house was full of Germans. ... I should tell you that we have a little boy. A German doctor brought him into the world. He was very kind. He spoke a little French. He looked after me well. We haven't got a midwife any more, Philomène left when the war started. Emile F. also has a child, a little boy. A German pastor baptized them at our house ... We've just got to hope you'll see [the baby] soon.

But these evacuees were luckier than many of those who spent all or part of the war in occupied territory. The larger towns – Lille, Roubaix,

Tourcoing, Douai, Laon, Saint-Quentin – all saw men, women and children interned in Germany as hostages for the good behaviour of those who stayed behind. Around 180,000 people were sent to camps such as those at Celle or Merseburg, and 30,000 died in captivity. Civilians who remained in France (just over two million) were subject to demands for forced labour on roads or railways. From 1916 this was formalized with the creation of Zivilarbeiterbataillonen (ZABs), made up of men between the ages of 14 and 60. Women between the ages of 14 and 45 were also liable for service. For those in the ZABs life was similar to that endured by prisoners of war – short of food and always liable to punishment. Frequent rule-breakers were sent to mine iron ore in a punishment company at Longwy, or to a prison (Sammellager des Streifsgefängnis) at Sedan, where the death rate was, on average, five or six per day.

Maria Degrutère was a teacher living in a suburb of Lille. In April 1916 the Germans announced they wanted volunteers to move to the country, to ease the pressure on food supplies in the city (caused, they claimed, by 'British attitudes'):

> These round-ups lasted all week in Lille. Each day German soldiers (twenty per house), bayonets fixed, arrived in an area around 3.00 am, got everyone out of bed and snatched some men, but in particular women and girls aged twenty to thirty-five, to take them who knew where. There were scenes of unspeakable anguish, agony for mothers whose children were torn away from them. Several people fainted, some went crazy, some made themselves ill trying to struggle with the officers ... It was a dreadful sight; they led us away like criminals going to the gallows.

Many of these 'volunteers' were sent either to the occupied Ardennes or to Germany, while those who remained at home were subject to ever more regulation. In Maubeuge, for example, inhabitants were reminded that 'in their own interest ... they should always demonstrate proper conduct towards officers'; those who had been in prison had to step aside when they met a German officer in the street; cats and dogs had to wear collars bearing the name and address of their owners, and dog ownership was taxed; each household had to register all its cattle, chickens and rabbits, and notify every change to the proper authorities within forty-eight hours; potatoes could not be fed to animals other than pigs, unless the creature was small or ill, nor straw used as animal bedding. In Sedan and Lille even mattresses were requisitioned. Streets were renamed: in Vouziers, for example, the Rue Gambetta became the Wilhelmstrasse. German time – one hour ahead of French time – was adopted, portraits of the Kaiser appeared everywhere, and German national celebrations, such as the anniversary of the Kaiser's accession, were celebrated.

There was little organized resistance of the kind later seen during the Second World War. At Roubaix a clandestine anti-German newspaper was published; meanwhile in Lille the Jacquet network organized escape routes for French and British soldiers caught behind the lines. In places like Noureuil (Aisne) hayricks were burnt. But, partly through lack of opportunity and leadership, and partly through fear of reprisals, most people had to content themselves with passive resistance.

Obtaining sufficient food was a constant problem throughout the occupied zone. Back in Beuvardes, Mayor Hue complained:

> On the plain the harvest of green wheat continues and soon there'll be nothing left to take. This morning we noticed that five rabbits had disappeared. Honest thieves! They left us seven ... the smallest [when] they could have taken the lot. We still have all our hens in the hen-house but the officers requisition the eggs they lay. 'We'll pay you for them,' one of them said to me. I'm sure they will. Just like they paid for Michel's cow, Leclère's hives, Pierre's wine, Joseph's cider, and all the household linen and goods of the poor souls they carted off to Germany.

But in mid-July Hue received some good news from a group of French and American prisoners: 'The big attack we'd been told about has begun ... The sky is on fire. The ground shakes. The officers are quiet in their mess this evening. One tinkles on the piano. The others go to bed early. Nothing suggests success.'

The Germans finally evacuated the village. After spending several sleepless nights in the cellar, shells bursting all around them, Hue and his family almost missed the actual moment of liberation during the night of 24/25 July. And when a French soldier arrived at their door they at first took him for a spy. But no – 'We really have been liberated! I'd hidden all our flags in the attic beneath the roof. I've brought them down. To-morrow we'll decorate all our windows!'

Hailed as the victor of the Second Battle of the Marne, Foch was created a Marshal of France. The Marne salient was cleared, shortening the front line by some forty-five kilometres and relieving the threat to Paris, as well as capturing many men and much equipment. The victory raised allied morale and undermined that of the Germans. Yet casualties were far fewer in areas where commanders followed Pétain's defensive doctrines than the more traditional approach favoured by Foch.

'We have got them' – the allied counter-attacks

With the arrival of the Americans, the allies had finally gained numerical superiority over the Germans, but Foch was not yet confident that he could launch a decisive attack in 1918. Instead, he envisaged a series of co-ordinated, sustained attacks all along the western front, as well as in Italy and Macedonia. While none of these was intended to be decisive in itself, together they would pave the way for what he hoped would be a final breakthrough offensive in 1919.

In the west Foch's ultimate objective was the town of Mézières, opening the way into the Ardennes. A giant pincer movement, with the British on the left and the Americans on the right, would attack towards the town, with the French holding the centre. Capturing Mézières would disrupt the three main railway lines running from Germany to France, and possibly force the enemy to abandon accumulated reserves of arms and ammunition. The first attack was launched in a combined Franco-British offensive at Amiens on 8 August. The French First Army formed part of the attacking forces, advancing eight kilometres on the first day and five on the second. On 10 August Third Army joined in and made eight kilometres across a twenty-five kilometre front. Although Foch achieved a decisive tactical victory over the Germans, the allies were unable to maintain the momentum of their advance and halted the following day after making substantial progress.

Lieutenant Joseph Tézenas du Montcel (5th Colonial Infantry) took part in the battle at Amiens. He and his men were aiming to take two small hills on the far bank of the river Avre, and he was pessimistic about their chances of success. To reach their objective, they first had to traverse open ground, then negotiate 300–400 metres of marsh by the banks of the winding river, cross a river of unknown width and depth, a main road, and finally another 300–400 metres of open ground. 'Madness,' he concluded.

British artillery provided the barrage, which was late, and the engineers could only construct one footbridge across the Avre. Carrying their comrades on their shoulders, some Senegalese troops forded the river, only to be cut down when they reached the opposite bank. Fortunately, other troops managed to cross elsewhere and turned the German position, allowing the 5th to get over as well. Montcel was immediately confronted by the bodies of the Senegalese, killed by a single machine-gun. The machine-gun crew stood beside their weapon, hands in the air, empty ammunition belts and cartridge cases strewn around them: 'They had sallow complexions, the same greenish colour as their uniform, their faces distorted by terror. I immediately understand why: their lives hung by a thread.' Montcel waited while his men and the remaining Senegalese passed by: '"Go! Get the hell out of here!" I told them bluntly. They didn't wait for me to repeat the invitation and scurried off to the rear while we ran ... to regain our place in the column.'

Montcel was then greeted by an unexpected sight:

> We couldn't believe it at first, but you have to bow before the evidence of your own eyes: a screen of patrolling cavalry was climbing out of the valley ... towards us! This spectacle was greeted with stunned silence, but it didn't last long. A few hundred metres behind the horsemen came lots of narrow infantry columns climbing the slopes we conquered yesterday. Behind them columns of artillery and lorries were appearing from all sides, snaking across the countryside using every possible route. It gave a sense of order and power. It was like a flood tide ... accompanied by the roar of aeroplanes.

The crossing of the Avre was accomplished with remarkable speed. Foch gave his orders on 24 July, and the French needed only two weeks to mount a complex operation which would have taken much longer earlier in the war. Here, as elsewhere in the final year of the war, the infantry no longer approached an action with its former élan, but a careful, methodical approach, backed up by reinforcements brought speedily to the point of the attack by road and rail, met with success. The reinforcements also included tanks – two battalions (600 machines) were moved on lorries to the front in two days. The artillery had managed to perfect predicted firing, no longer relying on ranging shots which inevitably gave away their intentions. The French had also improved their operational security, preventing details of their plans from leaking out in advance, as they had so often done before – sometimes, as in April 1917, with disastrous consequences.

The plan for the offensive involved a shifting point of attack, with each of the four corps of First Army taking its turn to lead, and the supporting artillery changing targets smoothly. The French had managed to assemble overwhelming air cover, all connected by radio, consisting of thirteen balloons, twenty-two squadrons of observation aircraft attached to the army corps, three attached to First Army's heavy artillery, and three for general reconnaissance. Escorting these were three groupements de chasse, about 150 machines in all. Also committed was part of the strategic bomber force – a group of long-range reconnaissance squadrons and three bomber wings. Over the winter and spring Pétain's training had created a flexible all-arms force, whose components were much more supple than the army of 1916, let alone that of 1914.

Although aerial reconnaissance had failed at Verdun in 1916, when it proved unable to identify dumps of German ammunition and stores, it was now an increasingly important tool. With new aircraft such as the powerful, radio-equipped Salmson 2A2, and more interpreters, by 1918 aerial photography had became one of the corner-stones of French intelligence gathering.

Of the pre-war arms-of-service, only the cavalry had failed to find a new role. With the introduction of the FT17 tank, there seemed little place for the massed use of horsed cavalry on the modern battlefield. A proposal to convert two cuirassier regiments currently serving as infantry into motorized units to accompany tank formations was rejected. But the men serving in tanks already felt they were the inheritors of the cavalry tradition. 'I was given eight fine lads, former dismounted cavalry, who must now become the machine-gunners and gunners in my tank,' wrote Marcel Fourier. 'For the moment they're finding their new circumstances quite bewildering. I can see it in their wide eyes, in their astonishment at the big steel beasts they'll be caring for. They don't bear much resemblance to the mounts they've looked after until now.' As one parliamentary deputy put it after the war, a modern army 'smells of petrol, not horse droppings'.

In mid-August the allies launched offensives on a number of fronts. On 20 August – another 'black day' for the German army – Mangin's Tenth Army attacked between the Aisne and the Oise, crossing the Oise and advancing twelve kilometres. First and Third Armies followed up on 27/28 August with attacks that resulted in the recapture of Noyon. Further north the British made similar progress, capturing Bapaume and Péronne. French and British advances both reached the series of defensive positions known collectively to the allies as the Hindenburg Line, where the British and Canadians broke through the Wotan Position (or the Drocourt–Quéant Switch), forcing the Germans to retreat and relinquish all the ground they had gained in March.

'What a pretty page in history. What a lesson in heroism for the whole world,' wrote a member of 70th Division. 'I've never seen such a fine offensive,' agreed a gunner (206th Artillery). 'It's great, even though life's a bit hard.' His final words were something of an understatement. Although the Germans were in retreat, the fighting was no less bloody. This was certainly the experience of 7th Tirailleurs: 'Out of one hundred and sixty men in the company, scarcely fifty returned. This will be the fifth time since January that the regiment's been reformed: in the end everyone will have passed through it!' Prior to an attack on 3 August, one soldier (11th Tirailleurs) reported that his company consisted of three officers, fourteen NCOs and 180 men. By that evening he was one of just a handful remaining, along with a Moroccan corporal and thirty men.

By the end of August both Foch and Haig had begun to believe they might after all defeat the Germans in 1918. On Foch's orders the Americans pinched out the Saint-Mihiel salient. As soon as the offensive had achieved its immediate objectives, Foch closed it down and turned instead to Mangin on the Aisne, who launched another attack, slowly pushing the Germans back. To one member of 1st Foreign Legion Regiment, the attacks on the Hindenburg Line in September were like 'a second Verdun'. A soldier from 152nd Division agreed: 'I went through the terrible days of Verdun all over again.'

On 8 October First Army accompanied the British in breaking through the main positions of the Hindenburg Line. Within days the French and Americans cleared the Argonne Forest, while the French retook Laon and positions along the Chemin des Dames, and began to advance beyond the Aisne. But the British and French were growing weary, and their slow, methodical advance permitted the Germans to withdraw in largely good order.

By now shortages of matériel were beginning to prevent France from playing its full part in the allied offensives. As well as meeting its own requirements for guns, tanks and aircraft, it was also called upon to supply the bulk of American needs. More than three-quarters of French production – 3,532 of 4,194 guns, 227 of 289 tanks and 4,874 of 6,364 aircraft – went to the American Expeditionary Force instead of the French army. On 19 August Pétain's chief of staff, General Buat, was grumbling about an order from Foch to supply the Americans with 24,000 horses: 'At times like this, you regret that the commander-in-chief of allied forces is French.' The diversion of much-needed equipment to their ally prevented Pétain from fulfilling his hopes of creating an army fully equipped for mechanized warfare.

By the end of the summer French troops were mentally and physically exhausted. 'Everyone is demoralized to a degree impossible to describe,' wrote Charles Auque (7th Chasseurs) on 3 September. Commanders looked instead to the Americans for the fresh impetus and energy needed to keep the offensives going. As Colonel Auguste Laure remarked to an American liaison officer: 'You have many of the characteristics we possessed in the early part of the war – dash and enthusiasm – you're willing to attack. Sadly the great losses we have sustained have forced us to become more conservative – probably too conservative – and your élan carries us along.'

Just as Foch was putting the finishing touches to his plans for another huge offensive, the Germans requested an armistice, and a ceasefire was finally announced on 11 November. In some sectors fighting went on until the last possible moment. One member of 46th Infantry offered to crawl out into no man's land to rescue a wounded comrade: '"You're mad," said the others. "Wait until 11 o'clock!" But I set off anyway and crawled up to the man. It was an Italian from a neighbouring regiment ... I pulled him towards some cover ... [and] settled him down as best as I could, telling him they'd come back for him. I crawled back but they'd seen me opposite and opened fire. Fortunately, I wasn't hit but it was a close-run thing.'

'Madelon fill up my glass' – Peace

The anti-war sentiments and strikes evident in Paris and the industrial areas of France in the previous year did not die away. A wave of strikes in support of an early end to the war had swept through many manufacturing towns and cities at the start of 1918. 'Comrades, the issue of wages concerns us little; the important thing is the war,' proclaimed a speaker at a meeting in the steel town of Saint-Etienne. 'To bring the conflict to an end it needs the soldiers in the front line to agree with us. There's only one thing for them to do: throw down their weapons and leave the front ... Comrades ... there's been enough blood spilt, enough men killed ... "Long live Peace! Down with War!"'

'Opinions are divided in my workshop,' commented one Parisian in February, 'but you've got to say that the idea of peace is gaining ground in people's minds, especially among women.'

Local officials were quick to blame anti-war sentiment on the influence of revolutionaries and pacifists, particularly refugees from Belgium and the Pas-de-Calais. Others blamed serving soldiers sent back to their factory jobs. In some towns the threat to recall them to the front was sufficient to get everyone back to work. But elsewhere, unions were unwilling to strike during wartime, and the strikes collapsed through a lack of leadership.

Unsurprisingly, the soldiers at the front were largely unsympathetic. 'Poor dears!' sniffed the writers of Le Filon, at news that union executives had to negotiate icy pavements on their way to a meeting. When metal-workers claimed they had 'borne the greatest weight of national defence ...

[and] did not want to miss out on the benefits of victory', only 'military discipline' prevented the soldier-journalists from responding with physical violence. Instead they contented themselves with an open letter, contrasting the life of the worker with that of the front-line soldier:

> Every day in your factory, from dawn to dusk, you file, you scrape, you lift huge weights, in other words they make you work harder than you've ever worked in your life ... and after an exhausting day you quite often envy the lot of the soldier at the front ... Rest assured, each one of us would much rather make shells in Bourges than be on the receiving end at Verdun ... Think, especially when you're kissing your wife and children, that all we have, poor exiles that we are, is the chilly kiss of an all-too-short letter ... Others give more to their country than manual labour, more than physical suffering, more than mental anguish, they sacrifice that which is most precious to them: their lives.

'I've had enough – more than enough,' wrote one soldier in 1917. 'When you think we're risking our hides for five sous a day while those in the rear making shells and the like earn fifteen to twenty, I swear it drives us crazy. Earning money, being with your family, living in safety, and plenty of pleasures the rest of us know nothing of – it's outrageous.' However, munitions workers were not completely immune from danger. On 1 May 1916 an explosion at the Vandier & Despret melinite works rocked the port of La Rochelle, with casualties numbering 176 dead and 138 injured. 'Everyone fled,' reported the *Echo rochelais,* 'houses collapsed, windows were shattered, walls were demolished. Conscious that something dreadful had just happened, people left their houses and headed into the countryside. Some got as far as the seashore; others, not daring to go far, took refuge on the Rossignolette heights.' Similar incidents took place in Le Havre, when an explosion at the Bundy works close to the town on 11 December 1915 killed at least 101 and injured 1,500, and at the powder works at Neuville-sur-Saône on 14 February 1917, when six were killed and sixty-two injured.

Although the issue of wages was of secondary importance to the speaker in Saint-Etienne, rising prices were also continuing to hit hard, particularly in rural areas. 'I'm not rich,' wrote one middle-class woman from the village of Blan (Tarn) in August 1917. 'If the war goes on much longer, many of us will be destitute.' The following May a mother from the Hérault was facing that very prospect. With her husband ill and unable to work, and her son in uniform, money was scarce: 'You can imagine how worrying it is when I couldn't [even] go out for bread this evening.' Her life became no easier as the summer wore on. Bread (as well as sugar and meat) was rationed, and bran, oats, rye, barley and potato flour began to replace wheat. Bread shortages became a regular occurrence: 'We've only had 300g of bread since Tuesday,' she wrote one Saturday in May; in June, 'things are just the same here – one or two days a week without bread'; and in August, 'there's been no bread for four days now, fortunately we'd brought some from Hérépian on Saturday'.

Yet reports from the departmental prefects indicated that morale in the country areas had recovered quickly after the reverses of the spring. 'I haven't noticed any worrying signs since May, despite the military actions since then,' wrote the prefect of the Puy-de-Dôme. 'People learned of the results of the last enemy offensive [and] of the threat to Paris and followed them anxiously, but at no time did it affect their morale.'

Some men wondered how women would react if peace were concluded: 'They can do without their husbands quite easily, and there'll be plenty of divorces and dramas once the war is over. Women who've done well out of deputizing for men in all kinds of jobs won't put up with their rebukes and advice any more.' And women certainly received advice aplenty from their menfolk at the front. 'Keep the shop clean, and take good care of sales and the customers,' wrote one shopkeeper from Albi (Tarn). '[Look out for] a little plot of land to buy. We'd be better putting our money into land because it always produces a return on your capital,' instructed a prisoner-of-war from his camp in Germany. Pierre G. even managed to run his family's small metalworks at Saint-Juéry (Tarn) from his prison camp.

But women had also showed themselves more than capable of managing the family farm or business. Delphine F., for example, ran her family's small vineyard near the remote village of Gabian (Hérault); her letters to her absent husband are full of the everyday details of her decisions, whether going into the village to buy seed onions, spraying the vines with sulphates or employing casual labour. Many men felt threatened by this. The writers of the popular song *Faut leur rentrer d'dans* ('We've Got To Get Them Back Indoors') were clearly in tune with popular male sentiment – 'Long live men, long live the Republic! / Stand up straight and pick up the cudgels / Danger threatens on all sides / We must take back our trousers / It's our honour they contain / Let's go, everybody up, let's be firm about this!'

By October public opinion in Paris appeared to be veering towards peace, although not everyone agreed how soon, or on what terms, it should come. 'There should be no talks until the Boche have surrendered or pulled out of France and Belgium completely,' commented one observer. But in a butcher's shop in working-class Alfortville, feelings were very different: 'They should make peace straight away and bring our soldiers home.' Two soldiers overheard at the Café des Princes were of the same mind: 'They should make peace straight away [and] stop any more pointless slaughter.' And so too was Lucien Cocordan: 'We're preparing for another big offensive. But we're hoping it won't take place. Perhaps the armistice will come first. How many lives that would save! We just have to wait and hope.'

   But these three soldiers were not necessarily in tune with the majority of their comrades. The postal censorship authorities sampled 9,593 letters at this time; 1,286 of them were in favour of an immediate armistice, but 2,142 wanted to hold out for a French victory, some adding that Germany's request for an armistice was a trick, that the Germans should be punished for their 'war crimes', or that they should not be allowed to start another war.

   With the end almost in sight, France also found itself facing a fresh enemy – Spanish flu. The onset of another catastrophe was almost unendurable: 'Why does this evil flu have to come and torment every home?' asked one soldier. 'As if bullets and machine-guns hadn't made enough gaps in our ranks ... now there's the flu ... doing damage, particularly at home,' wrote a member of 129th Infantry. 'You may well ask if it isn't the end of the world.'

   By September the pandemic was running amok in Mende: 'First our cousin Mimi Lafon ... she was twenty-six, and her brother was killed three years ago in the Dardanelles; then one of our Pistre cousins, the mother of nine children. There are plenty of cases here and some people have died, especially in the countryside.' Sergeant Georges Roumiguières (343rd Infantry) was touched by the unfairness of it all. 'Right now you can visualize men dying, but not women,' he wrote to his wife. 'Since we've been called to be slaughtered, you've got stay alive to look after the children and take our places in their lives.'

   Soldiers who went home on leave were also becoming increasingly reluctant to return to their regiments. Like many of their comrades, two young recruits had different tricks up their sleeve. One member of 153rd Infantry routinely came back late. He received eight to ten days leave every four months but 'used to spin them out a little ... and one time ... ended up spending fifteen days in prison'. Another soldier (116th Infantry) later recalled that 'once home you tried to make yourself ill' and get a certificate of extension. But the authorities soon got wise to this and ordered local mayors not to issue certificates under any circumstances.

   More and more men chose not to come back at all. Estimates suggest that between 10,000 and 15,000 men a year deserted between 1914 and 1916, a number which almost doubled in 1917. In the year beginning 1 May 1918 the gendarmerie in the department of the Gironde alone arrested 547 men for desertion, while in the Bouches-du-Rhône 678 men were captured between January and November of that year. Edward Morlae, the American legionnaire, was among those who fled in 1916, declaring that 'he'd had enough of fighting and would now like some glory'. Dressed in civilian clothes, he escaped across the border to Spain, caught a boat home and, much to the disgust of his former comrades, wrote what they considered a highly exaggerated account of his time at the front.

Many others followed him across the leaky border of the Pyrenees. Wounded in action, Joseph N. was deemed unfit for combat duty, but fit enough to work at a mine up in the mountains at Escaro (Pyrénées-Orientales): 'On 19 May 1916 the mayor ... told me I had to report to my depot before returning to the front ... In a moment of weakness ... I left for Spain instead, crossing the frontier at Prats-de-Mollo on 29 May 1916.' A lot of men aimed for Llívia, a small Spanish exclave high in the Pyrenees, entirely surrounded by French territory. The local police complained to the departmental prefect that 'a good number of the deserters currently in Barcelona and Seo de Urgel claim to have crossed the frontier via Llívia. This shows yet again that the soldiers ordered to keep the exclave under surveillance are failing in their duty.'

In October 1918 *La Mitraille* asked its readers to consider what they would do after the war. Did they think the soldier would prefer 'a very active life, full of pleasures, where he looks for distractions, the theatre, all kinds of parties ... or ... [would] he long for peace and quiet, and seek happiness in a quiet life, his loved ones close by, in the warm intimacy of his own home?'

Many of those who replied to *La Mitraille* – perhaps the family men – opted for peace and quiet. 'After the war everyone can bugger off and leave me in peace,' wrote Sergeant Pierre Graveson. 'The love of my family will suit me better than all the hypocrisy unleashed by the acts of men.' Marcel Plan, an artillery maréchal des logis, agreed: 'Other people's lives will no longer be of interest to us. We'll live for ourselves and our families. That's all.' But Paul Marcel was looking forward to the peace for very different reasons. 'I'm a lad from the class of 1916,' he replied.

> I went to war without having ever really lived ... and I hope to get out of it in the prime of life ... I was ignorant of the pleasures of life. Tucked away in my Alpine hamlet, I worked the land, knowing nothing of Paris, or those charming dolls, women ... But since then

> ... I've learned [a lot] ... and I've made up my mind. I'm going to
> leave my old Provençal home and head for this Paris I've heard so
> many wonderful things about. I'll go there to live, to enjoy myself
> and have a jolly time. I'll live there with all the ardour of youth. And
> after that ... who cares what happens!

'Don't go overboard on the grounds you're near Madame F.,' one gunner
(3rd Artillery) warned a friend, 'and especially don't try to make up for lost
time – you wouldn't manage it and you'd only wear yourself out.' Paul
Henriot adopted a sterner tone when writing to his son Lucien, stationed
at the big camp of La Courtine (Creuse): 'On your postcard you mentioned
nineteen dives. Are you talking about ... "convents"? If that's the case,
don't frequent [them]. They always contain women who steal away your
health; it's better you should know. There's less danger playing piquet. I
hope I've made myself clear enough ... Don't put what I'm thinking about
where I wouldn't put my walking stick or your mother the tip of her
umbrella.'

A month later, on 11 November, Maurice Laurentin (219th Infantry)
had just left the front lines:

> The battalion was heading towards the rear and had arrived at
> Guignicourt, where we found the whole village still asleep. A cyclist
> went past and said, 'The armistice has been signed.' God, let it be
> true! 7.30 am – 'Armistice, armistice!' That's what everyone was
> saying. People were congratulating each other, asking each other,
> 'Who told you?'. 'A cyclist', 'A cuirassier lieutenant', 'A
> telephonist'. The soldiers had no need to ask more. Then a group of
> 93rd Infantry arrived from the front, muddy and tired. 'It's over!'
> we shouted to them. 'It's signed!' Broad smiles lit up their faces.
> 'Thanks, old chap!' was all they could say. There was none of the
> noisy show of enthusiasm which greeted the declaration of war.
> They didn't throw down their weapons. They didn't break ranks;
> they just lifted their heads, the happy faces of brave men, incapable
> of disorder and excess, even in the midst of victory. My beloved
> France!

Others also found themselves unable to speak. Charles Laquièze (55th
Infantry) was a prisoner in Germany: 'There was no shouting, no
exuberance – we were all struck down by intense emotion. Our joy was too
great to sing out loud ... Can it be so? Can it be so?!' 'The end of hostilities
produced a kind of stupor,' recalled Abbé Marcellin Lissorgues (287th
Infantry). 'No shouting. No drinking sessions. We went up to each other to

shake hands. Our joy was too profound, too sombre to be expressed in a babble of words.' Roland Dorgelès (Aviation Service) was similarly affected: 'No, I didn't sing ... Perhaps I should have done, but I was choked by my memories. There were too many ghosts marching across the starless skies.'

But Ernest Brec and his comrades in 77th Infantry eventually celebrated with a glass of wine:

> Damn! A wave of joy swept over us. I don't know if I'd tears in my eyes. Like the others, I must have shouted 'Vive la France!' For a moment we were left breathless with happiness. Great sorrow is silent; so too is great joy. Then the shock passed; we recovered our power of speech and with it the reflex common to all Frenchmen, 'We'll have to drink a toast to that!' Yes, but with what? There was no red wine in this poor little place, just a bottle of lousy sparkling wine Bebert dug up in a shop where the bastard made us pay fifteen francs. We split it sixteen ways, hardly enough to wet your whistle! And that was how, on 11 November 1918, my battalion celebrated victory in a little town in the Meurthe-et-Moselle.

So too did Max Barthélemy (338th Infantry) and his comrades, who doubled into the nearest village, singing at the top of their voices: 'This untimely invasion brought out all the locals to see what was going on. We called out the news to them [and] they threw themselves around our necks, kissing us, weeping with joy.' But, advancing hot on the heels of the Germans, André Pestourie (60th Infantry) was in no position to celebrate: 'No food has reached us while we've been chasing after the Boche, apart from that provided by our mobile cooker. We'll drink a toast later.'

Meanwhile Louis Barthas heard the news at his regimental depot in Guingamp: 'We were overcome with happiness and joy; we couldn't find enough room for it in our hearts and we just stood there looking at each other, dazed and silent.' But the army allowed no time for celebration: 'We were soon brought back to reality by cries of "Fall in!" and the whistle-blasts of the duty adjutants calling us to go to drill as usual. Drill! On a day whose date would be remembered down the centuries. They were just bullying us. Grumbling away, we took the path to the parade ground, and so too on the day after.'

'Great catastrophe!' screamed the headline in *Le Bulletin désarmé*. 'Peace has broken out. The explosion has been heard throughout the world. Many victims. General consternation. We hear of strikes among shopkeepers and arms manufacturers etc. The nouveaux riche are committing suicide. Shirkers are running for the frontiers. The inventor of the hook on which hostilities have been suspended has been awarded the Grand Cross of the Légion d'Honneur.'

Firmin Bouille was in Paris on 11 November: 'Yesterday we celebrated the armistice with appropriate ceremony. My only regret is that I didn't finish the war in the front line. It's a regret shared by everyone at the depot who'd been at the front.' Six days later Georges Ripoull, a regimental bandsman, took part in a parade in the capital and described the scenes there in a letter to his brother: 'Before leaving Paris, I must tell you that yesterday was unforgettable for us and for the people of the city. Impossible to parade. The crowd carried us along. "Long live the poilus," was the cry all around. And at night the boulevards had never been so crowded. All the soldiers found themselves a friend.'

When the news reached the small Pyrenean town of Mauléon, people also rushed out into the streets to celebrate:

> As soon as the news leaked out ... people ran from the square to the church, wanting to storm the bell-tower ... Workshops closed straight away, everyone left work, noisy groups poured into the main square from every street ... everyone wanted to join in the celebrations. We hurried to put up flags and bunting. Along came the war orphans, Basque hunters in their elegant costumes, the flags and banners of various societies, then poles bearing the heads of Clemenceau and Foch ... all were greeted with enthusiastic cheers. Then came the heads of the Kaiser and the Crown Prince ... these caricatures were roundly booed. Finally, the town council all in a bunch. Mr Mayor addressed the crowd and garnered some hearty applause ... These were unforgettable moments. It was St Martin's Day and we'd driven the Boche out of France.

Others took a more restrained approach. In Mende the church bells started ringing at half-past midday. Someone opened a window and shouted down to a neighbour in the garden below: 'What's that they're ringing? Is it the armistice?' 'Maybe,' replied the gardener, eyes fixed on the potatoes he was planting. 'Peasant, shopkeeper, bourgeois or landowner, the man from the Lozère understands two things: firstly increasing his fortune [and] secondly keeping himself safe and sound,' commented one local woman. 'Apart from that nothing will move him and Alsace-Lorraine can stay as it is. "The Alsatians are all Boches [anyway]," a policeman said recently to my father. You won't be surprised to hear that his old Alsatian soul was outraged.'

In Senones (Vosges) the parish priest recalled 'the explosion of joy' when peace was declared: 'Some of the more eager started putting out the flags, something you didn't want to see when the enemy was still in charge. The Boche watched askance! The next day the same thing happened. The Germans were leaving in small groups. Some were wearing cockades on their caps in French colours and shouting "Vive la France!"'

But after the war there was a reckoning to come for some. The mayor of Senones, accused of being 'pro-Boche', was eventually cleared, but not so other 'collaborators' who were found guilty of denouncing 'patriots' or of profiting from their relationship with the Germans. Throughout the former occupied zone 123 people were brought before military tribunals accused of aiding the enemy, 83 in the department of the Nord alone. Punishments were severe. A woman from Saint-Quentin who betrayed two British soldiers received detention for life in a military fortress, while the so-called 'Laon informers', three men and a woman who had revealed the whereabouts of French soldiers, and the identities of those who had helped them, were executed.

A vengeful populace shaved the heads of women who had struck up relationships with German soldiers, horrifying Ephraim Grenadou: 'When we arrived in that area, they were settling their accounts – old quarrels from the time of the Germans. Good women had their heads shaved. What a circus! It wasn't to our taste at all.' Many women who found themselves in this predicament were first removed by the authorities to one of three camps and then sent on into the interior.

Prisoners of war began to head for home almost immediately. 'No triumphant welcome for them,' noted Edouard Déverin (GQG), 'no flowers and music. No grand parade, nor any sympathy. Still in uniform, they seemed more like a band of suspects or convicts. Off they went, gaunt, staring straight ahead, laden with bundles and boxes. A strange sort of procession with all kinds of uniforms mixed up together; some soldiers – those from the beginning [of the war] – were still wearing faded red trousers and kepis.' Any soldier declared fit to travel was directed to a repatriation centre in his home area, and then sent off on thirty, forty-five or sixty days' leave, depending on when he was captured (those taken prisoner in 1914 or 1915 receiving the maximum amount). Joffre had made harsh provisions for returning POWs in November 1914: 'On his return from captivity, every unwounded soldier taken prisoner will be subject to an enquiry to determine if disciplinary measures should be taken against him or if he should be court-martialled.' But in the event few men seem to have undergone an intensive interrogation.

After several months in German hands Yves Tourmen (12th Cuirassiers) had a treat in store when he finally arrived at his repatriation centre in Thionville (Moselle): white bread. 'At last,' he thought, 'proper French soldiers' food.' Many men had suffered extreme hardship when the allied blockade hit German food supplies during the last years of the war. Despite the food sent by his wife Marthe during his four years of captivity, Benoît B. was always hungry, always tired, and 'resigned to his fate'. He returned to France weighing just 55kg.

The pre-war classes were eventually demobilized during the spring and summer of 1919, while men called up between 1914 and 1917 were discharged between August and October 1919. This was not soon enough for some. Disturbances took place in Toulouse, where men of 117th Infantry and 57th Artillery demanded immediate demobilization, to cries of 'Down with war! Down with Clemenceau! String up the officers!' In Tunisia ships in Bizerta harbour mutinied in the same cause. Each man received a demobilization grant of 250 francs, plus an additional 20 francs for every month spent in uniform; he was also given a suit of clothes or the sum of 52 francs in lieu – and, if he wished to take it, his helmet.

Most soldiers were glad to be free of military life, 'this lousy regime', although 'after four years of mindless exhaustion' many found they 'needed a bit of time to readjust to the pleasures of civilian life'. Yet those who had been demobilized still had to earn a living. 'What I really want to do is cultivate the vines at Entraygues [Aveyron], with mother in charge,' confessed one officer a few days before his discharge. But he also had more practical concerns: 'I'm beginning to give serious consideration to the possibility of staying in the army to earn my living.' There was every chance that he would be able to do so, for French troops would soon be involved in Russia, Syria, Silesia and Morocco, as well as providing occupation forces for Hungary, the Rhineland and the Saar. Men from the classes of 1918 and 1919 had to complete their three years' service, and cruelly some found themselves involved in the fighting. But still more men were needed. 'How ironic,' wrote Lucien Cocordan in December. 'They're asking for men to re-enlist to go to Salonika (and they say they'll find some!) but I think it's more likely to be Russia.'

Among those performing garrison duties in occupied Germany were the men of 12th Infantry, so their return to their home town of Tarbes was postponed until 1919. The local newspaper, *Le Républicain*, recorded their arrival: 'Flowers covered every soldier's greatcoat and rifle. [They] also smothered the harness of the horses, as well as the machine-guns they were pulling. The whole town was there, forming a line two, even three, deep. Women and girls broke through the barriers to throw themselves into the arms of the soldiers; the rhythm of the line lost some of its allure but it only made the spectacle more beautiful.' A similar welcome awaited 10th Hussars and 24th Artillery, the other two regiments based in the town, when they returned later that year.

A law passed on 22 November 1918 offered some protection for the recently discharged soldier. Companies were forced to reinstate employees at current rates of pay, irrespective of their pre-enlistment wages, provided they applied within fifteen days of demobilization. The Chemins de Fer du Nord, for example, took back their former railwaymen at a rate of 4.25 francs per day. Louis Cavaillès travelled to Bordeaux from his home town of Castres to take up his old job on the railways: 'It went very well. I went to the office the following day. I've just been interviewed this morning and of course I was accepted ... I went back to my old landlord, who was glad to let me have a little room ... and to the same restaurant as well, where my old pals from the workshops were very happy to see me again.'

But in return the employee was obliged to fulfil his contract of employment. When one former soldier left the railway to take up a job elsewhere, he was pursued by the gendarmes, arrested and tried as a deserter, given six days in prison and forced to return to his old position. Women workers were quickly dismissed, sometimes without the compensation which was their due. One woman wrote to the pacifist newspaper *La Vague:* 'My husband has been in the army for the last six years. I worked like a slave at Citroën during the war. I sweated blood there, at the cost of my youth and my health. In January I was fired and since then I've been poverty-stricken.'

Despite developments in the surgical skills of army doctors, the huge number of disabled ex-servicemen produced by the war faced a particular challenge in resettling back into civilian life. Lucien Pitolet spent the war as a medical orderly:

> In 1914 a man hit in the knee by shrapnel would almost certainly be condemned to die of gangrene in the hospital to which he had been evacuated; in 1915 he would almost certainly be condemned to have his leg amputated at the thigh at a field ambulance near the front; in 1916 he would almost certainly be condemned to have his circulation resected as a possible cure, with his leg permanently stiff through ankylosis; finally, in 1918 he could be almost certain of keeping his leg and thigh, with almost complete mobility of the joint.

The pre-war system for dealing with disabled soldiers, involving review by the regiment and the ministry of war, almost collapsed under sheer pressure of numbers in 1914. Only in 1916 was the process finally streamlined. Four centres were set up in each military region, where two doctors, one of them a ministry appointee, subjected each man to a physical examination and an interview. Those who passed were returned to the army in an office job; those who failed were invalided out, with any who needed special equipment being sent for physiotherapy and mechanotherapy before final discharge.

Men invalided out of the army received a lump sum and/or a pension. But a soldier seeking a pension or end-of-service grant still faced many a bureaucratic twist and turn. Success or failure depended on two factors. Was he able to earn a living in civilian life? And had his military service simply exacerbated a pre-existing condition? During the first two years of the war the rules were harsh. If a soldier was judged to have died from, or been rendered unfit for service by, a pre-existing condition – for example, pneumonia – neither he nor his family would be entitled to a pension, grant or separation allowance, even if he died in a military hospital. In September 1916 these rules were amended to fall into line with existing labour legislation. Any man passed 'fit for service' on entering the army was judged to be precisely that; any subsequent illness or injury was therefore a result of his military service.

In the Ariège the sub-prefect noted that while a small number of men opted to attend a rehabilitation centre and learn a new trade, those from a farming background simply wanted to get home again and live off their pension, supplemented by work in one of the state monopolies – either as a postman, a forester or a tobacconist. 'All these poor devils were once heroes, celebrated everywhere,' commented an official from the armaments ministry, 'today they're nothing more than cripples. It's enough to make you weep!' Working in the offices of the ministry of pensions, P.-J. Mézières witnessed the continuing inefficiencies of the system at first hand:

> I was able to study the different parts of an administration which remained antiquated and flawed, where the work was entrusted to a few disabled ex-servicemen and a small number of war widows. But, as usual, most of the interesting and remunerative positions were handed to the incompetent, or to the relatives and protégés of various departmental heads, at the expense of these two categories of war victims ... As a result the work was performed poorly and slowly, despite the continual complaints of thousands of ex-servicemen.

But even for those who emerged sound in body the conflict continued to cast a long shadow. 'After being so wound up ... we find it hard to sit still,' wrote one young sous-lieutenant in March 1919. 'We can still feel the effects of the powder in our blood and on our nerves.' But, serving with the occupation forces at Dachsenhausen in the Rhineland, he was just beginning to relax a little: 'Last night the weather cleared; it was a lovely evening and we were able to cover fifteen or sixteen kilometres together. We've stayed inside since all that fresh air on Sunday, I'm feeling more at ease.' Paul Tuffrau – now a *former* major and battalion commander of 208th Infantry – also appreciated the healing effects of sunshine and landscape: 'The weather was beautiful. Seeing the familiar countryside again, the small town rather quiet, brought me deep joy ... Life goes on, things are just the same, only we have changed.'

Two years after the armistice Jean Norton Cru was walking along a street thinking about the war, when he thought he heard a sudden burst of machine-gun fire close by. Crouching down by instinct, he soon realized that the sound was simply that made by a pair of pigeons taking flight. Paul Flamant, once a company commander in 332nd Infantry, was continually drawn back to his old battlefields. On one occasion he met a fellow officer: 'Last year ... a lieutenant, a former officer like you ... came this way. He was looking for the grave of a soldier so he could show it to his widow. By nightfall, he still hadn't found it. He told me he'd rather sleep in an old sap than leave without finding his pal.' And Louis Althusser's father, 'while still asleep, would very often howl endlessly like a cornered wolf, with a violence which would drive us to the foot of the bed. My mother could never wake him from these nightmares. For us, for me at least, the night became a thing of terror and I've always lived in fear of those unbearable animal cries.'

The horrors of war certainly made it difficult for soldiers to reintegrate themselves into the family home. One infantryman (322nd Infantry) kept a journal during his time at the front so his wife might understand something of what he went through. But he never gave it to her. 'She wouldn't have understood,' he later commented. 'She read the newspapers.' Another man found himself a reluctant divorcee: 'Like so many [of my] disillusioned comrades, I would one day become familiar with the bitterness and surprise of divorce, that painful torture which for months on end marks those whose home has been broken and whose poor bruised soul is like some poor thing breathing its last, killed by the war.'

Many ex-soldiers joined a veterans' organization. The first general organization was formed in September 1916 for those who had fought with

Sixth Army at the battle of the Marne. But the very first such organization – the Association Générale des Mutilés de la Guerre – was founded for disabled ex-servicemen in August 1915 at the Maison Blanche, a Paris hospital specializing in prostheses. By 31 December 1918 it was also the largest of all, with 13,875 members. In the years following the war many similar societies appeared, particularly in the republican areas of southern France. This gave the voice of the veteran in France a distinctive left-wing slant, which perhaps explains why French fascism in the 1930s recruited well among ex-officers but not among former private soldiers, and remained a relatively small movement in consequence.

However, the ties that had bound men in wartime did not always survive the peace. 'Campaign life gives us comrades, companions,' thought Sergeant Georges Bonnet (5th Dragoons, 29th Artillery, 1st Artillery). 'We chat with them in familiar terms today but will take our leave of them tomorrow with no regrets. They will never know anything of our private thoughts [or] our hearts; we will leave them with nothing but memories of our outward appearance. Some show immense loyalty. [But] we do not necessarily give them the precious gift of our friendship.' Robert Fermer discovered the truth of this when he ran into an old comrade some years later: 'I saw V. again in Dijon in 1935 ... he was a railwayman at Nuits-Saint-Georges. Sadly, after a quarter of an hour, we had nothing more to say to each other.'

Looking towards the peace, *L'Horizon* envisaged nothing less than a brand new society: 'One reforged in the fire of battle, so transformed that nothing remains of the old structures, old-fashioned laws and outdated customs which for us nonetheless constituted the fabric and the spirit of the fair, free, pre-war France, which wasn't such a bad place to live.' But some men found that the inequality of sacrifice they had perceived during the conflict persisted long after the war. An angry Abel Moreau wrote:

> Soldiers, who for so long had been 'suckers', were soon seen as 'schemers'. They were blamed for joining big organizations ... accused of pursuing political ends, for wanting to occupy too prominent a place in the life of the nation – they who for four years had carried the cowardly hopes of the rear – for reminding people at every opportunity that they had saved the country, that they had not been compensated for their injuries, and that a grand old man [i.e. Clemenceau] had said: 'They have rights over us.' They were reproached for having too many rights, when for four years all they had were duties and tough duties [at that] ... France was divided: on the one hand, the soldiers, suffering, struggling, working to win the peace after winning the war; and on the other the shirkers, living [the

good life], enriching themselves, betraying [the soldiers] to get rich quicker, and spluttering blasphemies about the nation and victory.

After long months and years of separation many women and girls were happily contemplating marriage. 'When will the wedding take place?' wrote one hapless fiancé. 'Coco says when the new wine is in the barrels, but I'm not a wine-grower so that doesn't tell me much.' Coco and her intended were not alone. In southern France the wine harvest was normally the season for festivals, and in 1919 it was also the time for marriages. Alice Boyer lived in Pouzolles (Hérault) and exchanged news with a friend in the neighbouring Tarn: 'Here I am with the harvest over ... What's new in Vielmur? Not much I bet! My grandmother has been here and told me about the wedding of my cousin Elie, and of Juliette. Here we're up to about thirty and there are already more to follow in October.' But in Mazamet (Tarn) another young woman was facing up to the fact that her fiancé would not be coming back: 'Rosalie is worried sick. Until now she's been hoping that the poor lad would arrive home any day. It hurts me to hear her talk about him, but it would hurt her more if I told her I no longer have any hope that he's still alive.'

No financial compensation was available to women who lost a fiancé, a son or a brother. But approximately 600,000 war widows were eligible for an annual pension of 563 francs if her husband died of illness, and 600 francs if he had been killed in action. In addition, she would receive a further 400 francs per child for their two eldest children and 300 francs for each additional child.

For some families the absence of a corpse made grieving difficult. Even when a soldier had a known grave, the government at first banned any exhumations from military cemeteries to allow him to be buried at home. 'Nothing I've asked for,' protested the father of the grieving Contenson family in 1915, 'can affect military operations. It seems only fair to me that, having sacrificed my son for his country, we might be allowed the ultimate consolation of having his body since we know where it is buried.' In their anguish some relatives and friends took matters into their own hands, performing a clandestine exhumation, like one which took place at St-Gilles (Marne). 'It's my duty to report the following case,' the mayor wrote to the prefect.

On 29 May last, Ascension Day, Madame Descoutis, headmistress of the school in Montluçon (Allier) had the body of her son exhumed from the [military] cemetery [in St-Gilles], and after placing it in a lead-lined coffin, transported it to Montluçon by car. Naturally, all this was done without any authorization, the law allowing neither the exhumation nor the transfer of a soldier's remains.

Entrepreneurs were quick to latch on to human grief, charging up to 15,000 francs for an exhumation, and anywhere between 2.5 and 10 francs a kilometre to transport the coffin to its destination.

Wiser counsel eventually prevailed, and in 1920 the government granted permission for any coffin to be reburied within a soldier's home parish at the expense of the state. In the Pyrenean town of Mauléon the return of the dead brought the whole community out to mourn.

> The body of Brigadier Jean Garses arrived [in the town] on 7 January. It was the sixteenth and last in a series of bodies of men killed in action whose remains have been claimed by their families, [each of which] has provoked a moving demonstration of piety and national solidarity. All the [town's] banners and a considerable crowd gathered around to express the admiration and gratitude of the public.

Within a few years virtually every commune in France would have its war memorial. In the words of the mayor of Lusignan: 'It is our duty to show our gratitude to our brave compatriots who died on the field of honour by raising a commemorative monument to their memory, upon which each of their names will be written for ever more.'

Healthy or wounded, single or married, volunteer or sucker, *poilu* or *bonhomme* – who, then, was the French soldier of 1914–1918? Pétain claimed he was 'just a man with all his strengths and weaknesses', but the soldier who went to war in 1914 was certainly not the man who celebrated the armistice in 1918. The enthusiasm of the first months of the conflict evaporated as failed offensive followed failed offensive. Many soldiers became cynical about the apparent incompetence of their leaders and the alleged indifference of civilians. Yet even in the darkest days of 1917, weary and discouraged, they remained determined to resist the invader and to defend their country. 'What we've ... done is truly more than you could have asked of men,' concluded Maurice Genevoix. 'Nevertheless we did it.'

Appendix

French and British Army Ranks

Maréchal de France	Field Marshal
Général de division	General; commander of a division, army corps, army or army group
Général de brigade	Brigadier General
Colonel	Colonel; a regimental CO
Lieutenant colonel	Lieutenant Colonel
Commandant	Major; a battalion commander in an infantry regiment
Chef de bataillon	Major; CO of a chasseur battalion
Chef d'escadron	Major in a cavalry regiment
Capitaine	Captain; a company commander
Capitaine adjutant-major	Captain acting as adjutant
Lieutenant	Lieutenant; a platoon commander
Sous-lieutenant	Second Lieutenant; a platoon commander
Aspirant	Man having passed officer's exams and serving as an officer, awaiting full commissioned status
Adjutant-chef	Warrant Officer 1st class; occasionally a platoon commander
Adjutant	Warrant Officer 2nd class; occasionally a platoon commander
Maréchal des logis-chef	Sergeant in a mounted unit (i.e. cavalry, artillery, transport) in charge of squadron administration
Sergent-major	Sergeant in charge of company administration
Sergent	Sergeant

Maréchal des logis	Sergeant in a mounted unit
Sergent fourrier	Quartermaster sergeant
Caporal	Corporal
Brigadier	Corporal in a mounted unit
Caporal fourrier	Quartermaster corporal
Soldat de 1re classe	Lance corporal
Soldat	Private

Medical services

Médecin inspecteur général	General; army senior medical officer
Médecin inspecteur	Brigadier General; corps or army senior medical officer
Médecin principal de 1ere classe	Colonel; corps senior medical officer
Médecin principal de 2e classe	Lieutenant Colonel; divisional senior medical officer
Médecin-major de 1ere classe	Major; commander of a field ambulance or a regimental MO
Médecin-major de 2e classe	Captain; regimental MO
Médecin aide-major de 1ere classe	Lieutenant; battalion MO
Médecin aide-major de 2e classe	Second Lieutenant; battalion MO
Médecin auxiliaire	Adjutant; assistant to the battalion MO

Bibliography and Sources

Archives
Archives Nationales, Paris
BB18–2531–128 A14 Correspondance générale de la Division Criminelle, Dossiers de la Division Criminelle. Case of Paul Petit, 4 August 1914
F7–12936 Police générale, Documents provenant de la direction de la Sûreté générale et des Renseignements généraux. Letters from the departmental prefect, Lot, 1914
F7–12937 Police générale, Documents provenant de la direction de la Sûreté générale et des Renseignements généraux. Letters from the departmental prefect, Aube, 1914
F7–12938 Police générale, Documents provenant de la direction de la Sûreté générale et des Renseignements généraux. Letters from the departmental prefects, Manche, Nièvre, Rhône, 1914
F7–12939 Police générale, Documents provenant de la direction de la Sûreté générale et des Renseignements généraux. Letters from the departmental prefects, Haute Vienne, Vaucluse, 1914

Service Historique de la Défense, Armée de Terre, Vincennes
J1910 63e DI, minutes de jugement 482, 27 juin 1917
1KT 86 Legentil, R., *Notes de campagne de 12 avril 1915 au 11 novembre 1918*
1KT 1063 Larché, Louis, *Campagne 14–18: ma vie pendant la guerre*
6N 23 Fonds Buat, documents diverses, 1914–15
6N 146 Etat moral, directives du général en chef, situation à l'intérieur: rapport de contrôle postal sur les causes d'agitation dans les troupes du 15 au 30 juin 1917
6N 152–3 Documents relatifs au parlement, 1916–19
7N 109 Etat-Major de l'Armée, 1er bureau: documents, 1912
7N 985 Bordeaux: rapports de la commission militaire, 1916–18
16N 254 GQG, 1er bureau: matériel roulant, demandes, dotations, envois, mai 1916–septembre 1918
16N 297 Service du contrôle postal, mai 1916–septembre 1918
16N 1392 Commissions de contrôle postal de la IIe Armée, 1916
16N 1394 Commissions de contrôle postal de la IIe Armée, 1917
16N 1401 Commissions de contrôle postal de la IIIe Armée, 1915–19
16N 1405 Commissions de contrôle postal de la IVe Armée, 1916–18
16N 1417 Commissions de contrôle postal de la VIe Armée, 1916–17
16N 1523 Rapports de l'inspection des Chemins de fer du Nord, 4 & 15 July 1917
16N 1551-1552 GQG, 2e bureau: lettres saisies de militaires, 1916–18
16N 1688 GQG, 3e bureau: deuxième bataille offensive de Verdun, 1917
17N 47 Relations avec les populations civiles, rapport de l'inspecteur Hourbette, Langres, mai 1918
22N 284 6e Corps d'Armée, 2e bureau: correspondance expédiée, 1914–15

24N 818 12e Corps d'Armée, 3e bureau: engagement dans la région de l'ouest de Souain, 1914–15
24N 992 42e Division, 3e bureau: mouvements 20–30 septembre 1916, bataille de la Somme
26N 511 56 Brigade, journal des marches et d'opérations
DGN 4Mu89 Faivre, Charles, *Mémoire sur les observations faites en campagne* (1920)

Archives de la Préfecture de Police, Paris
BA/1587 Rapports de recherches et de renseignements émanants de la Police de Sûreté et de la Police de Renseignement 1918

Archives départementales des Deux-Sèvres, Niort
4M 6/79 Police et Sûreté générale, 1 December 1916

Archives départementales de la Gironde, Bordeaux
4M 337 Police des moeurs

Archives départementales des Hautes-Pyrénées, Tarbes
R422 Rapport, commissaire de police (Tarbes) au préfet, 26 février 1915

Archives départementales de la Marne, Châlons-en-Champagne
2R 212 Lettre, maire de Saint-Gilles au préfet, 14 juin 1919
2R 213 Lettre du famille Contenson, 20 avril 1915

Archives départementales de la Pyrénées-Orientales, Perpignan
1M619 Rapport, commissaire de police (Bourg–Madame) au préfet, 23 janvier 1918

Archives départementales de la Somme, Amiens
KZ591 Lettre du commissaire central au commandant d'armes, Amiens, 14 octobre 1914
Archives de la Justice Militaire, Le Blanc
Tribunal militaire de Marseille. Jugement 305/3097, 20 juin 1938

Centre d'Etudes Edmond-Michelet, Brive-la-Gaillarde
Fonds Lapouge 1 CEM 61 Correspondance, 10 mars 1916

Newspapers and Magazines
Le Commerce de Sablé (Sablé)
Le Correspondant (Paris)
La Croix des Côtes-du-Nord (Rennes)
L'Echo de Paris (Paris)
L'Echo rochelais (La Rochelle)
L'Est républicain (Nancy)
L'Express du Midi (Toulouse)
Le Figaro (Paris)
La Guerre sociale (Paris)
L'Illustration (Paris)

Le Journal (Paris)
Journal paroissiale (Mauléon)
Le Lannionais (Lannion)
Le Matin (Paris)
Le Messager du Millau (Millau)
Le Midi socialiste (Toulouse)
L'Œuvre de Paris (Paris)
Ouest-Eclair (Rennes)
Le Petit Marseillais (Marseille)
Le Petit Parisien (Paris)
Le Républicain (Tarbes)
La Vague (Paris)

Trench Newspapers
Le 120 court (120th Chasseurs)
L'Argonnaute (25th Infantry)
Boum! Voilà! (401st Infantry)
Les Boyaux du 95 (95th Infantry)
Brise d'entonnoirs (82nd Infantry)
Le Bulletin desarmé (44th Chasseurs)
Le Canard du boyau (74th Infantry)
Le Canard poilu (XV Corps)
La Chéchia (1st Zouaves)
Cingoli-gazette (17th Artillery)
Le Crapouillot (405th Infantry)
Le Crocodile (63rd Field Company, 3rd Engineers)
L'Echo des marmites (309th Infantry)
L'Echo de Tranchéesville (258th Brigade)
La Femme à barbe (227th Infantry)
Le Filon (34th Division)
Gazette du crénau (134th Territorials)
L'Horizon (4th Army)
Hurl obus (12th Territorials)
La Marmita (267th Infantry)
La Mitraille (64th Division)
La Musette (37th Infantry)
Nos filleuls (35th Division padres)
On progresse (9th Dragoons)
Le Pépère (359th Infantry)
Le Périscope (88th Infantry)
Poil des tranchées (409th Infantry)
Poil ... et plume (81st Infantry)
Le Poilu (305th Infantry)
Le Poilu saint-emilionnais (36th Division)
La Saucisse (205th Infantry)
La Vie poilusienne (142nd Infantry)
Le Voltigeur (12th Division)

Books and Journal Articles

Alain (i.e. Emile Chartier), *Correspondance avec Elie et Florence Halévy* (Paris, Gallimard, 1958)

Aldrich, Mildred, *A Hilltop on the Marne* (New York, Houghton Mifflin, 1915)

Alléhaut, Emile, *Le combat de l'infanterie: étude analytique et synthétique d'après les règlements, illustrée de cas concrets de la guerre 1914–1918* (Paris, Berger–Levrault, 1924)

Alléhaut, Emile & Goubernard, Commandant, 'A propos d'un jugement allemand', *Revue militaire française*, 15 (April–June 1925), 58

Althusser, Louis, *L'avenir dure longtemps* (Paris, Stock, 1992)

Amicale des 155e–355e RI, *La Sainte-Biffe: histoire du 155e régiment d'infanterie de Commercy pendant la guerre 1914–1918, évoquée par les survivants* (Nice, Don-Bosco, 1976)

André, François, *Les raisins sont bien beaux: correspondance de guerre d'un rural,1914–1917* (Paris, Fayard, 1977)

Annuaire statistique de la ville de Paris 1915–18 (Paris, Préfecture de la Seine, 1921)

Anon., 'Criticise account of Foreign Legion', *New York Times*, 14 March 1916, 4

Anon., *La dernière lettre écrite par des soldats français tombés au champ d'honneur 1914–1918* (Paris, L'Union des Pères et des Mères dont les Fils sont morts pour la Patrie, 1921)

Anon., 'La vie des prisonniers allemands au pays de France', *Je sais tout*, 121 (12 December 1915)

Anon., 'Récit d'un habitant de Noyon', *L'Illustration*, 31 March 1917

Antier, Chantal, 'Les lendemains qui ne chantent pas pour les permissionaires!', *14–18*, 16 (Oct–Nov 2003), 54–61

Antona, Antoine-Toussaint, *Ceux du 173e: les Corses au combat, 1914–1918* (Aleta, Collonna Editions, 2005)

Arnaud, René, *La guerre 1914–1918, tragédie–bouffe* (Paris, France–Empire, 1964)

Arnoult, Pierre, *Liaisons de 75: 2 mai 1917–11 novembre 1918* (Paris, Les Livres des Deux Guerres, 1939)

d'Arnoux, Jacques, *Paroles d'un revenant* (Paris, Plon, 1925)

Aubagnac, Gilles, 'Le camouflage à l'honneur', *Cahiers du CESAT*, 6 (2006), 69–75

Audoin-Rouzeau, Stéphane, *1914–1918, les combattants des tranchées: à travers leurs journaux* (Paris, Colin, 1986)

Auret, Camille, *Deuxième classe* (Paris, Figuière, 1933)

Auvray, Lucien, *Sous le signe de Rosalie: souvenirs d'un garçon de vingt ans – guerre 1914–1918, Verdun, Chemin des Dames et la suite* (Orléans, Lhermitte, 1986)

Bacconnier, Gérard, et al., *La plume au fusil: les poilus du Midi à travers leur correspondance* (Toulouse, Privat, 1988)

Bach, André, *Fusillés pour l'exemple, 1914–1915* (Paris, Tallandier, 2003)

Baldin, Damien, 'De la contiguïté anthropologique entre le combattant et le cheval', *Revue historique des armées*, 249 (2007), 75–87

Bally, Capitaine, 'Le commencement de la poursuite', in Ginisty, Paul & Gagneur, Maurice (eds), *Histoire de la guerre par les combattants, vol. 4 La victoire 1916–1918* (Paris, Garnier, 1922)

Barber, William M., 'Verdun to Bras', in *History of the American Field Service in France, 'Friends of France,' 1914–1917, Told by Its Members*, vol. 2 (New York, Houghton Mifflin, 1920)

Barrès, Philippe, *La guerre à vingt ans* (Paris, Plon, 1924)

Barreyre, Pierre, *Carnets de route, 1914–1919* (Bordeaux, CRDP d'Aquitaine, 1989)

Barthas, Louis, *Les carnets de guerre de Louis Barthas, tonnelier, 1914–1918* (Paris, Maspero, 1978)

Barthélemy, Max, *La fin de la riflette* (Paris, Eds de la Revue du Centre, 1934)

Barzini, Luigi, *Scènes de la Grande Guerre* (Paris, Payot, 1916)

Basty, Fernand, *Les parias de la gloire, 1914–1918* (Paris, Fournier, 1928)

Baudrillart, Alfred, *Les carnets du cardinal Baudrillart, 1er août 1914–31 décembre 1918* (Paris, Le Cerf, 1994)

Bec, Jean, 'Campagne 1914–1918: notes journalières du sergent Bec', *Bulletin des Amis de Montagnac*, 50 (October 2000), 3–46 and 51 (February 2001), 11–47

Becker, Annette, *Journaux de combattants et civils de la France du Nord dans la Grande Guerre* ([Villeneuve d'Ascq], Presses Universitaires du Septentrion, 1998)

Becker, Jean-Jacques, *Les Français dans la Grande Guerre* (Paris, Laffont, 1980)

Belmont, Ferdinand, *Lettres d'un officier de chasseurs alpins, 2 août 1914–28 décembre 1915* (Paris, Plon, 1916)

Bénard, Henri, *De la mort, de la boue, du sang: lettres de guerre d'un fantassin de 14–18* (Paris, Grancher, 1999)

Berger, Marcel & Allard, Paul, *Les secrets de la censure pendant la guerre* (Paris, Eds des Portiques, 1932)

Bernard, Jean-Pierre, et al., *'Je suis mouton comme les autres': lettres, carnets et mémoires de poilus drômois et de leurs familles* (Valence, Peuple Libre, 2002)

Bertrand, Georges, *Carnet de route d'un officier d'Alpins* (Paris, Berger–Levrault, 1916)

Bès, Victorin, 'Quelques extraits des carnets de guerre de Victorin Bès: un Castrais "combattant involontaire"', *Archives du Tarn*, 196 (2004), 673–90

Bessières, Albert, *Le train rouge: deux ans en train sanitaire* (Paris, Beauchesne, 1916)

Birnstiel, Eckart & Cazals, Rémy, *Ennemis fraternels 1914–15: carnets de guerre et de captivité* (Toulouse, Presses Universitaires du Mirail, 2002)

Bizard, Léon, *Les maisons de prostitution de Paris pendant la guerre* (Poitiers, Société Française d'Imprimerie, 1922)

Bizard, Léon, *Souvenirs d'un médecin de la préfecture de police et des prisons de Paris, 1914–1918* (Paris, Grasset, 1925)

Bloch, Marc, *L'histoire, la guerre, la résistance* (Paris, Gallimard, 2006)

Bloch, Marc, *Souvenirs de guerre, 1914–1915* (Paris, Masson, 1997)

Boasson, Marc, *Au soir d'un monde: lettres de guerre, 16 avril 1915–27 avril 1918* (Paris, Plon, 1926)

Bobier, Louis, *Il avait 20 ans en 1913: un poilu de Bourbon dans la grande tourmente, 1914–1918* (Bourbon-L'Archambault, Ed. l'Echoppe Bourbon, 2003)

Bodley, J.E.C., *Cardinal Manning and Other Essays* (London, Longmans, 1912)

Boillot, Félix, *Un officier d'infanterie à la guerre: lettres, ordres, notes de service d'un officier d'infanterie au cours de la campagne de 1914–1918* (Paris, Presses Universitaires de France, 1927)

Boitreaud, Solenne, *Les carnets de guerre (1914–1917) de Justin Giboulet, sergent mitrailleur dans les Vosges* (Mémoire de maîtrise, Université de Toulouse Le Mirail, 2000)

Bonnamy, Georges, *La saignée* (Paris, Chiron, 1920)

Bonnet, Georges, *L'âme du soldat* (Paris, Payot, 1917)

Bonnet, René, *Enfance limousine* (Paris, the author, 1954)

Botti, Louis, *Avec les zouaves: de Saint-Denis à la Somme, journal d'un mitrailleur, 1914–1916* (Paris, Berger–Levrault, 1922)

Boudon, Victor, *Avec Charles Péguy, de la Lorraine à la Marne, août–septembre 1914* (Paris, Hachette, 1916)

Boulanger, Philippe, 'Les conscrits de 1914: la contribution de la jeunesse française à la formation d'une armée de masse', *Annales de démographie historique* (2002/1), 11–34

Bourguet, Samuel, *L'aube sanglante: de La Boisselle (octobre 1914) à Tahure (septembre 1915)* (Paris, Berger–Levrault, 1917)

Bousquet, Joseph, *Journal de route, 1914–1917* (Bordeaux, Eds des Saints Calus, 2000)

Boutefeu, Roger, *Les camarades: soldats français et allemands au combat, 1914–1918* (Paris, Fayard, 1966)

Bouvereau, Henri, *Devant la mort* (Coulommiers, Brouillet, 1919)

Bréant, Pierre, *De l'Alsace à la Somme: souvenirs du front, août 1914–janvier 1917* (Paris, Hachette, 1917)

Brec, Ernest, *Ma guerre 1914–1918* (Maulévrier, Hérault, 1985)

Bridoux, André, *Souvenirs du temps des morts* (Paris, Albin Michel, 1930)

Brunelot, Virginie, '1914–1918: les Guyanais de la Grande Guerre', *La Semaine guyanaise* (8–14 November 2008)

Brunon, Raoul, *Lettres d'un soldat de la Grande Guerre, 1914–1917* (Marseille, Jouvène, 1920)

Campagne, Colonel, *Le chemin des croix, 1914–1918* (Paris, Tallandier, 1930)

Campana, Roger, *Les enfants de la 'Grand Revanche': carnet de route d'un Saint-Cyrien, 1914–1916* (Paris, Plon, 1922)

Carles, Emilie, *Une soupe aux herbes sauvages* (Paris, J.-C. Simoens, 1977)

Carlotti, François, 'In memoriam', *Actes de la recherche en sciences sociales*, 62–63 (1986), 111–14

Carpentier, Marcel, *Un cyrard au feu* (Paris, Berger–Levrault, 1963)

Carré, Jean-Marie, *Histoire d'une division de couverture: journal de campagne (août 1914–janvier 1915)* (Paris, La Renaissance du Livre, 1919)

Cassagnau, Ivan, *Ce que chaque jour fait de veuves: journal d'un artilleur, 1914–1916* (Paris, Buchet–Chastel, 2003)

Castex, Anatole, *Verdun, années infernales: lettres d'un soldat au front, août 1914–septembre 1916* (Paris, Imago, 1996)

Castex, Henri, *L'affaire du Chemin des Dames: les comités secrets* (Paris, Imago, 1998)

Caubet, Georges, *Instituteur et sergent: mémoires de guerre et de captivité* (Carcassonne, FAOL, 1991)

Cazals, Rémy & Loez, André, *Dans les tranchées de 1914–18* (Pau, Cairn, 2008)

Cazals, Rémy, et al., *Années cruelles, 1914–1918* (Villelongue d'Aude, Gué, 1983)

Cazin, Paul, *L'humaniste à la guerre: Hauts de Meuse 1915* (Paris, Plon, 1920)

Cendrars, Blaise (i.e. Frédéric Sauser), *La main coupée* (Paris, Gallimard, 1974)

Céran, Olivier, *Du sabre à la baïonette* (Paris, Albin Michel, 1930)

Chaine, Pierre, *Les mémoires d'un rat* (Paris, Payot, 1917)

Chambe, René, *Adieu cavalerie!: la Marne, bataille gagnée, victoire perdue* (Paris, Plon, 1979)

Chenu, Charles, *Du képi rouge aux chars d'assaut* (Paris, Albin Michel, 1932)

Chérel, Albert, 'Les territoriaux au fort de Vaux', *Revue historique* (1917)

Chevallier, Gabriel, *La peur* (Paris, Stock, 1930)

Christian-Frogé, René, *1914–1918: la Grande Guerre vécue, racontée, illustrée par les combattants* (Paris, Quillet, 1922)

Claeys, Louis, 'Marius Piquemal, souvenirs de guerre: "Ce que je voudrais redire et raconter"', *Bulletin de la Société ariégeoise des sciences, lettres et arts* (1996), 21–65

Clout, Hugh, *After the Ruins* (Exeter, University of Exeter Press, 1996)

Clozier, René, *Zouaves: épopée d'un régiment d'élite* (Paris, Plon, 1931)

Cochet, François, *Survivre au front: les poilus entre contrainte et consentement* ([Saint-Cloud], 14–18, 2005)

Cochet, François & Porte, Rémy, *Dictionnaire de la Grande Guerre* (Paris, Laffont, 2008)

Cochin, Augustin, *Quelques lettres de guerre* (Paris, Bloud & Gay, 1917)

Colombel, Mme Emmanuel, *Journal d'une infirmière d'Arras: août, septembre, octobre 1914* (Paris, Bloud & Gay, 1916)

Compagnon, J., 'La chevauchée héroïque de Berry-au-Bac: le chef d'escadron Bossut (16 Avril 1917)', *Revue historique des armées* (1984/2), 57–63

Coudray, Honoré, *Mémoires d'un troupier: un cavalier du 9e Hussards chez les chasseurs alpins du 11e BCA* (Bordeaux, Coudray, 1986)

Croste, Bernard, *Pour la France ou pour des prunes: souvenirs et réflexions d'un poilu pyrénéen* (Sorèze, Denis, 1999)

Cru, Jean Norton, *Témoins* (Nancy, Presses Universitaires de Nancy, 1989)

Cubero, José, *La Grande Guerre et l'arrière, 1914–1919* (Pau, Cairn, 2007)

Cuvier, Georges, *La guerre sans galon: à l'aventure avec le Cent-Six-Deux – des révoltes, à la victoire* (Paris, Eds du Combattant, 1920)

Cuzacq, Germain, *Le soldat de Lagraulet: lettres de Germain Cuzacq écrites du front entre août 1914 et septembre 1916* (Toulouse, Eché, 1984)

Daguillon, Jean, *Le sol est fait de nos morts: carnets de guerre, 1915–1918* (Paris, Nouvelles Editions Latines, 1987)

Darmon, Pierre, 'Des suppliciés oubliés de la Grande Guerre: les pithiatiques', *Histoire, économie et société*, 20 (2001), 49–64

Darrow, Margaret A., *French Women and the First World War: War Stories of the Home Front* (Oxford, Berg, 2000)

Delvert, Charles, *Histoire d'une compagnie: Main de Massiges-Verdun, novembre 1915–juin 1916, journal de marche* (Paris, Berger–Levrault, 1918)

Delvert, Charles, *L'erreur du 16 avril 1917* (Paris, Fournier, 1920)

Delvert, Charles, *Carnets d'un fantassin* (Paris, Albin Michel, 1935)

Denizot, Alain & Louis, Jean, *L'énigme Alain-Fournier, 1914–1991* (Paris, Nouvelles Editions Latines, 2000)

Dervaux, Anne-Marie, *Dans la tourmente de la Grande Guerre: gens du Hainaut* (Joué-lès-Tours, Sutton, 2001)

Desagneaux, Henri, *Journal de guerre 14–18* (Paris, Denoël, 1971)

Désalbres, Louis, *Mon carnet de route, 1916–1918* (Dax, Dumolia, 1958)

Desaubliaux, Robert, *La ruée: étapes d'un combattant* (Bloud, 1920)

Desbois, Evelyne, 'Les permissionaires', *14–18*, 2 (June–July 2001), 40–3

Deverin, Edouard, *RAS 1914–1919: du Chemin des Dames au GQG* (Paris, Les Etincelles, 1931)

Deville, Robert, *Carnet de route d'un artilleur: Virton, la Marne* (Paris, Chapelot, 1916)

Dorgelès, Roland (i.e. Raymond Lecavalé), *Le croix de bois* (Paris, Albin Michel, 1919)

Dorgelès, Roland (i.e. Raymond Lecavalé), '11–Nov–18', *Almanach du combattant* (1968), 47

Dorgelès, Roland (i.e. Raymond Lecavalé), *Je t'écris de la tranchée* (Paris, Albin Michel, 2003)

Doughty, Robert, *Pyrrhic Victory* (Harvard, Belknap Press, 2005)

Draën, Alphonse, *L'arrière 1914–1919 par un embusqué* (Toulon, Boucher, n.d.)

Dubut-Masion, Georges, *Journal d'un bourgeois de Maubeuge avant, pendant le siège et l'occupation allemande, 1914–1918* (Tourcoing, Duviver, 1923)

Ducasse, André, et al., *Vie et mort des Français, 1914–1918* (Paris, Hachette, 1962)

Duclos, Jacques, *Mémoires vol. 1, 1896–1924* (Paris, Fayard, 1968)

Duhelly, Jacques, *Philosophie de la guerre* (Paris, Alcan, 1921)

Dunn, J.C., *The War the Infantry Knew* (London, Abacus, 1988)

Dupont, Marcel (i.e. Marcel Béchu), *En campagne: l'attente, impressions d'un officier de légère 1915–1916–1917* (Paris, Plon, 1918)

Dupont, Marcel (i.e. Marcel Béchu), *Sabre au poing! Dix combats de cavalerie* (Paris, Berger–Levrault, 1931)

Duroselle, Jean-Baptiste, *La Grande Guerre des Français* (Paris, Perrin, 1994)

Escholier, Marie-Louise, *Les saisons du vent: journal août 1914–mai 1915* (Carcassonne, GARAE/Hésiode, 1986)

Escholier, Raymond, *Le sel de la terre* (Paris, Malfère, 1924)

Esnault, Gaston, *Le poilu tel qu'il se parle: dictionnaire des termes populaires récents et neufs employés aux armées en 1914–1918, étudiés dans leur étymologie, leur développement et leur usage* (Paris, Bossard, 1919)

Eve, Prosper, *La premiere guerre mondiale vue par les poilus réunionnais* (St Denis de la Réunion, Editions CNH, 1992)

Faget, Henri, *Lettres de mon père, 1914–1918* (Cassaignes, author, n.d.)

Faleur, Georges, *Journal de guerre* (Metz, Centre Régional Universitaire Lorrain d'Histoire, 2007)

von Falkenhayn, Eric, *The German General Staff and Its Decisions, 1914–1916* (New York, Dodd & Mead, 1920)

Fauconnier, Henri, *Lettres à Madeleine, 1914–1919* (Paris, Stock, 1998)

Fayolle, Emile, *Cahiers secrets de la Grande Guerre* (Paris, Plon, 1964)

Fels, Florent, *Voilà* (Paris, Fayard, 1957)

Ferro, Marc, et al., *Meetings in No Man's Land* (London, Constable & Robinson, 2007)

Ferry, Abel, *Carnets secrets, 1914–1918* (Paris, Grasset, 2005)

Fiolle, Paul, *La marsouille* (Paris, Payot, 1917)

Flamant, Paul, *Le réveil des vivants: la bataille de l'Aisne et les régiments de Champagne et du Nord-Est* (Reims, Eds du Nord-Est, 1924)

Florian-Parmentier, Ernest, *L'ouragan* (Paris, Eds du Fauconnier, 1921)

Fonck, René, *Mes combats* (Paris, Flammarion, 1920)

Fonsegrive, George, 'Dans un village du Périgord', *Le Correspondant*, 10 September 1914

Fourier, Marcel, 'AS31: la prise de Plessier-Huleu par les chars d'assaut 21 juillet 1918', in Ginisty, Paul & Gagneur, Maurice (eds), *Histoire de la guerre par les combattants, vol. 4 La victoire 1916–1918* (Paris, Garnier, 1922)

France. General Staff, Section Historique, *Les armées françaises dans la Grande Guerre* (Paris, Imprimerie Nationale, 1922–39)

France. Ministère de la Guerre, *Conduite des grandes unités* (28 October 1913)

France. Ministère de la Guerre, *Instruction au combat des petites unités* (8 January 1916)

France. Ministères de la Guerre et du Travail. Sous-Secrétariat d'Etat à la démobilisation, *Conseils aux démobilisés* (Paris, Imprimerie Nationale, 1919)

Franconi, Gabriel, *Un tel de l'armée française* (Paris, Malfère, 1926)

Fridenson, Patrick (ed.), *The French Home Front, 1914–18* (Oxford, Berg, 1992)

Gagneur, Maurice & Fourier, Marcel, *Avec les chars d'assaut* (Paris, Hachette, 1919)

Galtier-Boissière, Jean, *En rase campagne 1914: un hiver à Souchez, 1915–1916* (Paris, Berger–Levrault, 1917)

Galtier-Boissière, Jean, *La fleur au fusil* (Paris, Baudinière, 1928)

Garnung, Raymond, *Je vous écris depuis les tranchées: lettres d'un engagé volontaire, 1915–1918* (Paris, Harmattan, 2003)

Gaudy, Georges, *L'agonie du Mont-Renaud, mars–avril 1918* (Paris, Plon, 1921)

Gaudy, Georges, *Les trous d'obus de Verdun, février–août 1916* (Paris, Plon, 1922)

Gaudy, Georges, *Le Chemin des Dames en feu, décembre 1916–décembre 1917* (Paris, Plon, 1923)

Gaudy, Georges, *Le drame à Saconin et l'épopée sur l'Ingon, mai–septembre 1918* (Paris, Plon, 1930)

Gaulène, Guillaume, *Des soldats* (Paris, Perrin, 1917)

de Gaulle, Charles, *Lettres, notes et carnets, 1905–1918* (Paris, Plon, 1980)

Genevoix, Maurice, *Ceux de 14* (Paris, Seuil, 1984)

Gilles, André, 'Notations de bataille: Champagne, septembre 1915', *Revue de Paris* (17 January 1917), 589–616

Giono, Jean, *Le grand troupeau* (Paris, Gallimard, 1931)

Giraud, Marcel, 'Carnet de route du sergent Giraud', in Bernard, Gilles & Lachaux, Gérard (eds), *Batailles de Champagne, 1914–1915* (Paris, Histoire & Collections, 2008)

Goutard, Lieutenant, 'L'offensive de La Malmaison avec un section du 30e RI', *Revue de l'infanterie* (Dec 1928)

Goya, Michel, *Le chair et l'acier: l'armée française et l'invention de la guerre moderne, 1914–1918* (Paris, Grand Livre du Mois, 2004)

Goya, Michel, 'La pensée militaire française de 1871 à 1914', *Cahiers du CESAT* (March 2008)

de Gramont, Elisabeth, *Souvenirs du monde* (Paris, Grasset, 1929)

de Grandmaison, Geoffroy, *Un caractère de soldat: le capitaine Pierre de Saint-Jouan* (Paris, Plon, 1920)

Grange, Philippe-Jean, *Philibert, engagé volontaire, 1914–1918* (Paris, Albin Michel, 1932)

Gras, Gaston, *Malmaison, 23 octobre 1917* (Paris, Vieillemard, 1934)

Grasset, Alphonse, *Vingt jours de guerre aux temps heroïques* (Paris, Berger–Levrault, 1918)

Greenhalgh, Elizabeth, '"Parade Ground Soldiers": French Army Assessments of the British on the Somme in 1916', *Journal of Military History*, 63 (April 1999), 283–312

Grenadou, Ephraïm, *Grenadou, paysan français* (Paris, Seuil, 1978)

Guéno, Jean-Pierre, *Paroles de Verdun* (Paris, Perrin, 2006)

Guéno, Jean-Pierre & Laplume, Yves, *Paroles des poilus: lettres et carnets du front, 1914–1918* (Paris, Librio, 1998)

Haig, Sir Douglas, *Les Carnets secrets du maréchal Douglas Haig, 1914–1919* (Paris, Presses de la Cité, 1964)

Hallé, Guy, *Là-bas avec ceux qui souffrent* (Paris, Garnier, 1917)

Harel, Ambroise, *Mémoires d'un poilu breton* (Rennes, Ed. Ouest-France, 1921)

Harrison, Marie, 'An Englishwoman in Paris', *Everyweek*, 25 April 1918

Henches, Jules, *Lettres de guerre: extraits de la correspondance du chef d'escadron Jules-Emile Henches, 14 septembre 1875–16 octobre 1916* (Cahors, Coueslant, 1917)

Henches, Jules, *A l'école de guerre: lettres d'un artilleur, août 1914–octobre 1916* (Paris, Hachette, 1918)

Henriot, Emile, *Carnet d'un dragon dans les tranchées, 1915–1916* (Paris, Hachette, 1918)

Hertz, Robert, *Un ethnologue dans les tranchées (août 1914–avril 1915): lettres de Robert Hertz à sa femme Alice* (Paris, CNRS, 2002)

Hourticq, Louis, *Récits et réflexions d'un combattant: Aisne, Champagne, Verdun, 1915–1916* (Paris, Hachette, 1918)

Huot, Louis & Voivenel, Paul, *La psychologie du soldat* (Paris, La Renaissance du Livre, 1918)

Joffre, Joseph, *Mémoires du maréchal Joffre, 1910–1917* (Paris, Plon, 1932)

Jolinon, Joseph, *Le valet de gloire* (Paris, Rieder, 1923)

Joubaire, Alfred, *Pour la France: carnet de route d'un fantassin* (Paris, Perrin, 1917)

Jouhaux, Léon, *À Jean Jaurès: discours prononcé aux obsèques par Léon Jouhaux* (Paris, La Publication Sociale, 1915)

Jubert, Raymond, *Verdun mars–avril–mai 1916* (Nancy, Presses Universitaires de Nancy, 1989)

Junod, Edouard, *Edouard Junod, capitaine à la légion étrangère (1875–1915): lettres et souvenirs* (Paris, Crès, 1918)

Kahn, André, *Journal de guerre d'un juif patriote, 1914–1918* (Paris, Simoën, 1978)

von Kluck, Alexander, *Die Marsch auf Paris und die Marneschlacht, 1914* (Berlin, Mittler, 1920)

Krémer, Louis, *D'encre, de fer et de feu: lettres à Henry Charpentier, 1914–1918* (Paris, La Table Ronde, 2008)

Laby, Lucien, *Les carnets de l'aspirant Laby: médecin dans les tranchées, 28 juillet 1914–14 juillet 1919* (Paris, Bayard, 2001)

La Chaussée, J., *De Charleroi à Verdun dans l'infanterie* (Paris, Figuière, [1933])

de La Gorce, Paul-Marie, *The French Army: a Military–Political History* (London, Weidenfeld, 1963)

de Langle de Cary, Fernand, *Les raisons du désastre* (Paris, Payot, 1935)

Laouénan, Roger, *La moisson rouge* (Paris, France–Empire, 1987)

Laouénan, Roger, *Les coquelicots de la Marne* (Spézet, Coop Breizh, 1994)

Laouénan, Roger, 'Les soldats bretons dans la Grande Guerre', *Ar Men*, 71 (October 1995)

Laponce, Nicolas, *Journal de marche d'un artilleur de campagne: 1 La guerre de position, 1915–1917* (Bois-Colombes, the author, 1971)

Laporte, Sous-intendant, 'L'Intendance pendant la Guerre 14–18: le problème de la réunion des ressources nécessaires aux armées', *Bulletin de la Société industrielle de Rouen*, 49 (1921), 66ff

Laquièze, Charles, *Volontaire: épisodes de la Grande Guerre par un fantassin de dix-sept ans* (Paris, Nouvelle Librairie Française, 1932)

Larcher, Commandant, 'Le 10e corps à Charleroi (20 au 24 août 1914)', *Revue militaire française*, 38 (October–December 1930), 174–5

de Lardemelle, Charles, *1914: le redressement initial* (Paris, Berger–Levrault, 1935)

Laure, Emile, *Au 3e bureau du 3e GQG, 1917–1919* (Paris, Plon, 1921)

Laurentin, Maurice, *Le sang de France: récits de guerre d'un officier de troupe* (Paris, Bloud, 1919)

Laurentin, Maurice, *Carnets d'un fantassin de 1914* (Paris, Arthaud, 1965)

Lefebvre, Gaston, *Un de l'avant: carnet de route d'un poilu, 9 octobre 1914–27 novembre 1917* (Lille, Journaux et Imprimeries du Nord, 1930)

Lefebvre, Jacques-Henri, *Verdun: la plus grande bataille de l'histoire* (Paris, Durassié, 1960)

Lefebvre, Raymond & Vaillant-Couturier, Paul, *La guerre des soldats: le champ d'honneur – conseils de guerre aux armées – l'hôpital* (Paris, Flammarion, 1919)

Lélu, Georges (ed.), *Grand livre d'or historique de la gendarmerie nationale*, vol. IV (Beaune, Girard, 1939)

Lemarchand, Lionel, 'Etude de la correspondance censurée au début de 1917: une nouvelle dimension des œuvres littéraires grâce au témoignage', *Romance Languages Annual* (1999), 56–62

Le Naour, Jean-Yves, '"Il faut sauver notre pantalon": la Première Guerre mondiale et le sentiment masculin d'inversion du rapport de domination', *Cahiers d'histoire: revue d'histoire critique*, 84 (2001), 33–44

Le Naour, Jean-Yves, *Misères et tourments de la chair durant la Grande Guerre: les mœurs sexuelles des Français, 1914–1918* (Paris, Aubier, 2002)

Libermann, Henri, *Ce qu'a vu un officier de chasseurs à pied: Ardennes belges, Marne, Saint-Gond, bataille sous Reims, 2 août–28 septembre 1914* (Paris, Plon, 1916)

Lintier, Paul, *Ma pièce: avec une batterie de 75 – souvenirs d'un canonnier, 1914* (Paris, Plon, 1916)

Lissorgues, Abbé Marcellin, *Notes d'un aumônier militaire* (Aurillac, Imprimerie Moderne, 1921)

McConnell, James R., *Flying for France: with the American Escadrille at Verdun* (Garden City, Doubleday, 1917)

Madeline, André, *Nos vingt ans* (Paris, Calmann-Lévy, 1925)

Maillet, André, *Sous le fouet du destin: histoire d'une âme aux jours héroïques, 1915–1916* (Paris, Perrin, 1920)

Mairet, Louis, *Carnet d'un combattant, 11 février 1915–16 avril 1917* (Paris, Crès, 1919)

Mangin, Charles, *Lettres de guerre, 1914–1918* (Paris, Fayard, 1950)

Marc, Lieutenant, *Notes d'un pilote disparu, 1916–1917* (Paris, Hachette, 1918)

Marot, Jean, *Belhumeur* (Chalon-sur-Saône, Imprimerie du Progrès, 1930)

Martinage, Renée, 'Les collaborateurs devant la cour d'assises du Nord après la très Grande Guerre', *Revue du Nord*, 309 (1995), 95–116

Masson, Pierre, *Lettres de guerre, août 1914–avril 1916* (Paris, Hachette, 1918)

Maufrais, Louis, *J'étais médecin dans les tranchées, août 1914–juillet 1919* (Paris, Laffont, 2008)

Maugars, Maurice, *Avec la Marocaine* (Paris, Albin Michel, 1920)

Maurin, Jules, *Armée–guerre–société: soldats languedociens, 1889–1919* (Paris, Publications de la Sorbonne, 1982)

Mayoux, Pierre, *Paul Doncoeur, aumônier militaire* (Paris, Presses de l'Ile de France, 1966)

Méléra, Timothée, *Verdun (juin–juillet 1916); la montagne de Reims, mai–juin 1918* (Paris, Eds de la Lucarne, 1926)

Meyer, Jacques, *La biffe* (Paris, Albin Michel, 1928)

Meyer, Jacques, *La vie quotidienne des soldats pendant la Grande Guerre* (Paris, Hachette, 1966)

Mézières, P.-J., *La voix des morts* (Paris, Figuière, 1927)

Michel, Marc, *Les africains et la Grande Guerre: l'appel à l'Afrique, 1914–1918* (Paris, Karthala, 2003)

Michelon, P., 'Souvenirs du colonel P. Michelon, sous-lieutenant en 1914', *Le Casoar,* 19 (October 1965)

Miquel, Pierre, *Mourir à Verdun* (Paris, Tallandier, 1995)

Mistre, Maurice, *La légende noire du 15e Corps: l'honneur volé des Provençaux par le feu et par l'insulte* (Saint-Michel-l'Observatoire, C'est-à-dire, 2009)

Monthil, Edith, *De la ferme du Causse aux tranchées de la Grande Guerre: itinéraires d'un couple de paysans quercynois, Dalis et Louis Lamothe* (Thesis, University of Toulouse-La Mirail, 2003)

Mordacq, Henri, *Le drame de l'Yser – la surprise des gaz, avril 1915* (Paris, Editions des Portiques, 1933)

Moreau, Abel, *Le fou* (Paris, Malfère, 1926)

Morel-Journel, Henry, *Journal d'un officier de la 74e division d'infanterie et de l'Armée française d'Italie, 1914–1918* (Montbrison, Brassart, 1922)

Morin, Emile, *Lieutenant Morin, combattant de la guerre, 1914–1918* (Besançon, Cêtre, 2002)

Morlae, Edward, *A Soldier of the Legion* (New York, Houghton Mifflin, 1916)

Mornet, Daniel, *Tranchées de Verdun, juillet 1916–mai 1917* (Paris, Berger–Levrault, 1918)

Muenier, Pierre, *L'angoisse de Verdun: notes d'un conducteur d'auto sanitaire* (Paris, Hachette, 1918)

Murat, Georges, *Souvenirs de campagne du 131e territorial: 'impressions vécues', 1914–1918* (Cahors, Marmiesse, 1924)

Naegelen, René, *Les suppliciés* (Paris, Baudinière, 1927)

Niclot, Max, 'Le 4 août dans le bled marocain', *Almanach du combattant*, 35 (1964), 61–2

Nicot, Jean, *Les poilus ont la parole: dans les tranchées, lettres du front, 1917–1918* (Bruxelles, Complexe, 1998)

Ninet, Jules, *Copains du front* (Paris, Hartois, 1936)

Nion, Bruno, 'Un artilleur de la première guerre mondiale', *Militaria*, 209 (December 2002), 48–54

Nobécourt, René-Gustave, *Les fantassins du Chemin des Dames* (Paris, Laffont, 1965)

Noé, Léopold, *Nous étions ennemis sans savoir pourquoi ni comment* (Carcassonne, FAOL, 1980)

Nordmann, Charles, *A coups de canon: notes d'un combattant* (Paris, Perrin, 1917)

Offenstadt, Nicolas (ed.), *Le Chemin des Dames: de l'évènement à la mémoire* (Paris, Stock, 2004)

Orthlieb, Jean, *L'aéronautique hier-demain* (Paris, Masson, 1920)

Paluel-Marmont, A., *Saint-Cyr* (Paris, Nouvelles Sociétés d'Edition, 1930)

Papillon, Joseph, Lucien, Marcel & Marthe, *'Si je reviens comme je l'espère': lettres du front et de l'arrière, 1914–1918* (Paris, Grasset, 2003)

Paraf, Pierre, *Sous la terre de France* (Paris, Payot, 1917)

Pascal, Maurice, *Sous les obus avec le 6–7* (Villefranche-en-Beaujolais, Eds du Cuvier, 1934)

Pedroncini, Guy, *1917, les mutineries de l'armée française* (Paris, Julliard-Gallimard, 1968)

Pellan, François, *Lettres de guerre* (Paris, La Pensée Universelle, 1982)

Perette, Jean-François, '16 avril 1917, les chars!', *Revue historique des armées*, 158 (March 1985), 48–60

Péricard, Jacques, *Verdun: histoire des combats qui se sont livrés de 1914 à 1918, sur les deux rives de la Meuse* (Paris, Librairie de France, 1936)

Perrin, François, *Un toubib sous l'uniforme: témoignage du médecin-major François Perrin, 1908–1918* (Parçay-sur-Vienne, Anovi, 2009)

Pestourie, André, *Mon carnet de guerre* (Brive, Maugein, 1968)

Pétain, Philippe, *La bataille de Verdun* (Paris, Payot, 1929)

Pézard, André, *Nous autres à Vauquois, 1915–1916, 46e RI* (Paris, La Renaissance du Livre, 1918)

de Pierrefeu, Jean, *GQG secteur 1: trois ans au grand quartier général par le rédacteur du Communiqué* (Paris, L'Edition Française Illustrée, 1920)

Pillon, Robert, *Ses lettres de 1914 à 1916* (Paris, Librairie Générale et Protestante, 1917)

Pitollet, Lucien, *Sept mois de guerre dans une ambulance limousine* (Paris, Mercure Universel, 1933)

Pomiro, Arnaud, *Les carnets de guerre d'Arnaud Pomiro: des Dardanelles au Chemin des Dames* (Toulouse, Privat, 2006)

Porch, Douglas, *The March to the Marne* (Cambridge, Cambridge University Press, 1981)

Porch, Douglas, *The French Foreign Legion* (London, Macmillan, 1991)

Poulaille, Henry, *Pain de soldat, 1914–1917* (Paris, Grasset, 1937)

Poupin, Benjamin, '3e et avant-dernier carnet de route de Benjamin Poupin, secrétaire d'Etat-Major du 13e corps d'armée', *La Grande Guerre magazine*, 14 (1996), 26ff

Pourcher, Yves, *Les jours de guerre: la vie des français au jour le jour, 1914–1918* (Paris, Hachette, 2008)

Prévost, Marcel, *D'un poste de commandement (PC du 21e CA), bataille de l'Ailette, 23 octobre–2 novembre 1917* (Paris, Flammarion, 1918)

Prost, Antoine, *Les anciens combattants et la société française, 1914–1939* (Paris, Presses de la Fondation Nationale des Sciences Politiques, 1977)

Prost, Antoine, 'La guerre de 1914 n'est pas perdue', *Le Mouvement social*, 199 (April–June 2002), 95–102

Raynal, Sylvain, *Le drame du fort de Vaux: journal du commandant Raynal* (Paris, Albin Michel, 1949)

Reclus, Maurice, *Le Péguy que j'ai connu* (Paris, Hachette, 1951)

Redier, Antoine, *Méditations dans la tranchée* (Paris, Payot, 1916)

Ricadat, Paul, *Petits récits d'un grand drame: 1914–1918, histoire de mes vingt ans* (Paris, La Bruyère, 1986)

Robert, Henri, *Impressions de guerre d'un soldat chrétien* (Paris, Fischbacher, 1920)

Rolin, Charles, *La défense du Couronné de la Seille: Nomény, Sainte-Geneviève, le Xon, 1914–1915* (Paris, Berger–Levrault, 1934)

Rolland, Denis, *La grève des tranchées: les mutineries de 1917* (Paris, Imago, 2005)

Rostin, Marcel, *Un officier du 15e corps: carnets de route et lettres de guerre de Marcel Rostin, 1914–16* (Saint-Michel-l'Observatoire, C'est-à-dire, 2008)

Roujon, Jacques, *Carnet de route: août 1914–janvier 1915* (Paris, Plon, 1916)

Roullet, Pierre, *La vie d'un meunier: la vie d'un meunier au moulin à vent de La Bigotière à la Belle Époque, en Anjou* (Marseille, Laffitte, 1983)

Rousseau, Abbé Louis, *Fleurs de Vendée, 1914–1915* (La Roche-sur-Yon, Yvonnet, 1915)

Rouvier, Frédéric, *L'Eglise de France pendant la Grande Guerre* (Paris, Perrin, 1919)

Roy, Jules, *Guynemer: l'ange de la mort* (Paris, Albin Michel, 1986)

Ruquet, Miquèl, 'Le contrôle de l'enclave de Llívia par les autorités françaises pendant le premier conflit mondial', *Ceretania*, 5 (2007), 247–62

Ruquet, Miquèl, 'Les déserteurs français de la première guerre mondiale et la guerre d'Espagne', *Le Midi rouge*, 10 (2007), 32–6

Saint-Pierre, Dominique (ed.), *La Grande Guerre entre les lignes: correspondances, journaux intimes et photographies de la famille Saint-Pierre* (Bourg-en-Bresse, Musnier-Gilbert, 2008)

Seeger, Alan, *Letters and Diaries of Alan Seeger* (New York, Scribner's, 1917)

Ségalant, Laurent, *Lignes de vie: des Gascons dans la Grande Guerre* (Orthez, Eds Gascogne, 2009)

Sem (i.e. Marie-Joseph Goursat), *Un pékin sur le front* (Paris, Laffitte, 1917)

Serrigny, Bernard, *Trente ans avec Pétain* (Paris, Plon, 1959)

Smith, Leonard V., *Between Mutiny and Obedience: the Case of the French Fifth Infantry Division during World War I* (Princeton, Princeton University Press, 1994)

Szajkowski, Zosa, *Jews and the French Foreign Legion* (New York, KTAV, 1975)

Tanty, Etienne, *Les violettes des tranchées: lettres d'un poilu qui n'aimait pas la guerre* (Paris, Italiques, 2002)

Tardy, Georges, *Un poilu dans la Grande Guerre: lettres et photos de Georges Tardy* (Fontaines-sur-Saône, Bruno Tardy, 2009)

Terrasse, Jacques, *Avant l'oubli: l'histoire vécue du 355e Régiment d'infanterie* (Nice, Don-Bosco, 1964)

Tézenas du Montcel, Joseph, *L'heure H: étapes d'infanterie 14–18* (Paris, Valmont, 1960)

Tézenas du Montcel, Paul, *Dans les tranchees: journal d'un officier du 102e territorial, 8 octobre 1914–2 avril 1917* (Montbrison, Brassart, 1925)

Tharaud, Jerôme & Jean, *Une relève* (Paris, Emile-Paul, 1919)

Thomas, Louis, *Souvenirs d'un chasseur* (Paris, Perrin, 1919)

Toinet, Paul, *Plateau zéro, tambour cent* (Paris, Berger–Levrault 1929)

Top, Gaston, *Un groupe de 75 (1er août 1914–13 mai 1915): journal d'un médecin aide-major du 27e d'artillerie* (Paris, Plon, 1919)

Torquat, Sous-lieutenant, 'La vie guerrière dans un secteur calme avec le 41e RI à la tranchée de Calonne durant l'été 1917', *Almanach du combattant*, 122 (1976)

Tuffrau, Paul, *Carnet d'un combattant* (Paris, Payot, 1917)

Vaillant, Jean-Paul, *L'enfant jeté aux bêtes* (Paris, Correa, 1935)

Valluy, Jean, *La première guerre mondiale* (Paris, Larousse, 1968)

Varenne, Joseph, *L'aube ensanglantée* (Paris, Revue Mondiale, 1930)

Veaux, Georges, *En suivant nos soldats de l'Ouest* (Rennes, Oberthur, 1917)

Vial, Francisque, *Territoriaux de France* (Paris, Berger–Levrault, 1918)

Villate, Robert, *Foch à la Marne: la 9e armée aux Marais de Saint-Gond, 5–10 septembre 1914* (Paris, Lavauzelle, 1933)

Vuillermoz, Léon, *Journal d'un poilu franc-comtois* (Sainte-Croix, Balcon, 2001)

Weber, Eugen, *Peasants into Frenchmen: the Modernization of Rural France, 1870–1914* (London, Chatto & Windus, 1977)

de Witte, Jack-François, *Lettres d'un mécréant (1909–1918): François de Witte* (n.pl., Olympio, 2001)

Websites

2batmarne.free.fr/ [Hue]

36ri.blogspot.com/ [Le Bailly]

74eri.canalblog.com/ [Dorgelès]

119ri.pagesperso-orange.fr/ [Martin]

147ri.canalblog.com/ [Ricadat]

www.1851.fr/

www.1914-18.org/temoins/combattants/vosges.htm

www.1914-18.org/temoins/corresp/poilus.htm

asdecoeur.over-blog.fr/pages/ [Bersot]

www.assemblee-nationale.fr/

www.atelca.fr/ [Coeurdevey]

ceuxdu106.over-blog.com/ [Herbin]

champagne1418.pagesperso-orange.fr/ [Villain]

www.cheminsdememoire.gouv.fr/

chtimiste.com/ [26e RI, Gaudon, Videau]

www.crid1418.org/ [Cocordan]

www.eke.org/ [Hastoy]

www.estrepublicain.fr/ [Baulard, Lor, Villemin]

www.grande-guerre.org/ [Barbusse, Berthion, Lambert]

grandeguerre56.over-blog.com/ [Carré]

www.guerredesgaz.fr/ [Pillon]

histoiredeguerre.canalblog.com/archives/k__verdun_mai_1916_la_cote_304/index.
 html
www.histoire-genealogie.com/ [Baillon]
www.insee.fr/
laurent59.canalblog.com/ [Bloch]
www.lesfrancaisaverdun-1916.fr/
www.loire-atlantique.fr/
musique-militaire.fr/
neuf-neuf.pagesperso-orange.fr/ [Pincon]
pages14-18.mesdiscussions.net/ [Morizet, Vatan]
perso.wanadoo.fr/ [Bochet]
philippe.demonchy.pagesperso-orange.fr/ [Demonchy]
poilu14-18.blogspace.fr/ [foy]
prisonniers-de-guerre-1914-1918.chez-alice.fr/
videlaine.canalblog.com/ [Gissinger]
vlecalvez.free.fr/ [Duché]
vinny03.perso.neuf.fr/ [Etienne]
en.wikipedia.org/
fr.wikisource.org/ [Duboin]

Index

Adam, Joséphin (112th Infantry), 13
Alain (3rd Heavy Artillery), 165
Aldrich, Mildred, civilian, 30
Allard-Meeus, Sous-lieutenant Jean (162nd Infantry), 9, 25
Althusser, Louis, veteran's son, 217
Amond, Pierre (19th Chasseurs), 116
André, Victor (111th Infantry), 14
Anthoine, General François (Fourth, later First Army), 154, 173
Arnaud, Sous-lieutenant René (337th Infantry), 101, 105
Arnoux, Jacques (116th Infantry), 158
Auque, Charles (7th Chasseurs Alpins), 53, 62, 204
Auvergnon, Lieutenant Colonel (72nd Infantry), 87
Auvray, Lucien (87th, later 119th Infantry), 83–4
Azan, Jean (414th Infantry), 66

B., Abel, soldier, 127–8
B., Benoît, soldier and prisoner of war, 42, 78, 92, 214
Bac, Sergeant Louis (8th Zouaves), 154–5
Baer, Rif (Foreign Legion), 136
Baillon, Angéline, nursing auxiliary, 128
Ballet, Charles (75th Infantry), 181
Bally, Captain (125th Infantry), 197
Baqué, Sergeant (288th Infantry), 35
Barber, William (SSU3), 126
Barbusse, Henri (231st Infantry), 84, 85
Barrès, Maurice, journalist and politician, 25, 93, 101
Barrès, Philippe (12th Cuirassiers, later 31st Chasseurs), 91, 120, 169
Barthas, Louis (125th Territorials, later 280th and 296th Infantry), 11, 42–3, 47, 67, 118, 167, 171, 211
Barthélemy, Max (338th Infantry), 211
Barzini, Luigi, journalist, 17
Bastien, Maréchal de logis (5th Hussars), 149–50
Battarel, Raoul, soldier, 80
Battles
    Allied counter-offensives (1918), 201–5
    Argonne, offensives in (1915), 49, 61–2
    Artois, offensives in (1915), 48, 55–6

Champagne, offensives in (1915), 48, 51, 56–61
Chemin des Dames, offensive on (1917), 143–59; German counter-offensive, 173
Flanders, German offensive in (1915), 54; Allied offensive in (1917), 173
Frontiers, Battles of the (1914), 17–28
Kaiserschlacht (1918), 186–95
Marne, First Battle of the (1914), 30–4
Marne, Second Battle of the (1918), 195, 197, 200–1
Somme, Battle of the (1916), 134–9
Verdun, Battle of (1916), 96–134
Vosges, offensives in the (1915), 49–50
Baudrillart, Father Alfred, cleric, 43
Baulard, Pierre (39th Artillery), 81
Bec, Sergeant Jean (96th, later 107th Infantry), 179
Bègue, Emile, soldier, 79
Belmont, Ferdinand (11th Chasseurs Alpins), 19, 50, 66
Bénard, Major Henri (236th Infantry), 37, 44
Bénard, Louis (272nd Infantry), 44, 131
Benoit, Doctor (155th Infantry), 152
Bersot, Lucien (60th Infantry), 69
Bertrand, Colonel (162nd Infantry), 178
Bertrand, Georges (6th Chasseurs Alpins), 18, 28–9, 80–1
Bervet, Augustin (135th Infantry), 91
Bès, Victorin (161st Infantry), 10, 129
Besson-Girard, Jules (27th Chasseurs Alpins), 12–13
Biesse, Antoine (143rd Infantry), 18, 40
Bizard, Doctor Louis (Paris police), 76
Blaise, Corporal (216th Infantry), 127
Blanc, General Auguste (73rd Brigade), 65–6
Bloch, Sergeant Marc (272nd Infantry), 7, 12, 16, 37, 49, 65
Boasson, Marc (414th Infantry), 71
Bobier, Louis (11th Chasseurs Alpins), 170, 192
Bochet, Joseph (51st Chasseurs), 43
Boillot, Captain Félix (43rd Infantry), 155–6
Bonnamy, Georges (131st Infantry), 147, 152, 154
Bonnet, Georges (5th Dragoons, later 29th Artillery, 1st Artillery), 218
Bossut, Major Louis (Tanks), 150–2

Botrel, Théodore, songwriter and performer, 93

Botti, Lieutenant Louis (1st Zouaves), 55

Boudon, Victor (276th Infantry), 26, 31

Bouille, Firmin (artillery, Moroccan Division), 72, 84, 144, 212

Boulle, Adjutant Henri (76th Infantry), 44–5

Bourdillat, Aspirant (2nd Chasseurs), 100

Bourguet, Samuel (51st Artillery), 37

Bourguet, Lieutenant Colonel Victor (116th Infantry), 63

Bousquet, Joseph (55th Infantry), 91

Bouvereau, Henri (276th Infantry), 55–6

Boylesve, René, novelist, 117

Branchen, Private (405th Infantry), 103

Bréant, Major Pierre (90th Infantry), 138

Brec, Father Ernest (77th Infantry), 18–19, 91, 125, 211

Bridoux, André (2nd Zouaves), 66

Brindejonc des Moulinais, Corporal Marcel (Aviation Service), 28

Bringuier, Pierre (358th Infantry), 86

British, British army, 6, 24, 27, 28, 34, 35, 40, 56, 61, 63, 67, 74, 75, 90, 124, 129, 134, 135, 137, 138, 139, 140, 144, 146, 147, 176, 184, 187–8, 189–90, 191, 193, 199, 200, 201, 203, 204, 213

Brunon, Raoul (6th Chasseurs Alpins), 173

de Cadoudal, General Henri (40th Brigade), 32

Caillaux, Henriette, murder trial defendant, 2

Calmette, Gaston, journalist, 2

Campagne, Major, later Colonel (107th Infantry), 65, 94

Campana, Sous-lieutenant Roger (151st Infantry), 116, 133

Cantalou, Baptiste (171st Infantry), 78

Capdevielle, Lieutenant (142nd Territorials), 64, 82

Capus, Alfred, journalist, 39–40

Cariou, Benjamin, soldier, 72

Carlotti, François, civilian, 39

Carpentier, Sous-lieutenant Marcel (90th Infantry), 13

Carré, Corentin (410th Infantry), 9

Carré, Jean-Marie (4th Division), 49, 68

Cassagnau, Ivan (57th Artillery), 99

de Castelnau, General Édouard, 100, 139

Castelnau, Jean (95th Infantry), 115

Castex, Anatole (288th Infantry), 49, 134

Caubet, Georges (214th Infantry), 141

Cazin, Sergeant Paul (29th Infantry), 67–8, 82

Cendrars, Blaise (Foreign Legion), 8, 62

Céran, Olivier (Chasseurs d'Afrique), 28, 29

Chaïla, Xavier (8th Cuirassiers), 152

Chaine, Lieutenant Pierre (351st Infantry), 67, 103, 119

Chainat, Adjutant André (Aviation Service), 121

Chambe, Lieutenant René (20th Dragoons), 34

Chenu, Charles (226th Infantry, later Tanks), 19, 84, 151

Chérel, Lieutenant Albert, soldier, 107

Chevalier, Private (261st Infantry), 42

Chevallier, Gabriel (163rd Infantry), 93–4, 120

Chirossel, Louis (261st Infantry), 88

Christophe, Victor (150th Infantry), 137, 139, 158

Civilians, as forced labour, 199–200

Civilians, as refugees, 28–29, 189, 198

Civilians, as war workers, 51–3, 141, 166–7, 205, 206–7

Civilians, attitudes
to the Germans, 16–17, 197–200, 213
to military service, 4–5, 52
to the war, 2–3, 8–11, 38–9, 62, 142, 165–7, 184, 188–9, 205, 207–8, 220

Civilians, in German-occupied territories, 143–4, 197–200, 213

Clemenceau, Georges, politician, 177, 191, 194, 195, 212, 214, 218

Clozier, René (1st Zouaves), 196

Cochin, Captain Augustin (146th Infantry), 104

Cocordan, Lucien (22nd Dragoons), 60–1, 137, 139, 160, 208, 214

Coeurdevey, Edouard (167th Infantry), 77, 142

Colombel, Madame Emmanuel, nurse, 28

Conan, Yves-Marie (41st Infantry), 23

Costes, Sergeant (144th Infantry), 157

Coudray, Honoré (9th Hussars), 79, 89

Croste, Aspirant Bernard (144th Infantry), 122

Cru, Jean Norton (250th Infantry), 93, 119, 217

Cuzacq, Germain (234th Infantry), 16, 71–2, 80, 91

D., Julien, soldier, 65, 66, 84, 127

D., Michel (147th Infantry), 70–1
Daguillon, Jean (3rd Artillery), 177
Debidour, Louis, soldier, 40
Degrutère, Maria, teacher, 199
Delvert, Captain Charles (101st Infantry), 104–5, 106–7, 108, 116, 118, 119, 122–3, 141, 142, 162–3
Demonchy, Georges (4th Zouaves), 88–9, 132–3
Denys, Lieutenant Raoul (155th Infantry), 75
Dervilly, Abbé Jean (47th, later 120th Infantry), 71
Desagneaux, Henri (359th Infantry), 62–3, 173
Désalbres, Louis (128th Infantry), 148, 174
Desaubliaux, Robert (11th Cuirassiers, later 129th Infantry), 60, 119
Déverin, Edouard (48th Chasseurs, later GQG), 144, 213
Deville, Robert (17th Artillery), 16
Diez, Carlos, soldier, 88
Donati, Louis (55th Artillery), 14
Doncoeur, Paul (28th Brigade), 90
Dorgelès, Roland (39th Infantry, later Aviation Service), 61, 87, 211
Driant, Colonel Emile, 97, 99, 120
Duché, Henry (28th Infantry), 67
Duchêne, General Denis (Tenth, later Sixth Army), 144, 192, 194
Duclos, Jacques, soldier, 7
Duhelly, Jacques, soldier, 132
Dunn, Captain J.C. (Royal Welsh Fusiliers), 4–5
Dupont, Marcel (7th Chasseurs Alpins), 112
Durosoir, Lucien (129th Infantry), 114–15

Escholier, Marie-Louise, civilian, 3
Escholier, Raymond (59th Infantry), 81
Etchegoyen, Jean-Pierre, soldier, 52
Etienne, Ernest (3rd Zouaves), 3, 40–1
Etienne, Eugène, politician, 85
Eychenne, Juliette, civilian, 141

Faget, Maurice (129th Territorials), 64, 82, 159
Faleur, Georges (52nd Division), 7, 38
Fauconnier, Quartermaster Corporal Henri (273rd Infantry), 89, 142
de Fayolle, Sous-lieutenant Alain (50th Infantry), 25
Fayolle, General Emile (Sixth Army), 134–5
Fels, Florent, soldier, 64

Ferry, Corporal Abel (166th Infantry), 90
Fiolle, Doctor Paul (4th Colonial Infantry), 40
Flamant, Paul (332nd Infantry), 217
Floch, Corporal Henri (298th Infantry), 69–70
Florentin, Léon (44th Territorials), 117
Florentin, Colonel Marc (164 Brigade), 108
Foch, General Ferdinand, 28, 32, 134–5, 139, 159, 177, 187, 191, 192, 200, 201, 202, 204, 205, 212
Fontanille, Paul (6th Chasseurs Alpins), 15
Foucault, Louis (120th Chasseurs), 114
Fourier, Lieutenant Marcel (Tanks), 159, 197, 203
Fournier, Lieutenant Henri (288th Infantry), 35
Foy, Joseph (265th Infantry), 135–6
Franchet d'Esperey, General Louis (Fifth Army, later Northern Army Group), 33, 139, 146
Franconi, Gabriel (272nd Infantry), 82
French Army
   Accustomization to war, 38, 63, 72–3
   Casualties, 39, 124–30, 152–3, 177, 215–16
   Departure for the front, 12–15
   Discipline, 68–71, 120–4, 130–1, 160–9, 177–8
   Food and drink, 44, 80–4, 115–16, 164, 188–90, 211, 214
   Leave, 73–4, 163, 171, 208, 213
   Mobilization, 2–8, 53, 131, 184; demobilization, 214–16
   Prisoners, 41–2, 213
   Recreation, 37, 71–2, 74–7, 79–80, 103–4, 172–3
   Recruitment, 6–7, 25–6
   Soldiers' attitudes
      to the Americans, 185
      to the British, 15, 134, 138, 187–8
      to civilians, 80–1, 141, 165–6, 168
      to combat, 118–24, 167–8
      to the Germans, 16–17, 37, 42–3, 43–4, 93–4, 131, 180–1
      to home, 72–4, 171
      to newspapers, 40, 92–3, 117, 140, 181–2
      to officers, 65–8, 88, 117, 118–19, 162–3, 178–9, 187
      to the rear areas, 88–9, 102, 124, 131–2, 141–2, 209–10
      to religion, 90–2, 98–9
      to the war, 8–10, 12–13, 37, 44–5, 61–2, 77, 94–5, 113–15, 117–18, 137, 142, 157, 170–1, 179–80, 186, 193, 208–9

to women, 74–7, 210, 217, 219
Strategy and tactics, 14, 15, 16, 23, 24,
    26–7, 47, 51, 63, 133–4, 145–6, 156, 169–70,
    176–7, 185, 192, 193, 195–6, 202–3
Training, 15, 24, 26–7, 38, 53–4
Trenches, 62–4, 117, 186
Uniform and equipment, 24, 84–8, 120–1
Veterans, 217–19
Weapons, 88, 132–3, 150, 158, 170, 195, 196,
    202–3
Widows, 219–20
French Army: formations
  Headquarters (GQG), 50, 63, 65, 77, 100,
    114, 140, 146, 161, 167, 185, 186, 194, 213
  Armies
    First, 17, 25, 48, 61, 173, 192, 201, 202,
        203, 204
    Second, 17, 25–6, 48, 61, 100, 139, 163,
        174
    Third, 17, 20, 27, 34, 38, 48, 61, 134,
        144, 147, 187, 192, 194, 201, 203
    Fourth, 8, 17, 20, 26, 48, 50, 57, 124,
        134, 154, 155, 176
    Fifth, 17, 27, 28, 33, 34, 111, 144, 149,
        150, 153, 154, 155, 156
    Sixth, 28, 30, 34, 35, 134–5, 144, 149,
        153, 155, 156, 175, 192, 217–18
    Eighth, 48, 61
    Ninth, 28, 32, 33
    Tenth, 48, 55, 144, 149, 156, 192, 195,
        203, 204
  Corps
    I, 196
    II, 26, 49
    III, 139
    VIII, 154
    X, 196
    XI, 196
    XIII, 188
    XIV, 51
    XV, 19–20, 25–7, 140
    XVI, 15
    XIX, 7
    XX, 196
    XXI, 176
    XXXIII, 56, 100
    XXXIV, 48
    Sordet's Cavalry Corps, 24
    I Colonial, 26, 153
  Divisions
    1st, 181
    3rd, 98

    4th, 49, 68
    6th, 100
    11th, 196
    12th, 180
    17th, 104
    19th, 196
    20th, 32, 196
    21st, 196
    22nd, 193, 196
    28th, 191
    34th, 124
    36th, 129–30
    37th, 65, 188, 196
    38th, 196
    39th, 196
    41st, 161
    43rd, 102
    45th, 55, 196
    47th, 50
    51st, 60
    52nd, 7, 38
    56th, 92
    63rd, 162
    64th, 120–1, 209–10
    68th, 79
    70th, 187, 203
    74th, 109, 122, 159, 162
    133rd, 173
    152nd, 204
    166th, 187
    Moroccan, 72, 84, 144, 154, 196, 212
  Brigades
    4th, 100
    28th, 90
    35th, 90
    40th, 32
    41st, 33, 161
    42nd, 33
    56th, 43
    57th, 130
    73rd, 65–6
    164th, 108
    258th, 58
    Naval, 14, 35
French Army: units
  Artillery, 5–6, 21, 22, 23, 32–3, 36, 47, 51,
    55, 56, 58–9, 61, 66, 67, 86, 89, 97, 100,
    104–5, 109, 111, 113, 118, 119, 132–3,
    135, 145, 156, 158, 169, 170, 187, 197, 202
  Individual regiments:
    1st, 218
    2nd, 57

3rd, 177, 210
5th, 7, 140
8th, 178, 181
17th, 16
22nd, 179
24th, 215
27th, 38, 48, 72–3, 213
29th, 218
32nd, 120
34th, 105
39th, 81
43rd, 105
44th, 22, 38, 65, 118
46th, 87, 120, 138
51st, 37
55th, 14
57th, 77, 99, 214
60th, 7
61st, 111–12
206th, 203
220th, 185
225th, 178
276th, 181
4th Foot, 55
5th Foot, 36
3rd Heavy, 165
107th Heavy, 116
Moroccan Division, 72, 84, 144, 212
Aviation Service, 28, 110–12, 121, 128, 158,
190, 211
Cavalry, 5, 7–8, 24, 26, 28, 34, 60–1, 80, 87,
139, 187, 190, 202, 203
Individual regiments:
4th Chasseurs à cheval, 94
11th Chasseurs à cheval, 60
Chasseurs d'Afrique, 7, 28, 29
5th Cuirassiers, 3
8th Cuirassiers, 152
9th Cuirassiers, 24
11th Cuirassiers, 24, 60
12th Cuirassiers, 24, 91, 120, 169, 193,
214
5th Dragoons, 218
9th Dragoons, 173
20th Dragoons, 34
22nd Dragoons, 60–1, 137, 139, 160,
208, 214
1st Hussars, 6, 90
5th Hussars, 60, 149–50
9th Hussars, 79, 89
10th Hussars, 215
Engineers, 5–6, 36, 43, 89, 133, 201

Individual regiments:
2nd, 12
3rd, 47–8
8th, 108
10th, 108
Gendarmerie, provosts, 2, 3, 10, 11, 17, 20,
29, 32, 41, 88, 93, 102, 104, 166, 189,
209, 215
Infantry, 5–8, 22–3, 27, 36, 51, 53, 58, 60,
61, 63, 71, 80, 92–3, 100, 102, 105, 110,
112, 113, 118, 119, 121, 131, 132–4,
135, 139, 145–6, 150, 156, 159, 169–70,
176, 184, 195–6, 197, 202, 203;
colonial infantry, 8, 26, 88, 147, 148
Individual regiments / battalions:
1st, 135, 149
3rd, 167
5th, 187
6th, 81, 91
9th, 9, 94
11th, 66, 94, 104
12th, 214
18th, 6, 178
19th, 3, 179
20th, 36, 122, 160
23rd, 50, 120, 161
24th, 99
25th, 149
28th, 67
29th, 67–8, 82
30th, 9, 43, 172, 173, 175–6, 180, 192
31st, 13, 20–2, 33, 124–5
32nd, 32
33rd, 34
36th, 56, 162, 167
37th, 56, 89
39th, 61, 71, 87
41st, 23, 177, 186
42nd, 90
43rd, 155–6
44th, 17, 89–90
46th, 82, 104, 205
47th, 71
48th, 171
50th, 25
53rd, 54, 79
55th, 91, 210
56th, 68, 69
57th, 128–9, 147, 153–4, 187, 189, 193,
194
58th, 9, 94
59th, 81

60th, 57, 69, 93,133, 211
61st, 36
64th, 115
65th, 33, 57–8
67th, 123–4, 129, 147, 148
68th, 123, 172
72nd, 87
73rd, 63, 139, 180
74th, 3, 9, 36, 54, 119, 138–9, 185, 186, 187
75th, 181
76th, 44–5
77th, 18–19, 35, 91, 123, 125, 210
81st, 6, 65, 79, 82, 84, 87, 116–17, 175, 212
87th, 83–4, 105
89th, 148, 150
90th, 13, 83, 138
91st, 131
92nd, 137–8
93rd, 13, 32, 210
94th, 140
95th, 73–4, 115, 124
96th, 2–3, 179
99th, 191–2
101st, 104–5, 106–7, 108, 116, 118, 119, 122–3, 141, 142, 162–3
103rd, 185
106th, 38, 48–9, 65, 77, 79, 118–19, 220
107th, 12, 13, 22–3, 65, 94, 179
108th, 178
111th, 14, 130
112th, 13, 27, 43–4, 53, 61–2, 63, 66, 94
115th, 122, 177
116th, 63, 158, 180, 208
117th, 171, 214
118th, 16
119th, 83–4, 107, 109–10, 128
120th, 71
122nd, 12, 29, 43–4
123rd, 98–9
124th, 94–5
125th, 197
127th, 101, 117–18, 134
128th, 148, 174, 178
129th, 6, 60, 62, 114–15, 119, 208
131st, 68, 147, 152, 154
132nd, 145
133rd, 161
135th, 91, 192–3
137th, 33
139th, 41–2

140th, 130
141st, 19–20
142nd, 105
143rd, 18, 40
144th, 122, 157
146th, 101, 104
147th, 70–1
149th, 179
150th, 137, 139, 158
151st, 116, 119, 133
152nd, 105–6, 168
153rd, 126, 208
155th, 75, 152
161st, 10, 54, 129
162nd, 9, 25, 161–2, 178
163rd, 73, 93–4, 120
166th, 90
167th, 77, 142
171st, 78
172nd, 76–7, 87, 103, 152–3
173rd, 26, 72
174th, 99, 125–6, 127
205th, 75, 91, 113–14, 130
206th, 101
208th, 217
214th, 141
215th, 123, 170–1
216th, 31, 127
217th, 131
219th, 210
222nd, 177, 181
226th, 19, 84, 190–1
227th, 83
229th, 161, 178
231st, 71, 73, 84, 85, 102, 115, 117
233rd, 197
234th, 19, 71–2, 80, 91
236th, 37, 44
240th, 86
246th, 67, 80, 119, 217
249th, 59–60, 153, 159
250th, 93, 119, 217
256th, 136
257th, 101
258th, 130
261st, 42, 88, 95
265th, 135–6
267th, 79
272nd, 7, 12, 16, 37, 44, 49, 65, 82
273rd, 89, 142
276th, 8, 26, 31, 55–6, 102, 117
277th, 90–1

280th, 67, 72
281st, 136
287th, 164, 210
288th, 35, 49, 134
289th, 194
290th, 118, 123
296th, 43, 118, 167, 171, 211
298th, 69–70
305th, 68
309th, 116
321st, 172
322nd, 20, 217
329th, 81, 82, 90, 119, 120, 136–7
332nd, 217
334th, 164
335th, 105
336th, 69
337th, 101, 105
338th, 91, 134, 211
339th, 6
343rd, 37, 64, 72, 75–6, 86, 91, 208
344th, 180
346th, 108, 181
347th, 108
351st, 67, 103, 119
352nd, 64
355th, 144
356th, 14, 37, 63
358th, 86, 112
359th, 62–3, 117, 173
363rd, 161
368th, 108
369th, 108
370th, 113, 116
401st, 81
405th, 103
408th, 180
409th, 186
410th, 9
414th, 66, 71, 121–2, 160, 169
3rd Algerian Tirailleurs, 101
5th Algerian Tirailleurs, 65
7th Algerian Tirailleurs, 203–4
11th Algerian Tirailleurs, 204
2nd Chasseurs, 13–14, 100, 149
4th Chasseurs, 100
6th Chasseurs Alpins, 15, 18, 28–9, 80–1, 173
7th Chasseurs Alpins, 53, 62, 112, 204
11th Chasseurs Alpins, 19, 43, 50, 66, 170, 192
17th Chasseurs, 150

18th Chasseurs, 114
19th Chasseurs, 116
24th Chasseurs Alpins, 29–30
27th Chasseurs Alpins, 12–13
31st Chasseurs, 91, 120, 169
44th Chasseurs, 81, 186, 189, 211–12
48th Chasseurs, 144
49th Chasseurs, 177
51st Chasseurs, 43
56th Chasseurs, 64–5
66th Chasseurs, 25, 141
69th Chasseurs, 57
107th Chasseurs, 110
120th Chasseurs, 114
4th Colonial, 40
5th Colonial, 149–50, 157, 201–2
36th Colonial, 68–9
Régiment d'Infanterie Coloniale du Maroc, 115, 120, 123, 175
Foreign Legion, 7, 8, 12, 59, 62, 120, 136, 184–5, 204, 209
Infanterie Légère d'Afrique, 4
Senegalese tirailleurs, 8, 156–8, 166, 201–2; 5th Battalion 157; 48th Battalion, 157
11th Territorials, 116
12th Territorials, 6
22nd Territorials, 108
24th Territorials, 108
44th Territorials, 9, 117
45th Territorials, 178
64th Territorials, 15, 16
98th Territorials, 108
102nd Territorials, 121, 140–1, 160
108th Territorials, 6
112th Territorials, 116
125th Territorials, 11, 42–3, 47
129th Territorials, 64, 82, 159
131st Territorials, 163, 164–5, 167, 180–1
134th Territorials, 186
142nd Territorials, 64, 82
330th Territorials, 108, 117
Vietnamese tirailleurs, 166
1st Zouaves, 55, 172, 196
2nd Zouaves, 66
3rd Zouaves, 3, 40–1
3rd bis Zouaves, 55
4th Zouaves, 88–9, 132–3, 158
8th Zouaves, 154–5
Medical Service
Doctors, 4, 7, 23, 38, 44, 84, 108, 125,

126, 129, 131, 148, 152, 178, 215, 216
Hospitals, 38, 40, 54, 93, 126–9, 141, 152–3, 158, 215–16, 218
Nurses, 28, 125, 127, 128
Tanks, 150–2, 158–9, 176, 195, 197, 203
Transport units
SSA226, 126
SSU3, 126–7
TM388, 100
French Red Cross, 127
Frère, Major Aubert (1st Infantry), 135

Gallieni, General Joseph, 97
Galtier–Boissière, Corporal Jean (31st Infantry), 13, 20–2, 33
Garnung, Raymond (5th Artillery), 7
Gaudin, Lieutenant (64th Territorials), 15, 16
Gaudon, Alexandre (32nd Infantry), 32
Gaudy, Georges (57th Infantry), 128–9, 147, 153–4, 187, 189, 193
Gaulène, Guillaume, soldier, 93
de Gaulle, Lieutenant Charles (33rd Infantry), 34
Gémeau, Major (BEF GHQ), 183–4
Genevoix, Lieutenant Maurice (106th Infantry), 38, 48–9, 65, 77, 118–19, 220
Gérard, General Augustin (II Corps), 49
Germany, German Army, 2, 3, 4, 8, 10, 15, 16, 17–28, 30–4, 36–7, 48, 49–50, 54–62, 96–134, 134–9, 143–59, 169, 173, 186–95, 197, 200–5
Giboulet, Sergeant Justin (215th Infantry), 123, 170–1
Gissinger, Lucien (174th Infantry), 99, 125–6, 127
Goldfarb, Pierre (Foreign Legion), 8
Gosset, Captain (48th Senegalese Battalion), 157
Goutard, Lieutenant (30th Infantry), 172, 173, 175–6
Grange, Jean–Philippe (30th Infantry), 9, 180
Gras, Sergeant Gaston (RICM), 123
Grasset, Captain Alphonse (107th Infantry), 12, 13, 22–3
Graveson, Sergeant (64th Division), 209
Grenadou, Ephraïm (27th Artillery), 72–3, 213
Grossetti, General Paul (XVI Corps), 117
Guilhem, François (296th Infantry), 43

Hallé, Guy (74th Infantry), 119, 138–9
Harrison, Marie, journalist, 188
Hastoy, Simon (6th Infantry), 81, 91
Henches, Captain, later Major Jules (46th, then 32nd Artillery), 87, 120, 138
Herbin, Louis (106th Infantry), 79
Herr, General Frédéric (Verdun Fortified Sector), 98, 100
Hertz, Sergeant Robert (44th Territorials), 9
Hervé, Gustave, writer, 10
Hounière, Désiré, garde civile, 16
Hourticq, Louis (330th Territorials), 108, 117
Hue, Alfred, mayor of Beuvardes (Aisne), 197–8, 200
Humbert, General Georges (Third Army), 144, 147
Huot, Doctor Louis, Colonial troops medical service, 75, 84, 120

Italy, Italian Army, 13, 17, 137, 184, 192, 201

Jaurès, Jean, politician, 2, 10
Joffre, General Joseph, 5, 15–16, 17, 23, 27–8, 30, 34, 37, 47, 50, 51, 54, 55, 57, 61, 68, 77, 87, 97–8, 100, 131, 132, 134, 138, 139, 144, 177, 213
Jolinon, Joseph (370th Infanry), 113
Joubert, Alfred (124th Infantry), 94–5
Jouhaux, Léon, trade unionist, 10
Jubert, Sous-lieutenant Raymond (151st Infantry), 119
Junod, Captain Edouard (Foreign Legion), 59

Kahn, André (37th Infantry), 56, 89
Krémer, Louis (231st Infantry), 71

La Chaussée, Captain Julien (39th Infantry), 71
Laby, Aspirant (249th Infantry), 59–60, 159
Lamey, Colonel (42 Brigade), 33
Lamothe, Louis (339th Infantry), 6
de Langle de Cary, General Fernand (Fourth Army), 26
Laquièze, Charles (55th Infantry), 210
Larché, Sergeant Louis, 84
Laure, Colonel Auguste, 204–5
Laurentin, Lieutenant Maurice (77th, later 219th Infantry), 35, 210
Le Bailly, Fernand (36th Infantry), 56

Le Lann, Sous-lieutenant François (65th Infantry), 33
Lélu, Georges (43rd Divisional Provost Squadron), 102
Legentil, Private (74th Infantry), 185
Lintanf, Joseph (19th Infantry), 3
Lintanf, Léonie, 11
Lintier, Paul (44th Artillery), 22, 38, 65, 118
Lissorgues, Abbé Marcellin (287th Infantry), 164, 210
Lyautey, General Louis, 146

Magnien, Abbé Joseph (66th Chasseurs), 141
Maillet, André (23rd Infantry), 50, 120
Mairet, Louis (127th Infantry), 117–18, 134
Maistre, General Paul (Sixth Army), 175
Malecot, Corporal (152nd Infantry), 105–6
Mangin, General Charles (Sixth, later Tenth Army), 109, 144, 156–7, 159, 162, 195, 203, 204
Marot, Jean (334th Infantry), 164
Martin, Sergeant Vincent (119th Infantry), 107, 109–10
Massignac, Clément (11th Infantry), 66, 94, 104
Masson, Sous-lieutenant Pierre (261st Infantry), 95
Maufrais, Doctor Louis (94th Infantry), 140
Mazel, General Olivier (Fifth Army), 144, 146, 150
McConnell, James (Aviation Service), 112
Médus, Philistall (4th Zouaves), 158
Méléra, Timothée (RICM), 115
Messimy, Adolphe, politician, 68, 85–6
Meyer, Bandsman (74th Infantry), 3
Meyer, Lieutenant Jacques (329th Infantry), 81, 82, 90, 119, 120, 136–7
Mézières, P.-J., writer, 216
Micheler, General Joseph (Reserve Army Group), 144, 146
Michelon, Sous-lieutenant (2nd Chasseurs), 13–14
Mordacq, Colonel Jean (3rd bis Zouaves), 55
Moreau, Abel (6th Foot Artillery, later 102nd Artillery), 218–19
Morel-Journel, Henry (74th Division), 109, 122, 159, 162
Morin, Sergeant, later Lieutenant Emile (60th Infantry), 57, 93, 133
Morizet, André, soldier, 179
Morlae, Edward (Foreign Legion), 59, 209

Mornet, Daniel (231st Infantry), 73, 102, 115, 117
Muenier, Pierre (SSA226), 126
Murat, Georges (131st Territorials), 163, 164–5, 167, 180–1

N., Joseph, soldier, 209
Naegelen, René (172nd Infantry), 76–7, 87, 103, 152–3
Nayral de Bourgon, General Alexis (3rd Division), 98
Ninet, Jules (89th Infantry), 148, 150
Nivelle, General Robert, 27, 100, 106, 109, 139–40, 141, 144–5, 146, 147, 148, 154, 156, 158, 159, 162, 177
Noé, Léopold (281st Infantry), 136
Nordmann, Corporal Charles (5th Artillery), 140

Odent, Lieutenant Colonel (68th Infantry), 123
Oudry, Lieutenant Colonel (152nd Infantry), 106

de P., Lieutenant Arnaud (Aviation Service), 111
Painlevé, Paul, politician, 146, 156, 177
Paoletti, Dominique (163rd Infantry), 73
Papillon, Marcel (356th Infantry), 14, 37, 63
Paraf, Pierre (92nd Infantry), 137–8
Pascal, Maurice (67th Infantry), 148
Pasquier, Pierre (67th Infantry), 129
Péguy, Charles (276th Infantry), 8, 26, 31
Pensa, Laurent (31st Infantry), 124–5
Perette, Corporal Jean-François (Tanks), 151
Perrin, Doctor François (36th Division), 129–30
Pestourie, André (60th Infantry), 211
Pétain, General Philippe, 27, 34, 56, 90, 100, 101, 104, 107, 110, 111, 131–2, 135, 139–40, 146, 147, 159, 168, 169–74, 175, 176, 177, 178–9, 183–4, 185, 186–7, 191, 192, 195–6, 201, 203, 204, 220
Peugeot, Corporal André (44th Infantry), 17
Petit, Paul, anti-war protester, 10
Pézard, André (46th Infantry), 82, 104
de Pierrefeu, Jean (GQG), 185, 194
Pillon, Robert (24th Infantry), 99
Pinar, Doctor Adolphe, 53
Pinçon, Captain (99th Infantry), 191–2

Poincaré, Raymond, politician, 10, 98, 141, 146, 159, 177
Portes, Corporal Jean (1st Infantry), 149
Poulaille, Henry, soldier, 75
Poupin, Benjamin (XIII Corps), 188
Prévost, Marcel (XXI Corps), 176

Raynal, Commandant Sylvain, 107
Redier, Antoine (338th Infantry), 91, 134
Rendel, Quartermaster Sergeant (20th Infantry), 122
Ribot, Alexandre, politician, 47, 146, 177
Ricadat, Paul (147th Infantry), 70–1
Rigaud, Gratien (122nd Infantry), 12
Ripoull, Georges (81st Infantry), 116–17, 212
Robert, Henri (123rd Infantry), 98–9
Rocca, Emile (24th Chasseurs Alpins), 29–30
de Rohan, Captain, 100
Rohan, Colonel (358th Infantry), 112
Rollet, Lieutenant Colonel Paul (Foreign Legion), 184–5
Ronarc'h, Admiral Pierre (Naval Brigade), 14
de Rose, Major Charles (Aviation Service), 111
Rostin, Lieutenant Marcel (112th Infantry), 27, 43–4, 61–2, 63, 66
Roullet, Pierre (277th Infantry), 90–1
Roujon, Jacques (352nd Infantry), 64
Roumiguières, Private, later Sergeant Georges (343rd Infantry), 72, 75–6, 86–7, 91, 208
Rousseau, Abbé (93rd Infantry), 13
Rousseau, Private (87th Infantry), 105
Russia, Russian army, 2, 15, 36, 47, 134, 137, 165, 167, 169, 184–5, 214

de Saint-Jouan, Captain Pierre (131st Infantry), 68
Saint-Pierre, Amand, soldier, 140
Sarrail, General Maurice (Third Army), 34, 38
Seeger, Alan (Foreign Legion), 8, 136
Sem, journalist, 101–2
Suteau, Private (91st Infantry), 131

Tabourot, Captain (142nd Infantry), 105
Tanty, Emile (129th Infantry), 62
Tardy, Georges (226th Infantry), 190–1

Tézenas du Montcel, Lieutenant Joseph (5th Colonial Regiment), 157, 201–2
Tézenas du Montcel, Lieutenant, later Captain Paul (102nd Territorials), 121, 140–1, 160
Thiais, Jean (64th Infantry), 115
Thomas, Louis (66th Chasseurs), 25
Toinet, Paul (2nd Artillery), 57
Top, Doctor Gaston (27th Artillery), 38, 48
Torquat, Sous-lieutenant (41st Infantry), 177
Tourmen, Yves (12th Cuirassiers), 193, 214
Touzet de Vigier, Lieutenant (9th Cuirassiers), 24
Trouilh, Major (5th Senegalese Battalion), 157
Tuffrau, Sous-lieutenant Paul (246th Infantry), 67, 80, 119, 217

United States of America, American army, 8, 30, 59, 112, 126, 136, 184, 185, 194, 200, 201, 204, 209

Vaillant, Jean-Paul, artilleryman, 105
Vaillant-Couturier, Aspirant Paul, soldier, 58–9, 133
Valle, Lieutenant Paul (74th Infantry), 9
Vandebeuque, Jacques (56th Chasseurs), 64–5
Varenne, Joseph (414th Infantry), 71, 121–2, 160, 169
Vartan, Abbé Gustave (107th Chasseurs), 110
Veaux, Doctor Georges (41st Infantry), 23
Veurpillot, Pierre (4th Foot Artillery), 55
Vial, Francisque (11th Territorials), 116
Videau, Henry (5th Cuirassiers), 3
Vilain, Camille (1st Artillery), 154
Vion, Louis (370th Infantry), 116
Viviani, René, politician, 10
Voivenel, Doctor Paul (257th Artillery, later 211th and 220th Infantry), 75, 84, 120
Vuillemin, Major (152nd Infantry), 168
Vuillermoz, Léon (44th Infantry), 89–90

Wolff, Major Henri (36th Colonial Infantry), 68–9

X., Raoul, soldier, 110

Ybarnégaray, Jean (249th Infantry), 153